The Split God

SUNY series in Theology and Continental Thought
———————
Douglas L. Donkel, editor

The Split God

Pentecostalism and Critical Theory

Nimi Wariboko

An earlier version of chapter 7 was published as "West African Pentecostalism: A Survey of Everyday Theology," in *Global Renewal Christianity: Spirit-Empowered Movements—Past, Present and Future, Volume 3: Africa* by Vinson Synan, Amos Yong, and J. Kwabena Asamoah-Gyadu (Lake Mary, FL: Charisma House, 2016): 1–18. Used by permission.

Published by State University of New York Press, Albany

© 2018 State University of New York

All rights reserved

No part of this book may be used or reproduced in any manner whatsoever without written permission. No part of this book may be stored in a retrieval system or transmitted in any form or by any means including electronic, electrostatic, magnetic tape, mechanical, photocopying, recording, or otherwise without the prior permission in writing of the publisher.

For information, contact State University of New York Press, Albany, NY
www.sunypress.edu

Library of Congress Cataloging-in-Publication Data

Wariboko, Nimi, author.
Title: The Split God: Pentacostalism and critical theory / Nimi Wariboko, author
Description: Albany: State University of New York Press [2018]
Series: A volume in the SUNY series in Theology and Continental Thought.
Identifiers: ISBN 9781438470191 (hardcover) | ISBN 9781438470207
  (pbk.) | ISBN 9781438470214 (ebook)
Further information is available from the Library of Congress.

10 9 8 7 6 5 4 3 2 1

To Mark Lewis Taylor

Contents

Acknowledgments — ix

Preface — xi

Introduction: Thinking at the Boundary — 1

1 Day of Pentecost: The Founding Violent Gesture of Splits — 21

2 Spiritual Discernment: Bathroom Mirror as Metaphor — 45

3 The Beauty, Skin, and Monstrosity of Grace — 65

4 The Sacred as Im/possibility: Expect a Miracle! — 83

5 The Impossible Possibility, Capitalism, and the Pentecostal Subject — 111

6 Worship as Pure Means — 133

7 Everyday Form of Theology: Between Pentecostal Apparatus and Prosaic Existence — 155

Conclusion: Ethical Implications of a Split God — 181

Notes — 195

Bibliography — 219

Index — 227

Acknowledgments

Authors write acknowledgments to publicly record their indebtedness to the living and the dead who helped them in the process of researching and writing their books. I have done a lot of this in my previous sixteen monographs and four edited volumes. Now that I am on my seventeenth monograph, it occurred to me that my acknowledgment should properly focus on the not-yet born. I expect their coming onto the academic scene, to carry forward the ideas in this book. I acknowledge their accomplishments of this task and the claim past scholarship has on them.

This approach to acknowledgment is very important for those of us who are Africans and/or Pentecostals. We write not only with an eye on the current intellectual questions and debates, but also with an ear on the distant sound of the footsteps of coming generations. We are building a body of work for the next generations, whose coming is expected and whose joy in inheriting and encountering works and ideas left for them by their own deeply excites me. I acknowledge here the inspiration I received from the generations of Africans and Pentecostals who are coming after me. I acknowledge the intellectual powers of those who come after me, the straps of whose sandals I am not worthy to untie. I have no greater joy than to expect that my brothers and sisters, my children, will be committed to the quest for truth rooted in the public intercourse of rigorous ideas.

Now let me turn to the past and present generations who assisted me in bringing the idea of this book to fruition. I salute Catherine Keller of Drew University, who read a draft of chapter 4 and blessed me with her gifts and insights that improved its quality. I am also grateful to Boston University School of Theology colleagues in the Track 2 Theology and Ethics colloquium who read and commented on chapters 1 and 4. Erica Ramirez, doctoral candidate at Drew University travelled all the way from New Orleans, where she was living with her family, to attend the colloquium on Wednesday, December 2, 2015 when I presented chapter 1. Erica, thanks for your enthusiastic support of my scholarship. The editors and staff of the State University of New York Press, Christopher Ahn, Chelsea Miller, Diane Ganeles, and Dana Foote did great service to the cause of publishing this book, a service that models what good editors should be. I also wish to thank Douglas L. Donkel, editor of the SUNY series in Theology and Continental Thought, for his support. Thanks to Ms. Itohan Mercy Idumwonyi of Rice University for finding time to prepare the index amid writing her dissertation.

I also acknowledge all my teachers, past and present, in formal and informal settings, who helped to form and inspire me to work at the uncomfortable intersectionality of disciplines. I am a scholar on the boundary. I work on the boundaries of economics and ethics, economics and religion, economics and philosophy, ethics and theology, philosophy and theology, social history and ethics, social sciences and theology, and present and not-yet-present knowledges. My thinking always functions at an interstitial site, wrestling in a contact zone of disciplines that is neither/nor. This is a site that opposes binary opposition, oscillating between spheres of knowledge. It is the fragile, fleeting, and slippery *para-site* of erotic, new, refreshing insights and lights. I am talking of the uncanny non-place that promises to birth the underivably new in history. My soul finds deep peace at this frontier, the edge of knowledge that is always approaching and withdrawing approach. This book reflects this orientation of my scholarship. And I thank you, the reader, for your forbearance in walking and working with me in this unhomely space.

Preface

This book exclusively appropriates critical theory as a lens to interpret Pentecostalism. It examines the construction of the notion of God among Pentecostals and brings it into conversation with a postmodern philosophy of religion, particularly the Marxist/psychoanalytic thread of critical theory rather than the existentialist or hermeneutic phenomenological one. Pentecostalism is one of the fastest-growing religious movements in the world (especially in the global south) and its conception of God, its ideas about ontology, epistemology, the sacred, human embodiment of the divine, and numerous other matters offer rich resources for deep philosophical reflection. Continental philosophy offers us varied and rich concepts, tools, and interpretative lenses for studying Pentecostalism as a social movement, religious tradition, and historical reality, and to aid in such reflection. In particular, the ideas of Slavoj Žižek, Jacques Lacan, Jean-Luc Nancy, and Giorgio Agamben, for instance, are significant sites in which to engage pentecostal thoughts and ideas to make connections between Pentecostalism and postmodern philosophy of religion. Besides, critical theorists like Žižek have engaged the theology and radical orthodoxy of John Milbank. Nancy has applied his deconstructive philosophy of religion to Christianity. Alain Badiou has engaged the figure of Saint Paul as militant revolutionary. Agamben has brought his formidable analytical skills to bear on Paul's Letter to the Romans and given us a fresh understanding of messianism. How might the insights, critical perspectives, and philosophies of these scholars help us to undertake a critical religious study of Pentecostalism? While this book will engage the philosophers mentioned here and many more, it is germane to add that our discourse enters into postmodern religious theory through the specific conversational thread of Žižekian critical religious theory (an alternative tradition in continental philosophy). He is a prominent player in the contemporary debates and his theory has become influential in postmodern religious theory. In spite of all these, the book does not make claim to be a work of philosophy per se—it is only a work in critical religious studies with a focus on Pentecostalism. Its aim is to bring to pentecostal studies the rich resources and critical tradition of continental philosophy of religion.

The data and issues that form the basis of our engagement with critical theory come from everyday practices of Pentecostals rather than from academic theologies and doctrines of God. The data and issues of our arguments are organized around the grassroots-derived notion of the split God. By this I mean that Pentecostals have opened up the traditional notion of God into new possible uses. The art and act of splitting *deactivates* the traditional (inherited) notion of God and radicalizes it. By splitting, the inherited notion is not only separated from its orthodox grounding without abandoning orthodoxy, but also "parts" and "attributes" of God are separated from Godself and are recombined and exhibited in their separation from Godself, becoming "spectacles." Pentecostals hold that this split God is forever interacting with a reality that is an internally inconsistent and incomplete whole. We want to grasp Pentecostals' splitting of the world and of God as they grapple to understand human existence spiritually. The book studies this epistemic orientation philosophically and critically, demonstrating how it structures and organizes everyday practices and how everyday practices in turn help Pentecostals to construct a practical, handy notion of God. The book then offers an intellectual reflection connecting pentecostal practices on the ground with continental philosophies in order to deconstruct the pentecostal philosophy of God.

This study clearly presents various dimensions of pentecostal practices and makes cogent connections with multiple elements of critical theory, showing how everyday theology questions dogmas and resists the conservative status quo even as, in many instances, it makes common cause with neoliberal capitalism. Though Pentecostalism is usually considered a conservative or fundamentalist movement, its operative everyday notion of God is radical and nonorthodox. Pentecostal spirituality not only locates itself in orthodox Christianity, but also challenges it. Indeed, in the everyday practices of Pentecostals, there is a profound indifference to the caesura between orthodoxy and nonorthodoxy. Under the pressure of everyday practices, the inherited notion of God is separated from its orthodox grounding without abandoning orthodoxy.

The book is not a work of systematic (constructive) theology, but an attempt to develop a "philosophy" at the intersection of Pentecostalism and critical theory. It aims to develop a pentecostal philosophy of God that is not beholden to theology and guild-theologians, but one that emerges out of a serious conversation with continental philosophy and critical theory. As some of the readers of this book well know, Pentecostalism as a worldwide movement with over 600 million adherents (including the charismatics) has no critical philosophy and has not registered much on the radar of continental philosophy and critical theory despite the recent turn of continental philosophers to religion. The works of Žižek, Agamben, and Badiou can enable pentecostal scholars to understand that Pentecostalism is not merely a theology, but also a social movement that has genuine revolutionary (subversive) potentials. This book, by drawing from the thoughts of scholars such Žižek and Badiou, hopes to make an impact on the literature of pentecostal studies and critical theory. In the final analysis, this study not only departicularizes the pentecostal notion of God, but also offers a pentecostal critical theory of God that may enter into critical dialogue with radical continental philosophy.

Pentecostalism is a worldwide religious movement that has captured the imaginations of hundreds of millions of people. Scores, if not hundreds, of perspicacious scholars are devoted to studying it. These scholars celebrate it as giving the lie to death-of-God philosophy and theology. Pentecostals, they say, embody, articulate, and celebrate the livingness and active presence of God in the world. This is a fair assessment. The only problem is that the God the Pentecostals worship, solicit, and celebrate has not been subjected to a sustained philosophical-critical theoretical analysis. This book undertakes such an exercise—on the terms of Pentecostals—and reveals that the God that "died" in the 1960s and the God who was "resurrected" in the 1980s are not the same. God *is* now a radically split God. Pentecostals have crafted from the materials of their everyday lives a notion of God that is not in (or cannot come into) full identity with Godself, and God is forever interacting with a reality that is ontologically incomplete. Time and again, we see Pentecostalism professing a traditional doctrine of God, yet its very practices continually set the stage for the unraveling, liquidation, or reconstitution of that doctrine. The dogmatic, doctrinaire edifice of a seamless God, constructed in giant granite without crack from top to bottom, is tottering. Pentecostals are quarrying it for parts and part-of-no-part to craft their imaginary of the divine. Before their hammer and chisel everything that is shakable is being shaken so that what cannot be shaken may remain. Everything is swaying in the wind (pneuma).

Our particular interest in deciphering the pentecostal God demands its own particular method of study. My approach is to dust off the movement's patina of trained theological talks, to scrape off the barnacles of inherited scriptural dogmas, to evade its leaders' pious proclamations that are unhinged from everyday life, and to reach beyond its crust of fundamentalism to the searing core of its radical metaphysics in order to unveil the God that stands behind and coordinates everyday pentecostal practices. In other words, the goal here is to uncover the God that Pentecostals presuppose, knowingly or unknowingly, in their everyday practices. The key question I ask and address is this: What is the Pentecostals' unvarnished theory of God as discernible from their everyday practices? The theory or answer (a notion of a split God) that emerges from the analysis and inquiry is then set into deep conversation with the work of major radical philosophical thinkers, past and present.

It is germane to quickly add that the concept of split here does not refer to the Trinity, the existence of three "persons" in the triune God. We are not adding the adjective "split" to God because there are three hypostases of one substance in the Christian notion of God or because there is a gap between essence and existence in God. The pentecostal partition of God that is implied in the notion of a split God is not the transcendental/immanent dualism of theologians or philosophers. God is radically split in himself. This is a fracture within God that cannot be reduced to polarities, negation, nonbeing, abyss within God. The split refers to a God that is divided. In simplest of terms, this means they are treating attributes and dimensions of God as self-standing that are in reality an organic whole. They have projected their epistemological limitation about knowing God, their knowledge of ontological incompleteness to God. The limitation of their knowledge about God is simultaneously the limitation of the very God that they worship. This gap, as we will show in the various chapters of this book, becomes a foundation for miracles in a universe that is itself incomplete. The notion of a split God gestures to the gap in the simple God, the gap at the purest or deepest level of monotheism or the One that divides, supplements, and causes to overflow the *mono* or oneness. The concept points to the cracks in the One that are gathered into one and as such destabilize the one from becoming complete, *One-All*. (Later we will return to this concept in more detail through examples and practices of Pentecostalism.) Indeed, this is the unacknowledged radicality of pentecostal metaphysics, which we hope to uncover or retrieve in this book. This is, however, not a radicalness that is a product of operations of abstractness, but one that is rooted in the immediacy of lived, experienced reality and intimately knows real, sensuous, physical human activity, practice.[1]

Before we proceed further, I need to add that the notion of the split God as deployed in this book involves four different, but related, dimensions. In the preceding paragraph, we have given a short overview of how this concept relates to God, the first of the four. In its functioning in the everyday forms of Pentecostalism it mobilizes and harnesses three other forms of split. The second dimension involves a belief in ontological incompleteness that conditions being or existence. Third, the subjectivity of the pentecostal believer is split; the pentecostal self is split between the desires and nomos of this world and the spiritual world he or she hopes to inherit. Finally, the pentecostal worldview is split between the noumenal and the phenomenal. Each of these distinct notions of split (they are actually dimensions of one notion) are interwoven together in the everyday form of Pentecostalism, and the practices we are analyzing will fall apart or lose significant relevance if any of these four dimensions are absent. Each of these dimensions will be studied as a case in the following chapters to show how it conditions and is conditioned by everyday practice.

What do these dimensions mean relative to the particular model of God operative in the lives of Pentecostals? Pentecostals (especially those in Africa) are continuously "tearing" God apart and then bringing parts of his attributes together into a new unity, into a contingent synthesis that the necessity of practice imposes on the manifold parts. Their ultimate interest is to invoke the synthesized attributes as partial organs that can perform miracles on hard reality (that is always incomplete) or to enable them to bypass the inaccessibility of the "Thing itself." The ultimate *perverse* vision of this view of God in everyday practice is that God is nothing but a combination of partial organs. These partial organs become means of jouissance and detachable tools to either attack one's enemies or to drive prosperity to oneself. For instance, African Pentecostals pray: "Thou glory [power, thunder, fire, hand] of God arise and consume my enemies."[2] While observing them "binding and casting" out demons in prayer, and hearing how God or God's attributes are deployed as subjectless partial organs, one gets the impression that the very unity of God's being (body) is magically dissolved. They are not perceiving God as a *One* or *All* but as a desubjectivized multitude of partial objects, not as a unified totality. God is a "kind of vaguely coordinated agglomerate of partial objects": here the power, there a hand, over there the glory, and close to it the consuming fire.³ Does this conception of God not surprisingly echo Hegel's conception of the radical negativity of the subject ("night of the world") or the negative power of understanding?⁴

With such separation and spectacularization of God's attributes, and yet the attributes are deemed to still carry God's power and presence, the partial organs are thrown alongside God or within the omnipresent God as divine in themselves. What we have, for instance, are Power-God, Hand-God, or Glory-God. These *parallels* (*para* + *allelos*, alongside one another) put God's essence itself in the hyphenation—"God-power-glory"—"which is a mark of union and also a mark of division, a mark of sharing that effaces itself, leaving each term to its isolation *and* its being-with-the-others."⁵ The Pentecostal God under this scenario is God-singular-plural.

This book tells the fascinating story of a pentecostal notion of God not as a theological text, but as a critical inquiry into the important dimensions of pentecostal life and spirituality that reveals how God and reality that "exist out there" are constructed (or more appropriately, *imagined*) to fit the everyday nitty-gritty materiality of the "here and now."⁶ It traces the splits and tensions in the concept of God that is forged amid the pressures and tensions of everyday pentecostal social existence. The abstract systematic theological noun "God" (as generally conceived in the pentecostal theological academe) often elides the splits and oppositions. Using the paradigm of split, this book offers a critique of pentecostal social life on a sophisticated critical-theoretical and philosophical basis.

The God of Pentecostals is split.⁷ This is because Pentecostals present God as divided, reality as a *not-All*, self as split, the sacred as separate from God, and their worldview is dangerously split. The split-God image of Pentecostals recapitulates on a small-scale God's split identity. The Godhead as decipherable from the specifics of divine-human relation flowing from pentecostal orthopraxis is marked by inconsistencies and splittings. This book shows that Pentecostalism's limitation to a split God, that is, the very practices, beliefs, rituals, and interactions that prevent Pentecostals from relating to or conceptualizing a harmonious, consistent God, is, at the same time, the positive condition to its access to a living, active, miracle-working God, and this partly explains its robust growth.

The analyses of Pentecostalism offered here extract this problematic kernel about God and spirituality that a doctrinaire, public pentecostal position simultaneously disavows and needs for its flourishing. As the Catholic writer G. K. Chesterton would put it, indeed, I am in this exercise approaching "a matter more dark and awful than it is easy to discuss; and I apologize in advance if any of my phrases fall wrong or seem irreverent touching a matter which the greatest saints and thinkers have just feared to approach."[8] In the story of Pentecostalism, which the cultured despisers disdain, there is a distinct philosophical suggestion that the Pentecostals' split-God image, in some unthinkable way, might just be reflected back into God Himself.

The pentecostal believer is a radically split entity. On one hand, she regards heaven as her real home; the contemporary world is full of sins and horrors of disobedience to God. She does not really belong to this world; she cannot find a home in the modern/postmodern world, so she thinks. On the other hand, the spiritual world is perfect. Spirit-filled life, global life dominated by the Holy Spirit lies ahead of the contemporary world, unattainable now. Instead of subordination of one to the other, the two are kept apart. They are separated by rotary motion of egotistic striving, "selfhood," or drives.[9] This split between the worlds, the fissure separating material home and spiritual home-to-come, is actually internal to the pentecostal self-identity and Pentecostalism itself.

Pentecostalism is an *idealist* "soul" invariably locked in a *materialist* body.[10] The main focus of idealism is to go from a confusing, fleeting phenomenal reality to the true reality. Pentecostals relentlessly simulate breaking the phenomenal veil for the hidden truths behind it—this is not too dissimilar to a dog on seeing its image going behind the mirror in search of the real dog behind it. Pentecostals' abiding interest of going beyond phenomenal reality to the permanent and true reality of the noumenal is idealism. Materialism, however, is concerned with how solid material bodies generate out of themselves "incorporeal" events.[11] Spiritual presences pervade and haunt Pentecostalism and are often generated by intersubjective relations, the interfacing of human bodies. The aesthetics of Pentecostalism is about how bodies generate "incorporeal" anointing events, noumenal events.[12] The coexistence of idealism *dispositif* and that of materialism in Pentecostalism marks a split, an unacknowledged gap in reality. There is a preexisting reality and its virtual one, a semblance created by idealism. Pentecostals' real life is somewhere *between*, a model of preexisting, material, real life and a semblance of a nonexistent life.[13] This split in pentecostal life or practices seems to have been transposed into the Absolute in a kind of Schellingian move.[14]

The God, qua a notion of Christian God, who inhabits this "between" with them is imagined by Pentecostals to be cracked, a real deity and its fantasmatic supplement; in him multiple, incompatible possibilities exist. From an infinite distance, the notion of pentecostal God is crafted to inspire awe. From a finite, immanent distance, it looks like something fabricated to be seen from an infinite distance away. At close range, one observes that the conceptual movement is not going to be from a holistic God to the split God and subsequently to a higher synthesis of the two opposing orientations. The inner logic of the pentecostal-conceptual fabrication is rather a radicalization of the split. God is living and active, not dead at all, but he is split. The split is not just phenomenal, it is ontological. Indeed, in the everyday life of Pentecostals, God is not an abstract universality but concrete universality.[15]

By this recognition, the book accomplishes a journey of moving from the God *of* Pentecostalism to God *in* Pentecostalism. The critical theoretical point in approaching God in *everyday pentecostal theology* is to ask what the functions of God and his external determinations or reflections are. The issue is not what God is, but what God Pentecostals want. The God that emerges in the picture teased together by these kinds of questions and issues takes a little getting used to from a nonpentecostal/charismatic perspective. The God in Pentecostalism is split. The split God acts in the stead of the simple God, acting as more God than the trinitarian God or the logically consistent doctrinaire God, while still positing itself to re-present the orthodox God.[16] (Pentecostals are not the trustees of Christianity, but seekers of the possibility of Christianity.)

The story or analysis of this discovery is told in a way akin to the cinematic format of *between two frames*, dealing with reflexive redoubling. The story of the split-God image is first taken as the full story (as given in the introduction), but it is reframed by the split orientation and ontologically incomplete reality of Pentecostals (as given in chapters 1–6). And what we see as Pentecostals' inconsistencies, unorthodox practices, and orientations to be explained is already a story of the split-God image. Pentecostals claim an immediate access to the true, essential functioning and character of the trans-phenomenal triune God. The problem is that when we examine their practices and readings of this God, there are conflicts and inconsistencies with the generally acceptable notion of God in the wider Christian world. How do we judge their claim? One approach is to say that only distorted reflections are accessible to them, wrong images of God deformed by their subjective perspective. No denomination can truly reflect God in its practices; a true correspondence between practices, rituals, beliefs, and interactions and the "essence" of God is unattainable.

But what if, in a way apropos to Hegel, the partial, distorted reflections—the fissure between practices and essence—are internal to the "essence" itself?[17] Whether we should limit the "true" meaning of God in/of Pentecostalism to a philosophy that limits itself to "external reflection" (all reflections of God in practice/appearance are only distorted and partial; the "true" functioning of God is in the unattainable beyond, and thus in crude analogy the economic trinity can never be the immanent trinity) or to a "determinate reflection." That is, the fissure between practices and appearance—the various readings, multiple interpretations, external determinations of the "essence"—is immanent to the essence itself. The split is internal; thus, from the human phenomenal standpoint the essence of any substance is appearance qua appearance. This book demonstrates that the multiplicity of practices in Pentecostalism strongly indicates that it has sided with the second approach. Ordinary Pentecostals (in the global south) may feel haunted by demons, but never by the specter of the unknowable God.[18] The unknowability of God is not an obstacle to their disposition to combine the attributes of God or to deploy them as partial organs in ways that affirm their view of reality and how to transform it. In mainstream academic theology, given the Kantian division between noumenal and the phenomenal, the unknowable God makes haunting possible within epistemological frameworks. This is generally not the case in Pentecostalism, as I have demonstrated elsewhere.[19] *Perhaps they know not what they do!*

The book also reveals the religious attitudes to the world that this approach (the notion of a split God) fosters among Pentecostals by examining the forms and contents of their practices and beliefs. We look closely at the following areas: spiritual discernment, divine grace, sacred sphere, day-to-day orientation to late capitalism, worship, and everyday theology. These practices and beliefs in turn enlighten, convince, and persuade Pentecostals about the reality, truth, and power of the split-God image. Studying Pentecostalism via the notion of a split God offers a distinctly new lens, which enables us to ground the abstract doctrine of God in concrete revelations, stories, and experiences of God's presence in the actual life-process of Pentecostals. What ordinary Pentecostals experience and know about God in humanity's planetary household offers a reliable guide to the immanent God. This new lens calls pentecostal theologians to a theory of God in which the material practices of Pentecostals express some truth about the one God of eternity. Such a theory should be made central to everyday pentecostal theology. This book, both as a form of inquiry and a methodology, focuses on the theoretical and philosophical significance of pentecostal practices.

There is no one Pentecostalism, but *Pentecostalisms*, and in a work like this invariably the following questions come up: What Pentecostalism do you have in mind in this book? What pentecostal context frames the discussions and analyses of this book? The primary social contexts are American and African frames, as these condition my interpretation of everyday folk engaged in pentecostal practice. I draw heavily from my experience and research in Africa and the United States to demonstrate how the specific sociocultural contexts in African countries in which the "microtheologies" play out are important to understanding the particularities of everyday theologies. Though Africa and America constitute my "constant points of reference, the conclusions from such are not intended for merely parochial uses, but can rather be taken as points of departure for an informed understanding of the varieties of [everyday forms of Pentecostalism or pentecostal microtheologies] within varying geographic and temporal frames."[20]

This book is dedicated to Dr. Mark Lewis Taylor, Maxwell M. Upson Professor of Theology and Culture at Princeton Theological Seminary, Princeton. He is my good friend and teacher. Taylor is my teacher in three ways. First, I took two doctoral seminars from him at Princeton Theological Seminary (Fall 2004: "Theory and Praxis in Theology," and Spring 2005: "Theology of Paul Tillich"). Second, he was my *Doktorvater*. (Thanks for your excellent guidance in 2006.) Finally, my thinking and approach to theology and social ethics are deeply influenced by the impact of his scholarship and teaching. I owe my love of radical continental philosophy and its deployment as a viable theological and social-ethical method in my own work to him. He was and he is still encouraging and cheering me on to always go beyond the deep originality and creativity, rigorous and finest standards, and exquisite and swift intellectual prowess of the scholarship of the leading thinkers of our time. He wants me to be the best. Professor Taylor, you are the greatest! This is the *Reader's Digest* version of the book for you: I uncovered what most Pentecostals are doing to (the notion of) God in God's holy name and I translated their doings into a theory, which I then set into conversation with some of the best minds in today's global philosophico-theoretical scene. While at this, I performed acts of both re-cognition and resistance on Pentecostalism, demonstrating how to departicularize pentecostal studies. This book affirms, invites, and challenges schools of thinking.

Behold, this book is set for the *fall* and *rising* of many theologies in Pentecostalism. It is destined to provoke into being a book that will cause the Copernican Revolution in pentecostal theology. This book is a sign that says: "What meanest thou, O sleeper? Arise, wake up from your dogmatic slumber, and write the book!"

—Nimi Wariboko
Westwood, Massachusetts
February 22, 2017

Introduction

The study of Pentecostalism is in the ascendancy. Scholars have used the lens of social theory to study global Pentecostalism. Theologians have taken to postmodern approaches to construct pentecostal theologies and others have called for postmodern engagements with Pentecostalism. And yet there is no book that specifically attempts to bring critical theory to examine or investigate the determinate practices and theologies of global Pentecostalism. This book fills that gap in scholarship. It fills the gap by bringing critical social theory to bear not on academic (systematic, constructive) pentecostal theologies, but on the everyday forms of theologies, lived pentecostal practices. Reading pentecostal practices in the light of critical theory will be meaningless unless pentecostal practices are also used, in turn, to interrogate critical theory and mainstream academic theologies. This is what we do in the context of the idea and practice (performance) of split God in Pentecostalism. The book adopts a transdisciplinary methodology to bring pentecostal studies, critical theory, theology, and social ethics together to investigate an everyday form of religion, to reflect on microtheologies occurring at everyday practices, and to make sense of global pentecostal identity. Within this methodological strategy, it privileges pentecostal sources at the grassroots.

Though I developed my ideas by interacting with a host of critical theorists (especially Slavoj Žižek, Jacques Lacan, Jean-Luc Nancy, and Giorgio Agamben), I always begin by citing pentecostal sources (data, worship, expectation of miracles, prayer, quest for prosperity and health, beliefs, behaviors, hopes, and ideas from everyday forms of practice) and then use critical theory (a tradition in continental philosophy) to rethink them. Without eschewing academic discourse, everyday forms of religious practice are here considered as adequate sources for philosophical, theological, and social ethical reflection. This preferential option for the practices of "ordinary" Pentecostals is what I call microtheology or microtheologies. Critical theory (especially when equipped with a social scientific/psychoanalytic/Marxist lens) of all the threads within continental philosophy, in my judgment, is most suitable for this kind of work because it easily lends itself to deep appreciation and interrogation of practices and discourses of global Pentecostalism.

The aim of this book is to reveal the operative notion of God in the everyday forms of Pentecostalism and to examine how it conditions Pentecostals' social-ethical behavior in different spheres of their lives. We will not be concerned with God in the abstract, but precisely with how a particular tradition understands and deploys the concept of God in concrete practices. There is no textbook or philosophical God to be found apart from the God that believers know and perform or is discernible from their daily practices. When examined through the lens of critical theory, the God that is discernible from pentecostal practices is a split God. The pentecostal God appears to distance himself from himself. For God to emerge as divine *subject* to Pentecostals, a certain move from "Substance to Subject must occur within God himself," as in the emergence of human subjectivity from substantial personality in Hegelian philosophy.[1] The God who is summoned in prayers and deliverance services, pressed to perform endless miracles, and solicited in daily lives is alienated, separated, split from his substantial content, from his divine attributes, properties. Then by the sheer power of faith, persistent prayers, and name-it-and-claim-it techniques, these attributes as carriers of God's power and presence are summoned as partial organs to work independently of God himself. God or God's universal substance is objectivized or particularized. God is split from God! For religious studies this is an important finding, and for theological studies it opens the door to compare classical doctrine of God in mainline denominations or theological tomes with the "God" that Pentecostals think they know or encounter in their daily lives.

In its functioning in the everyday forms of Pentecostalism, the split-God model teams up with three other forms of split: split reality (ontological incompleteness), split selves (split subjectivity), and split worldview (dualism/"en-spirited matter"[2]). First, there is a belief in ontological incompleteness, which is a condition of being or existence. The second form relates to the subjectivity of the pentecostal believer as split; the pentecostal self caught between the care of the soul (the spiritual world they want to inherit) and the care of external material things, the desires and nomos of this world. Finally, the pentecostal worldview is split between the noumenal (invisible) and the phenomenal (visible), but the noumenal could also be considered as an intensification of phenomenal perception. Each of these distinct notions of split (they are actually dimensions of one notion) constitute a rhizomatic network in the everyday form of Pentecostalism. The network not only accounts philosophically for each of the others, but also provides each of them a broader basis of their fitness within the practices we are analyzing. Part of the work of this introduction is to make the pentecostal everyday notion of a split God clear and coherent. Also, in every chapter of the book, further explanations are provided of the notion of split as applied in the context of the discussions in the chapter, so the reader can easily keep in view which dimension of the notion of split is in focus and how it is interacting with others.

The Notion of a Split God

For a hundred years now it appears there is always an ongoing debate on the living condition or the existential status of God. A debate that structures how we perceive reality. There was a time in history when everybody believed that God is alive and exists. Then Friedrich Nietzsche and some theologians came along and told us that God is dead. Not long after Nietzsche declared his medical verdict, the Pentecostals arrived almost from out of the blue with fury, enthusiasm, and dedication to proclaim that God is alive, he exists, but he is split. Their practices also suggest that they (implicitly and explicitly) believe in an ontological incompleteness in reality, being. And now we have the maverick Slovenian philosopher Slavoj Žižek ardently arguing that God is dead and split; his violent splitting occurred when Jesus Christ (God-become-man) cried on the cross: "Father, why hast thou forsaken me?" According to Žižek, the cry not only revealed God's impotence, but also brought God to realize his own impotence: "The gap that separates the suffering, desperate man . . . from God is transposed into God Himself, as His own radical splitting or, rather, self-abandonment."[3] Žižek's main point of interest in his argument is that the "death of God" compels human beings to face reality as an internally inconsistent and incomplete whole.

My book examines in depth the various ideas, concepts, beliefs, and actions Pentecostals take to demonstrate their investment in the notion of a split of God and cracks in reality. Pentecostal practices of discernment, relating to the work of grace, and technology of subjectivation, understanding of the working of the sacred, pure worship, and the modulation of an everyday form of theology cannot be adequately grasped within the framework of reality as a consistent, harmoniously ordered whole. Reality (and by extension their notion of God) is full of cracks, and those who want to understand it must think in terms of dialectics of gaps.

The scholars and those death-of-God theologians who have made a volte-face to acknowledge the resurrection of God amid the public resurgence of religion are overlooking a problem. The problem is that the dead-and-revived God that academics now celebrate or ponder in their ivory towers is not the same God that "died." The God the Pentecostals have resurrected, so to speak, is not the transcendental, holistic, philosophers', systematic theology God, but a split God. The God walking the streets and eating fish with Pentecostals at various campgrounds, passing through walls into storefront churches, and stooping to enter chicken coops as cathedrals is cracked, incomplete. Pentecostals have introduced a gap/cut into the traditional notion of God; certain attributes and dimensions of God are mobilized in practices or prayers as if they are self-standing instead of being an organic whole. This gap is eventually inscribed into God. Pentecostalism first tears apart God and then brings the manifold parts together into a contingent synthesis for their pragmatic, utilitarian purposes. If Nietzsche's mad man in the market shouted, "We have killed him," and theologians in the 1960s bellowed in hallowed academic halls, "God is dead," Pentecostal believers or thaumaturgists are today shouting in the public square, "God is split."

Here, to use Giorgio Agamben's philosophy, by split I mean the opening up of the inherited, orthodox notion of God—its aims and modalities—into new possible uses. The activity of splitting deactivates the traditional notion of God and radicalizes it, disposing it toward a new use without abolishing the old use that "persists in it and exhibits it."[4] In the practice of splitting, Pentecostals not only separate—without abandoning orthodoxy—the inherited notion of God from its orthodox grounding, but also "parts" and "attributes" of God are separated from Godself and are exhibited in their separation from Godself, becoming *spectacles*. It is precisely through the mode of "consuming" the spectacles that the gap that separates suffering, desperate humans from God is transposed into God as a split within Godself or God's own splitting and the deactivation of the traditional notion of God is effected. In all this there is a heedlessness toward clear differences between orthodoxy and nonorthodoxy.

The starting point for grasping the Pentecostals' view of God as split is to focus on their inclination toward the non-All, non-whole, of reality. Because Pentecostals believe that there are cracks in reality, tears in the phenomenal curtain over the noumenal that allow "miracles" to eventuate or spirit-filled believers to access things-in-themselves, their actions cannot reflect a harmoniously ordered God. Many philosophers maintain that the non-whole structure of reality—ontological incompleteness—implies that there is no master-signifier guaranteeing the harmonious order of reality. So when we perceive the God behind the everyday actions of Pentecostals and structure of belief, what comes out is an inconsistent one, with splits and cracks all over his being.

The Pentecostal God is a running skein of threads and parts, flung and scattered among several practices like divided messiah's garments at Calvary. Thus a simplistic traditional reading of the biblical God into the pentecostal vision of God as actualized in practice will wind up not making sense of their everyday theo-talk. Pentecostals confess with their mouths: "God, God, God of Abraham, Isaac, and Jacob," but their actions reflect a God or reality that is incomplete, a not-All. The Pentecostal God is not the God of the philosophers and theologians that died, he is not the Orthodox (Bible-only defined) God, but a particular way of structuring the relation between orthodoxy and lawful (Christianly) transgression of orthodoxy. Far from being the solution to the problem of death-of-God theology, the Pentecostal God is rather the name of an impasse, a useful problem. "It is precisely as an enigma that the [Pentecostal split God] can today help us to grasp certain unthought dimensions of our [religious] situations. As Chesterton says in his *Orthodoxy*, 'man can understand everything by the help of what he does not understand.'"[5]

The essence of a split God is not thought-induced. It did not originate from careful theological ruminations, but in Pentecostals' social practices. This does not mean that it is merely a practical tool. It is an objective form through which Pentecostals grasp their world. The abstraction of a split God from the harmonious God is not metaphorical in meaning. It is literal and ultimately foundational for pentecostal religious consciousness. The religious notion of God resulting from the abstraction is characterized by a complete absence of holism, a differentiation purely by separability (partial, limited, non-All) and by applicability to every kind of intercourse that occurs in the divine-human relation.[6]

This means that the God Pentecostals "see" is never whole, not because they lack the mental capacity to comprehend a comprehensive and systematic (notion of) God, but because they are always in the picture that bears witness to their God-world relations. Their position is not that of an external observer who can grasp the whole of God, divine-human relations, or objective reality. Their notion of a split God is a "reflexive twist by means of which [they] are included in the picture [of God] constituted by [them]. It is in this reflexive short circuit, this necessary redoubling of [themselves] as standing both outside and inside"; that is, their picture of God that bears witness to their notion of a split God. God is split and never "whole," or reality is split and non-All because it "contains a stain, a blind spot which mediates [their] inclusion in it."[7]

Only a few practical persons ("fundamentalists") can claim to have a comprehensive (All) notion of reality or God. The God we claim to know ("see") is always split. Adrian Johnson makes this point well when he says, "What appears as external reflection (i.e., the gaze of the subject on the substance) is not confined to an epistemological field separated off from the reflected-upon reality of being. Rather than being external, this reflection is inscribed in the reality of being upon which it reflects as an internal inflection, an immanent folding-back of substance on itself; the gaze of the subject upon the substance is substance-as-not-all gazing upon itself."[8]

It is in this sense of a split God (juxtaposition of holism—All—and separability (partial, non-All) that we venture to say that all religious views of God are "commodified." Karl Marx taught us that at the heart of commodity fetishism or abstraction is the separation of quality (use value) from quantity. The natural intercourse of commodities in the market pivots around their exchange value (quantity, monetarily quantifiable value), and use value is what belongs to them as objects. In the market commodities stand face-to-face, talk and exchange glances as objects characterized by total abstraction from use value. The God we encounter in various religions or forms of Christianity has been abstracted from wholeness, God-intrinsicness. The God of a religion reflects only "quantity" (institutionally/doctrinally quantifiable value such as the sacrifice to end all sacrifice or murder of innocent victims, the lamb for our sins, a good harvest, or bringing rain during a drought, and so on). "Quantity" is a performance we can measure against other gods, technology, or political powers and their value-as-performance, value-as-responsiveness—and as an intrinsic quality. Just as in the market the merchant is not interested in the use value of commodities but in their exchange values, we are not also interested in the use "value" (the in-itself quality, which we cannot know) of God, but in God's performance. Both the performance value and the split God that results from it are born of "fetishistic inversion." Enjoy your truth!

Pentecostals, perhaps, overenjoy this truth. In their way of seeing, the gap, cut, split between subject and substance, subject and object, human and God is reinscribed into being, substance, into God. God is split. The external limitation (the limited conceptualization of God amid the divine-human relation) turns into God's self-limitation. Or rather, more precisely, the split God that emerged out of multiple processes of practices is retroactively inscribed into God.

In the philosophical sense, we might argue the gap/split that Pentecostals see in God is perhaps the place where God is exposed to human beings and human beings are exposed to God. The gap represents gestures to divine existence between two sites: immanence and transcendence; the wound of transcendent immanence. The gap represents a border unto experience of divine-human relation, the spot where divine aloofness confronts human suffering and vulnerability. This border experience is inscribed unto the transimmanent Holy Spirit as a form of space, so to speak.

The gap is the exteriority of God, the spacing of experience of contact with human beings, of the outside, the outside-of-self, to use Jean-Luc Nancy's language.[9] God is posed in exteriority. The gap gestures to "an outside *in the very intimacy* of an inside."[10] It is important to further clarify what is meant by gap as space. The space is not a place, but the sharing of the edges of Being and beings, their spacing. It is a locus or nexus of mutual interactions: a condition of possibility for the existence of interactions. Conceptually speaking, where is this space or locus to be located? There are three possibilities: a space outside of God, a space within God in some sense, or the space as identical to divine-human relation. The first is not acceptable because it means that Godness is grounded in an external source. Nor can the space be identical to God, since it is itself the result of interactions between God and human beings, an other. Thus, I suggest that it is within (as being-with, "an outside in the very intimacy of an inside") God, more precisely *within* divine-human relation, where God and humans are not just juxtaposed but are actually exposed to one another. The space is the basis of interactions, inseparable from divine-human relation, to be sure, but nevertheless distinguishable from it. So when we say the gap is inscribed into God, it does not mean it is a laceration in the being of God. God (God's body) remains in his (its) most intimate trinitarian folds exposed to the outside. Like an open mouth,

Godness or God's body "exposes to the 'outside' an 'inside' that, without this exposition, [divine-human relation] would not exist."[11]

The pentecostal notion of a split God, as we shall demonstrate in the chapters ahead, is not merely an epistemological exercise. It both "ontologizes" and "deontologizes" the critical construct of God that has come to reign in the modern church and the implicit notion of God that is behind God-is-dead theology. It is important to pay attention to the tensions of ontologization and deontologization in the pentecostal construct of split God as we can glean from the practices of Pentecostals, not from their academic theological tomes. The notion of God in the modernist church and among the death-of-God theologians pivots around an epistemological scheme. The God that died in academe or melts away in the pews was inaccessible, not knowable, and this non-knowability as part of reality was never questioned. God was an external inaccessible entity, and the gap that separates human beings from God was mainly an epistemological obstacle as the noumenal realm was left as inaccessible and all that was needed was to ignore it. While still believing in their capacity to penetrate the noumenal realm, conservative Pentecostals did what the liberal Christians could not do; they transformed the epistemological obstacle to positive ontological condition: the gap between us and God has now become a positive feature of God. Our incomplete knowledge of God or reality becomes a positive feature of God or reality, which is itself incomplete.[12] In this respect the pentecostal notion of God emanating from an everyday form of theology is both ontologizing and deontologizing. By not supposing that the gap is merely epistemological as in presupposing reality as a whole and thus "introducing a gap into the very texture of reality" and God, their notion of a split God deontologizes the modernist or death-of-God-theology notion of God. But by still believing in "a fully constituted noumenal realm existing out there," they at the same time ontologize the modernist or death-of-God-theology notion of God.[13] In other words, the pentecostal notion of God not only negates the theme of God's death, but also redescribes the God that supposedly died. God is not dead; he is split. Pentecostals' everyday form of theology is both subtractive and multiplicative. On one hand while they took away some of the metaphysical ballast of modernist theology by collapsing the distinction between appearance and true reality of traditional ontology with the notion of split reality and God, on the other they invested more in the domain of noumenal things-in-themselves that is anchored by the split God.[14] Pentecostal everyday theology is full of contradictions, and we cannot grasp it unless we work carefully through tensions to reconcile opposites. The contradictions and their dialectics conceal the creative impulse of the Pentecostal movement.

The task of pentecostal philosophy for pentecostal scholars is in unearthing this creative impulse, articulating the ideas of the new, the Pentecostal principle inherent to the movement and betrayed by their actualizations in practice. The way forward is to *repeat* these ideas so as to redeem their failure. By repetition I do not mean the reproduction of the old, but the emergence of the new through a reworking of the *virtuality* inherent to old ideas and revisiting paths not taken as we attempt to do in this book. As Žižek argues, far from being opposed,

> [t]he emergence of the New, the proper Deleuzian paradox is that something truly New can ONLY emerge through repetition. What repetition repeats is not the way the past "effectively was," but the *virtuality* inherent to the past and betrayed by its past actualization. In this precise sense, the emergence of the New changes the past itself, that is, it retroactively changes (not the actual past—we are not in science fiction—but) the balance between actuality and virtuality in the past. Recall the old example provided by Walter Benjamin: the October Revolution repeated the French Revolution, redeeming its failure, unearthing and repeating the same impulse. Already for Kierkegaard, repetition is "inverted memory," a movement forward, the production of the New, and not the reproduction of the Old. "There is nothing new under the sun" is the strongest contrast to the movement of repetition. So, it is not only that repetition is (one of the modes of) emergence of the New—*the New can ONLY emerge through repetition*.[15]

So how do we repeat an idea from everyday theology of Pentecostalism in critical religious studies such as this book? It is by staying close to the structure and dynamics immanent in the position of the idea. We need to "trace the trajectories that are 'extimate' (i.e., intimately and internally external, endogenously exogenous) with respect to" everyday Pentecostalism insofar as they are consequent extensions of everyday theology in pentecostal everyday theology more than pentecostal everyday theology itself.[16]

Piety and danger are extimate in pentecostal everyday theology. The Pentecostal worldview is essentially split from within. There is a part that is faithful to the received tradition of Christian faith or conservative biblical orientation and there is always another part that threatens to exceed the bounds of the faith, make common cause with liberal, secular forms of explanation or understanding. These two are at the heart of the pentecostal worldview and co-constitute a tension that is always at the brink of breaking loose but not quite getting there yet. There is a core and there is an excessive core. There is always already what is in Pentecostalism more than Pentecostalism itself, more than its explicit theology. There is always the danger of overidentifying with the inherent and excessive core, and the excess escaping as a monstrosity. This excess is not external to pentecostal piety; it is a logical and integral counterpart of it, on the arc of being a faithful Pentecostal. As we have already shown, the pentecostal notion of God is orthodox but at the same time immanently related to a notion of God outside orthodox Christianity. This notion, like many other ideas and practices in the worldwide Pentecostal movement, stands inside and outside the Christian tradition. It appears that in the movement's practices there is no fundamental distinction between core and excessive core. None of them possess an existence independent of the other. There is unity and identity between them as they are parts of one single principle: the *Pentecostal principle*, the capacity to begin, to initiate something new. No operation of the core lacks an excessive dimension, just as the excessive core does not lack a manifestation of the core. The Pentecostal principle in reality is the result of the union of the core and excessive core.

Let us, for example, consider one of the issues as it relates to the subjectivity of God. For Pentecostals, the *emergence* of God's subjectivity is dependent on the belief that the Holy Spirit is persuaded to give the very substance of his being (his creative power) as an exchangeable value on the altar (market) of prayers and offering. There is no subjectivity of God without the kenotic emptying of God's substantial-positive being to mortal, sinful, fragile creatures, to human beings. We are dealing with a split between God Almighty—the sovereign, omnipotent ruler of heaven and earth—and God the benevolent giver, who is persuadable. If God the giver is to emerge at the level of God the Almighty, he must pour out his creative powers on demand. ("Name-it-and-claim-it theology" is only one example.) This is to say that God in pentecostal practice must already be persuaded by the logic of exchange or submitted to the norms of reciprocity.[17]

The place to understand the powerfulness of God is not the form of power but in its very content. From the pentecostal understanding of

God's subjectivity, it appears God not only maintains a vague distance to his sovereignty, but enacts its disavowal in relating to human beings, saying as it were, "I use my sovereignty, but I am not performatively bound by sovereignty." God appears not to believe in his sovereignty—he is split from his omnipotence. There are Christians who do not believe in the sovereignty of God; however, only in the virulent form of wealth-and-health Pentecostalism does God not believe in his sovereignty. The "unplugged" character of God's sovereignty makes the contents of the Spirit's creative power available to everyone who can ask. The "unplugged" stance permits "faith-filled" Christians to "indulge in some extra-legal pleasures." The Almighty God is split at the altar of Pentecostals and he is put back together as an all-purpose giver. This is the ultimate logic of the pentecostal "name-and-claim-it" practice.[18]

The pentecostal construction of God's subjectivity is the obverse of its notion of pure substanceless subjectivity at the individual believer's level. As John the Baptist said of Jesus Christ, "He must increase, but I must decrease" (John 3:30 NIV), so the Pentecostal believer decreases in her substance (so to speak) as she grows in faith, becomes a subject of God. For the believer, her subjectivity is dependent on being reduced to the "almost nothing" of an abject beggar. Is the Pentecostal believer the true subject/substance then? No. The Pentecostal's self-effacing, almost self-erasure is only a pathway into intercourse or exchange with a God emptying his creative goods on her. This is why Paul's willingness to become disposable excrement (Phil. 3:8) so he will attain the resurrection from the dead (Phil. 3:8, often read out of context) appeals to many a Pentecostal. Dung—making the self a dung—incorporates one into the economy of divine exchange.

In this way the formulations of God's subjectivity and the believer's subjectivity enable Pentecostals to enjoy "pagan pleasures" (believing that God incites his subjects to enjoy). Their access to jouissance depends on their ability to separate God's sovereignty and God's creative power, to violate the simplicity of God. Pentecostals give a positive accent to God's omnipotence and sovereignty but actually act or desire to transgress it. Pentecostalism valorizes the "unplugged" stance of God toward his sovereignty, but it is combined with the love of "pagan pleasures." This is the "perverse core" (in the Lacanian sense) of Pentecostalism, and the work of many defenders of Pentecostalism is to find a nonperverse way to explain this innermost kernel of the movement's understanding of divine-human relation.

What do all these tensions about the idea of God in pentecostal everyday theology suggest? Do the tensions (contradictions?) put Pentecostals outside the ballpark of rational theology? Or do they raise new questions that beg for answers or responses? They suggest at least three things. First, the transcendental, God does not completely structure the practices and performances of the different worlds of different groups of Christianity. Second, the tensions raise the thought that there is no consistent totality that Christianity can name as God. Third, it may well mean that the tensions (the elusiveness of characterization) of pentecostal interpretation of God belong to God himself. It is necessary to think, practice, and perform God but yet impossible to decide what God is in a *logocentric* style. And it is impossible to decide on the basis of the Bible (an experience) that the dimensions or aspects of God accented by Pentecostals are not of God. The question remains undecidable and yet calls for the necessity of a decision on how to think and practice God. This originary decision, the place of impossible possibility of a decision, is part of any faith in God or any particular Christian denomination's orientation to (belief in) God. Pentecostalism like any other denomination or movement is a *truth procedure*; "that is to say: it is something relying on something undecidable . . . which necessitates a decision that then produces consequences brought about by a faith subject."[19]

The decision we so make constitutes not only a theory of God, but it is also constitutive of our epistemology and ontology (insofar as, Hegel demonstrates, it is impossible to have an epistemology without an ontology).[20] As we have shown in the foregoing pages, the tension-ridden experience and practices are ultimately based on an inconsistent realm of non-All, which is the *Real* of reality. Pentecostalism is a Christianity of the non-All. It shows that there is no consistent (meta) doctrinal standpoint from which the relation between the idea (or ideas) of God and practical (phenomenal) inconsistency could be explained. Not only is the idea of God incomplete, inconsistent, but also the practices, phenomena, of any denomination (including Pentecostalism) are inconsistent. And the relation between idea and practice is also inconsistent. Pentecostalism is a performing symptom, a display of these consistencies, of a non-All reality. The inconsistency reminds us that there is no complete chain of causality that runs between idea and phenomena. If the chain of causality is complete, harboring no gap, the new will not happen. The new occurs only when there are gaps in the chain of causality. For the new to occur, the force of becoming, actualization, cannot be totally tied to the confines of the idea. In any case, there are even gaps at the level of the idea, so the chain of complete causality cannot even take place with the most faithful practice. The paradox of Pentecostalism is that it maintains fidelity to the founding religious belief in the complete chain of causality by not obeying it. In the nitty-gritty of daily material life, Pentecostals express solidarity with the complete potency of the chain while gaining access to jouissance by violating it.

The paradoxes, tensions, or the incessant dancing of Pentecostals at the boundary of "heresy" are bound to give those who are not very familiar with Pentecostalism the impression that it is almost theologically promiscuous, expressing "the threatening image of a community with uncontrolled boundaries."[21] They weave in and out of Christian tradition or orthodoxy in their expectation of the new and surprises of the Holy Spirit.

Pentecostal everyday theology is a *paleonomic* gesture in the sense that it simultaneously erases and preserves the Christian tradition. Paleonomy, according to Jacques Derrida, is the "maintenance of an *old name* in order to launch a new concept."[22] It is a strategy of the person who wants to conquer from within a system. "A paleonomic gesture requires us to stand inside and outside a tradition at the same time, perpetuating the tradition while breaking with it, and breaking with the tradition while perpetuating it."[23] In this gesture is the piety and danger that I mentioned earlier. But at the same time, the perspective of piety and danger enables us to investigate the pentecostal notion of God, which eludes theorization, as a paleonomy. In this way, I hope to present the current study as critical theoretical engagements with the practical and as practical engagements with the Žižekian critical religious theory, slipping and sliding between religious critical theoretical critique of pentecostal religious thinking and production of new thinking about pentecostal religion.

So this book is a work of tracing out the paleonomy, piety and danger, and tensions in pentecostal everyday thought. Paul Tillich in his *The Protestant Era* says, "Those who want to know the power of reality in the depth of their historical existence must be in actual contact with the unrepeatable tensions of the present."[24] In the following chapters I raise a series of tensions, which should be of interest to social scientists, pentecostal theologians, and religious studies scholars.

The Structure of the Book

The point of departure of this study is the observation that God is split; that pentecostal practices suggest that there is a primordial crack both in

God and reality itself. In the preceding pages we have addressed systematically the theoretical questions regarding this observation emanating from the biblical, pragmatic, and psychological contexts of Pentecostalism. The theoretical-analytical responses are further developed and substantiated through case studies and modes of conceptualization of pentecostal practices in the chapters ahead. Each of the case studies offers a different perspective on how the implicit or explicit belief in a split God threads through empirical pentecostal practices. There are six case studies—constituting six chapters (2–7) of the book—and they represent six modes or conceptualizations of practices: discernment, grace, sacred, subjectivity, worship, and the everyday form of theology. The case studies analyze different patterns of performing a presentation of the (notion of) a split God. It is true that the six chapters illustrate how the notion of a split God is embedded in everyday pentecostal practices, but nevertheless the case studies transcend the mere theoretical-analytical construct of the split God. I have tried as much as possible to respect the richness and complexity of the six practices, even as they illuminate different contexts of action of the one split God in the social reality of lived Pentecostal practice. The ultimate test of the relevance of any of the case studies is the ability to throw new light upon Pentecostals' collective self-understanding of themselves and their God. The case studies cannot prove our theoretical-analytical construct of the split God. While the practices amply illustrate the notion of the split God, we cannot say one is the cause of the other because of the inherent reflexivity of pentecostal practice. On one hand, the Pentecostals may be seen as the effect of applying the notion of a split God to their everyday existence; on the other hand, the notion may itself be the condition of possibility of the practices. Pentecostals, like any other religious believers, are simultaneously the subjects and objects of doctrines or notions.

Let me now offer a rationale for choosing these six particular case studies. They each serve to illustrate instances of various types of the split of God or reality. Chapter 2 on discernment shows that Pentecostals desire to pierce the phenomenal veil over reality and this presupposes a cracked reality. What gives them the impression that they can see through to "things-in-themselves"? They believe the ability comes from a heady abundance of the grace of God—or anointing—in their lives. We examine grace (in chapter 3) as an empowerment that "opens up" already existing gaps in reality that they exploit for their own flourishing and for *performing* of salvation or presentation of miracles. Based on the belief in cracked, split reality and unmediated access to the powers of the noumenal realm, chapter 4 (on the sacred) crafts a pentecostal theory of sacrality. The theory of sacrality revolves around Pentecostals' understanding of miracles, which is very complex as miracles are deemed to arise both from phenomenal and noumenal realms and raises the question whether God is the sacred or the sacred is split between an Other-God and an immanent dimension. Chapter 5 throws light upon pentecostal subjectivity, which is fidelity to the crack opened up by divine grace in the believer's life, liberating the self from forms of power that inhibits human flourishing and economic prosperity by exploiting the powers of the sacred. Next, we consider worship. Worship is not only the pentecostal perennial festival of grace, but it is also the energizing and defining core of the pentecostal lifeworld. It is the site in the daily encounter with God where all the other practices integrate and cohere as a crazy quilt of pulsating divine-human relation. Chapter 6 presents the pristine pentecostal idea of worship as pure mediality, where the pulsating mass of divine-human relations floats above calculations and the instrumentality of the nitty-gritty materiality of everyday life. Chapter 7 ("Everyday Form of Theology: Between Pentecostal Apparatus and Prosaic Existence") shows how everyday Pentecostals consume and produce their own theology. It shows how folks appropriate the sermons and prescriptions for disciplining their bodies that come out of the pulpits to creatively produce their own *wearable* theology to further fit their "bodies," their lifestyles in the here and now, or to circulate meanings and pleasures. We see how folks collect a bricolage of resources to produce meanings and pleasures and to resist or evade the containment or disciplinary efforts of the pulpit or social system. The chapter ends with a brief methodological discussion on how to reconstruct the everyday theology of believers in their lifeworlds dealing with and reinventing the notion of a split God. Finally, the concluding essay reveals the "theological excess," religious "too-muchness," that informs the everyday life of Pentecostals. This discussion is not really a conclusion; it is rather an unconcluding postscript.

Now the careful reader would have already noticed that we skipped introducing chapter 1. This chapter is not a case study; it is rather a foundational theoretical analysis of the day of Pentecost (Acts 2). It shows that the notion of the split God is rooted in the inaugural, "originary" event of Pentecost, the very *ur*-moment of the Christian church. The stories of the practices, rituals, beliefs that we relate in chapters 2–7 are the tracing, rearticulations, and reticulation of the *primordial* split in the life of Pentecostals.

While the foregoing states the point of departure for this study, it does not relate the impulse behind the study. It also does not tell us how the connections between the chapters are not just linear, proceeding from one practice to another as if each one is in a silo. Together the chapters perform the production of knowledge via the woof and warp of interconnections, helping us to come to terms theoretically and practically with the story of God or the lens with which God is viewed in a certain Christian community. During my research, there was a realization that the dominant philosophers or theologians of Pentecostalism were of little help when it comes to telling the story of a split God in everyday Pentecostalism and making philosophical sense out of it.

This book tells the story of how Pentecostals at the grassroots perceive God, rather than as doctrine or a systematic theological figure finely decorated and proportioned by scholars. It puts the Christian God in a radically new perspective, which appears to be resisting learned notions of God that seem bookish, cold, or contrived. For all the recent scholarly attention given to the study of Pentecostalism, surprisingly little effort has been devoted to the movement's bottom-up notion of God. What is the portrait of God deep in the grain of the extraordinary, creative practices and popular imaginations of Pentecostals and what do they reveal about their perceptions and working of God? I tease out here a portrait of God as discernible from varied practices and daily engagement with the sacred, practices of discernment, appropriation of divine grace, and subject-formation. Each practice has "plowed all the Bible and cut it [in] holes," and each has its God at the end of its trace, molded by the nitty-gritty materiality of everyday needs, fears, and hopes.[25]

What kind of God will a person encounter if she goes into a pentecostal church and, instead of asking "tell me who God is," observes how God is talked about, approached, courted, performed, and enacted as a real presence? What will emerge is not an impressionist painting of God, but an expressionist one. God comes out neither as a photograph of Godself in the Bible nor as the idealized image of God in systematic theological tomes. The type that emerges attempts to convey to an observer Pentecostals' deepest levels of engagement with and profound participation in the transimmanent Holy Spirit and reality. This expressionist portrait, as we have already demonstrated, distorts the reality or traditional notions of God in order to accent other features that resonate more with them in their intensive participation in the divine being.

This expressionist picture of God is the fertile ground for everyday Pentecostals' "theological" understanding of discernment, grace, the sacred realm, subjectivity, and worship, which often does not fail to leave an *impression* of the power and reality of the Holy Spirit even on the most skeptical observers.[26] This book offers a glimpse of this picture of God, painted by people who are fervently committed to Jesus Christ and are grasped by the Holy Spirit.

Its chapters are, therefore, arranged to enable the reader to see the portrait's major brush strokes and their interconnections. The six case-study chapters of the book are finely related in two pairs (chapters 2 and 5, and 3 and 6); two single chapters act as either a node/"ground" or as the "roof" of ideas expressed in the other chapters. Chapters 2 and 5 represent two ways of looking at the pentecostal subject. In chapter 2 ("Spiritual Discernment: Bathroom Mirror as Metaphor"), we see him or her discerning (judging and making distinctions in life situations and then reaching decisions based on evaluation) on issues based on the belief of split (non-All) reality. Here we see how the notion of a split God produces subjects in the combined sense of being subjected *to* and being subject *of* a particular belief. In chapter 5 ("The Impossible Possibility, Capitalism, and the Pentecostal Subject"), we examine the subject turning the split in reality, an impossible possibility into a make-believe economic space for relating and conniving with late capitalism. In the pentecostal articulation, it is the belief in split reality that provides the dialectical link between subjectivization and "abundant life" in capitalism.

Chapter 3 ("The Beauty, Skin, and Monstrosity of Grace") dwells on grace, the pentecostal *logic of sense* as grace that dances on and off bodies of believers, and the monstrosity of grace. The Absolute or God that Pentecostals say they can access through the crack in reality is fragile, as flashes or bursts of energies in the matrix of bodies. In the hands of Pentecostals, grace works like dark energy. Unlike other kinds of matter that pushes away, dark energy pulls together. The difference is that most other kinds of matter are under pressure, whereas dark energy is under tension. But when the tension increases enough, dark energy does the opposite; instead of pulling the universe together, it leads to an acceleration of the expansion of the universe.[27] Pentecostals' firm belief in the work of grace pulls them close to the rest of Christians, but their exuberant stance on the miraculous appears to be pushing them away from Christianity into the unChristianity core of Christianity. Pentecostalism inhabits a space that undermines distinction between Christianity and non-Christianity. This occurs in the same vein as when we say a "person is inhuman" instead of "he is not human," a new space beyond humanity and its negation is opened up. "'He is not human' means simply that he is external to humanity, animal or divine, while 'he is inhuman' means something thoroughly different, namely that he is neither human nor not-human, but marked by a terrifying excess which, although negating what we understand as 'humanity,' is inherent to being human."[28]

Grace as pure means (as we shall see later) not only supports the peculiar subject formation of Pentecostals—subjects subjugated to capital—but also undergirds the pure form for worship. Pentecostal worship is a pure means (the subject of chapter 6: "Worship as Pure Means"). Grace in the form of labile, malleable divine power is not means but pure manifestation. As Ruth Marshall puts it, "As the figure of ultimate sovereignty and historical agency, the power of God through the Holy Spirit takes the form of a pure manifestation, rather than simply a means to whose end is salvation."[29] In my 2012 book, *Pentecostal Principle*, I argue that the pentecostal attitude "allows" miraculous divine grace to float between the serious matter of saving the soul and ordinary, ephemeral, bodily, existential matters, relieving it of the weight of eternal life. Divine grace in the hands of the Pentecostals has become a pure means, means without ends. Thus Pentecostalism becomes part of the gigantic apparatus of late capitalism that converts every object into means. In this way, Pentecostalism and its subject formation make common cause with late capitalism.[30]

The "monstrosity" of pentecostal grace is also discernible in its worship or the idea of worship as pure mediality (medium), not as something instrumental, but as free selfless offering to God. We often hear Pentecostals express the view that their worship service is pure, or at least they aspire toward a pure worship, *just worship*. But this supposedly noble idea or orientation to worship (the splitting of means and ends) expresses a "perverse core" of pentecostal everyday form of theology. Perversity "is what remains embedded, coiled, and concealed within the very illusions of normativity."[31] The condition of worship as pure means is radical freedom, the freedom of worship from its *situation* as worship directed to a purpose. Worship becomes *eventual* (in the Badiousian sense) like grace. What remains coiled within normativity of service to God is the now-familiar pentecostal inclination to radical freedom, the spontaneity that disengages from tradition (past) and from the chain of causality.

Worship as pure means is free, which is to say it is ultimately grounded in itself, and we cannot attribute to it any purpose or any network of causal instrumentality or scheme. There is a discontinuity in the texture of purpose. This thus implies a hole in the fabric of social relations or divine-human relation, an incompleteness in the texture of the phenomenal reality of religion. Worship as pure means in Pentecostalism somewhat approximates the Kantian notion of freedom. Is this not what grace is all about? Is grace not ultimately grounded in itself, and apart from the natural or social causes? Is worship as pure means as an ambition of "pious" Pentecostals not that of recipients of divine grace wanting to become givers of such grace?

As you might have noticed, chapter 4 ("The Sacred as Im/possibility: Expect a Miracle!") separates the two sets of chapters (2 and 5, and 3 and 6). It is the proper matrix for contextualizing the problematic addressed in chapters 2, 3, 5, and 6; and it also provides the bridge for each of the pairs to connect. The pentecostal understanding of the sacred informs how these practices (such as discernment and worship) perform the representation of God in everyday life. The notion or theory of the sacred is a powerfully integrating and structuring force for the currents of ideas about discernment, grace, subjectivity, and worship as well as being their "ground."

This introduction and chapters 1–6 put up the foundation and walls of the architecture of a pentecostal everyday form of theology, so to speak. Chapter 7 erects the roof. Hovering over the lines and fibers of connections we have constructed in the course of the earlier chapters, the chapter affords the reader a bird's-eye view of everyday theology constructed in this book. Besides, as erected over an "area" bigger than the space required by the preceding chapters, chapter 7 provides the reader an uncommon view of an everyday form of pentecostal theology. A view not captured by an academic theological lens, but by a participant observer.

The size of the roof I have erected over the six chapters owed its size to the fear that the roof could become too small too soon. Indeed, the "ecclesiastical walls" may be erected almost any time without proper measurements. Walk into a typical small church at a barn, camp, or storefront and you will notice a sign displaced above the space designated as altar, "Jesus is Lord." By appealing to this high (abstract) Christological theme, the members of these small churches are doing something remarkable in the architecture of religious institutions or theological systems. They have constructed their roofs over their heads. But they lack "the ecclesiastical walls of liturgy, governance, and instructions that are normative in a given church tradition."[32]

Often, literally, there are no physical walls, only roofs over the heads. And in some cases, there might not even be a roof. I was once part of a pentecostal church in Victoria Island, Lagos, Nigeria, that had neither roof nor walls—and we were exposed to the tropical sunshine or rain as we worshiped Jesus as Lord. Real, useable theologies issued from the tongues, bodies, cries and moans, and testimonies and celebrations of the hard-bitten followers of Christ in that place. How do we capture or retrieve the theologies in such small places? The concluding section of chapter 7 offers a brief discussion on what I call *microtheology*. Microtheology is an interpretative analysis of everyday embodied theological interactions and agency at the individual, face-to-face level. It is a study of everyday social interactions of individuals or small groups that demonstrate the linkages between spirituality (practices and affections) and embodied theological ideas (beliefs).

1

Day of Pentecost

The Founding Violent Gesture of Splits

Introduction

When the day of Pentecost came, they were all together in one place. Suddenly, a sound like the blowing of a violent wind came from heaven and filled the whole house where they were sitting. They saw what seemed to be tongues of fire that separated and came to rest on each of them. All of them were filled with the Holy Spirit and began to speak in other tongues as the Spirit enabled them. Now there were staying in Jerusalem God-fearing Jews from every nation under heaven. When they heard this sound, a crowd came together in bewilderment, because each one heard their own language being spoken. Utterly amazed, they asked: "Aren't all these who are speaking Galileans? Then how is it that each of us hears them in our native language? Parthians, Medes and Elamites; residents of Mesopotamia, Judea and Cappadocia, Pontus and Asia, Phrygia and Pamphylia, Egypt and the parts of Libya near Cyrene; visitors from Rome (both Jews and converts to Judaism); Cretans and Arabs—we hear them declaring the wonders of God in our own tongues!" Amazed and perplexed, they asked one another, "What does this mean?" Some, however, made fun of them and said, "They have had too much wine." Then Peter stood up with the Eleven, raised his voice, and addressed the crowd: "Fellow Jews and all of you who live in Jerusalem, let me explain this to you; listen carefully to what I say. These people are not drunk, as you suppose. It's only nine in the morning!" (Acts 2:1–15 NIV).

The thesis I want to pursue in this chapter is the idea that the current pentecostal notion of a split God and the practices, rituals, and interactions articulated around this notion are (partly) rooted in the inaugural event of Pentecost. I want to show that when the event of Pentecost is approached at its most theoretically accessible point—which is not necessarily its strongest theological point—the violent gesture of splits lies at the origin of the movement. Here I develop an analysis of Acts 2 that illuminates the startling function of the split nature of speaking in tongues and freedom of life-in-the-Spirit in Pentecostalism. The analysis also demonstrates that while at one level the story of Acts 2 illustrates basic religious belief in a complete chain of causality, in fact, the event exemplifies the transgression of this belief. With this chapter, the analysis begun in the preface and introduction reaches a decisive point, profoundly grounding the split-God image of Pentecostals in the *ur*-moment of the church.

The Violent Gesture of Language

The founding event of Pentecostalism—language, speech in tongues in Acts 2 or here in America (Azusa Street, Los Angeles; or Topeka, Kansas) "bars" (in the Lacanian sense) subjectivity of both God and human beings. For the disciples or the faithful to step into the new era of the Spirit, into the new symbolic order, so to speak, they had to speak a new language. The disciples at Jerusalem did not understand the language they were speaking at the inaugural event, but their hearers did. Speakers and listeners at Azusa/Topeka did not understand what was spoken. As Jacques Lacan teaches us, language designates the entire symbolic order, and the price of acquiring it is the splitting of the subject—subjectivity is barred. Disciples and believers were torn from the psychosocial forces of the old order and the codes that regulated their flow and nourished them, and they were thrown into the new one. Language at least introduced symbolic division between subject (disciples, believers) and the old order (mater, mother, M-Other).

Glossolalia is the language of the other. The "of" here is polyvalent. The language of the other is the Other's language, and it is *speaking* through "I." It might be speaking the desire in me that I am unconscious of. It may well be that my language is the language of the other, "that is the unconscious itself." The "language of the other" also means my language *for* the Other and it can also be understood as the desire *for* the Other.[1] Glossolalia represents the experience of the Other, the divine as an "outside that is inside, that forever faulting [the speaker's] identity."[2] Identity is not oneness.

There is also a split for the Other, the Spirit. The language (desire) *for* the Other is the desire for the Spirit. To speak the language or fulfill the desire, I would have to do or to be what the Spirit desires. What does the Spirit want (lack)? I guess it is human beings (flesh) who can worship God in spirit and truth (John 4:23–24). This want, desire, lack opens up a gap, a split, between aim and goal, an in-between in the path toward the end and the end itself, between drive and desire.

The language of the Other as well as the Other in language is a game of cleavage, which inevitably splits God, as it were. The Other in language is *difference*, which in the words of Martin Heidegger is the temple of everything. Building on Heidegger's idea of language being the temple of Being, Mark C. Taylor states, "Language exhibits the contrasting rhythms characteristic of all cleaving. The *poiesis* of language both joins and separates. . . . While language holds together opposites usually set apart, it also holds apart the opposites it brings together. In this way, language eternally returns to the difference—the difference that is the . . . temple of everything that is."[3]

On the day of Pentecost, the Holy Spirit united the disciples and three thousand others into a new community, but each person remained singular, and linguistic difference marked the whole group. Commenting on the place of language on the day of Pentecost, political theorist Anne Norton says, "At the moment in which they recognize themselves as the *demos*, the people are united by the *heilege geist*, that common mind and spirit that realizes itself in language, more precisely in linguistic difference. . . . Their work is in language and through language: not one language but in the diverse forms that language takes. They are all to speak, to write, to bear witness; each is to do so in a particular language, a particular tongue."[4]

On the day of Pentecost, language was both the unifying medium of the immanent community and its extension to include the other, and the distinguishing marker of the persons/groups in the commons. Diverse tongues, each person speaking to others and being understood, became the symbol of the interplay between likeness and difference. Norton notes, "Language is a human capacity, but it appears in wildly diverse forms among human beings. One does not learn language, one learns a language, and so becomes human in a distinctive and particular manner. That which is common to all is achieved only in ways that are not common to all."[5]

Let us get back to Heidegger to further theoretically ground the observations of Taylor and Norton. Language's key role is to articulate "the between" where communication can take place. The between keeps alive the ceaseless oscillation of difference; it does not allow difference to turn into identity. In one of Heidegger's articulations of the differential between that mediates Being and being, he states,

> For world and things do not subsist alongside one another. They penetrate each other. Hence the two traverse a mean. In it, they are one. Thus at one, they are intimate. The mean of the two is inwardness. In our language, the mean of the two is called the between. The Latin language used *inter*. The corresponding German term is *unter*. The intimacy or inwardness of world and things is not a fusion. Intimacy obtains only where the intimate—world and thing—divides itself cleanly and remains separated. In the midst of the two, in the between of world and thing, in the *inter*, division prevails: *dif-ference*. The intimacy of world and thing is present in the boundary of the between; it is present in the dif-ference. The word difference is now removed from its usual and customary usage. What it now names is not a species concept for various kinds of differences. It exists only as this single difference. It is unique. Of itself, it holds apart the mean in and through which the world and things are at one with each other. The intimacy of the difference is the unifying element of the *diaphora*, the carrying out that carries through. The difference carries out world in its worlding, carries out things in their thinging. Thus carrying them out, it carries them toward one another. The dif-ference does not mediate after the fact by binding together world and things through a mean added on to them. Being the mean, it first determines world and things in their presence, i.e., in their being toward one another, whose unity it carries out.[6]

The sum of what we have stated in this section is that language as the characteristic feature of the day of Pentecost, both as "language of the Other" or "language for the Other," causes a splitting in the subjects. This is the implicit violent gesture that is often missed in the theological analysis of the xenolalia, and by extension glossolalia, of the inaugural event of Pentecostalism. This is because they are not approached at their theoretically most accessible point. Let us now examine another type of split that occurred on the day.

Tongues-Speech as Revelation and Reveilation

Speaking in tongues (glossolalia), uttering mysteries in the Spirit (1 Cor. 14:2), is both a revelation and reveilation.[7] It conceals communication (*communicare*, to make common) or the commons (the interspace of persons) by uttering only what the Spirit understands. By withdrawing from the community, interspace, the tongues-speaker is neither a person nor a nonperson. By this (non)placement she is one who is "set apart." Note that "set apart" is polyvalent. It means in the usual sense that she is "holy," touched by the Spirit, the one who is privileged, though many will come to be so privileged. In another sense it means she is set apart because she is uttering "secrets" that the others in her immediate community cannot understand. This second sense plays on the etymology of the word "secret," which is *secernere*; *se*, apart, on one's own, plus *cernere*, to separate. Tongues that reveal divine presence amid believers only by not revealing harbor the secret of division in the body of Christ, splitting the body from within. Speaking in tongues is that which "set apart" true believers as classical Pentecostals understood so well. But what was unthinkable by them and what is unsaid in their position is that the secret of tongues, the secret they cherish, is also the secret of God. In descending into the human realm (in immanence), God is also "set apart." God's position is both an ex-position and "parting" of God's self. God turns to human beings at Pentecost by turning away from God's self. Similarly, a turning to sinful human beings at the moment of the cross means God turning from God, God forsaking God, God withdrawing from himself (Matt. 27:46). The secret of the cross is also the secret of Pentecost.

Let us put things differently. Glossolalia, the founding event of Pentecostalism, enables the communication between humans and God by "withdrawing" from language. This withdrawal creates a hole in both human beings and God, so to speak. This hole represents the "originary lack" that births Pentecostalism—at least at Azusa/Topeka. This lack, which marks humans and God alike (or mimics God withdrawing from himself), "is neither the absence of a presence nor the presence of an absence, is not the *arche* but an *anarche* that re-moves the ground that once seemed secure. This unground that undercuts every *Ungrund* is always lacking and hence is ungraspable and incomprehensible."[8] The excess of Pentecostalism and its imbrication in the split-God image—the undercutting of orthodoxy and unsettling of theological grounds—can be traced to this "originary" lack. This tendency to re-move the grounds that seem secure will be further illustrated in the analysis of the various kinds of speaking in tongues.

Three Types of Speaking in Tongues

There are three types of tongues-speech in the Bible: xenolalia (Acts 2, and possibly Acts 10:44–48, 19:1–7), interpreted glossolalia (1 Cor. 14:13), and noninterpreted glossolalia (1 Cor. 14:6–10, 23). I will use these three terms to name some kind of agency that nudges Pentecostal believers, God's subjects, to act ethically, even as it splits them (their identity). In the first case, the ecstatic speaker does not (necessarily) understand the language, but his or her audience does.[9] In the second case, the unknown spiritual language is interpreted for the speaker and audience and it becomes a prophecy. In the final case, both the speaker and the audience (if any) do not understand what is being said. Paul in this case says, "Unless you speak intelligible words with your tongue, how will anyone know what you are saying? You will just be speaking into the air [empty space]. . . . So if the whole church comes together and everyone speaks in tongues, and inquirers or unbelievers come in, will they not say that you are out of your mind [crazy, mad]?" (1 Cor. 14:9, 23 NIV).

I want to read these three forms of tongues-speech in accordance with Lacan's triad of Imaginary, Symbolic, and Real (I-S-R)—only as a heuristic device.[10] In simple terms, the imaginary refers to identification with ideals (including dreams, imitation of another person, the ego ideal, idealized self-image, some supreme good, some positive determination of the paramount goal of society/institutions/god) in lived experience. The symbolic order refers to the laws, regulations, meanings of our community, institutions, or culture. In fact, it is the so-called "society" that structures a person's experience of reality. It is the whole trans-subjective symbolic order that conditions a person's existence. It stands to a person as an external reality. It also refers to a subject's point of symbolic identification in community. The Real is the enigmatic, impossible demand of the symbolic order, the "Big Other" that eludes symbolization or representation and thus fills the subject with uncertainty and anxiety. As it is not directly observable, experienceable, or symbolize-able, a person is only able to discern through its effects. There is no guarantee that a person gets it right or wrong, which raises a lot of anxiety and marks the person as guilty even before he or she acts.

Table 1. Forms of Speaking in Tongues and Lacan's Triad

Forms of Speech	Lacan Triad	Ethical Suggestion
Xenolalia	Imaginary	Separate
Interpreted Glossolalia	Symbolic	Incorporate
Noninterpreted Glossolalia	Real	"Speak up"

Table 1 summarizes upfront the analogy I am making between three forms of tongues-speech and the Lacan triad. The Acts 2 event, where the disciples spoke to the people who had come to the holy city Jerusalem from more than a dozen countries / linguistic groups, exemplifies the ideal of forming a new (ecclesial) community. At that moment the promised ideal of giving of the Holy Spirit had come and now the church was formally born. Jesus had asked the disciples not to leave Jerusalem and to wait for the gift of the Holy Spirit. Their speaking in tongues, among other gifts, fulfilled this promise and brought into being the church. The kind of tongues they spoke on that day enabled them to reach this positive good. The attainment of this good was through a subtractive process, a new community had to be formed by separating (or beginning the separation of) followers of Jesus Christ from Judaism. Those who had faith in Christ were separated from those who did not by a new line of separation within the Jewish ethnic group or within Israel. The tongues spoken on that fateful day were an instrument of drawing a new line of identity to build up the remnants of Christ working in anticipation of his second coming, a project Peter and company identified with. This kind of separation is at the heart of the Gospel message. The audience in Jerusalem heard the message for them to betray their tradition, split from their organic community, turn away from their generation, and come into a new one, to a new universal truth. Peter implied that in this new community, the Jews in Jerusalem were asked to cut or separate themselves from their "tradition" and participate in Christ who has already overcome all separations and cuts. Put differently, they were being asked to enter into a new humanity by literally excising themselves from their old humanity—a point Paul made explicit and elaborated upon in Galatians 3:28: "neither Jew nor Greek . . ."

The overall lesson here is that the form of tongues-speaking that best identifies with the supreme good of Christianity (or the emerging ecclesia) is the type the listeners understand, and it calls them to become followers of Jesus Christ by subtracting from their particular lifeworlds. But let us not forget that this operation on the day of Pentecost and even today is a violent gesture of creating a new community, of separating people from their own communities. When the people heard Peter's sermon, they were cut to their hearts, as the Bible says, and asked Peter what they needed to do (Acts 2:37). This cut was not just about the pain of sinfulness, doubt, failure, or unpreparedness for the new thing God was doing in their midst or what the message provoked in them, but they were being asked to split from their "ethical substance," the norms and theological ethical practices and prescriptions that constituted the Jewish tradition.

The violent gesture of separation that the first form of tongues-speaking initiated seems to be countered by the second form, which incorporates believers back into their communities. This second form is the translated glossolalia. As Paul noted in 1 Corinthians 14, a person speaking in untranslatable or noninterpreted glossolalia is constrained into his or her private space while in the midst of the church community. The person is in fact speaking into an empty space, for her "language" is not part of the symbolic order (in the Lacanian sense) of the church community. But interpretation or translation incorporates the speaker and the meaning of her tongues-speech into the community and into social discourse and signification. For Lacan, language not only incorporates its speaker into the symbolic order, but it is synonymous with the symbolic order or the domain of culture.[11] So precisely, the demand for glossolalia to be interpreted, to be translated into known language, is to incorporate the speaker into the symbolic order (the law and structure) of the new (church) community.

This incorporation may imply also "reincorporation" to the bigger (more-than church) community, and if this is the case, the reincorporation balances the earlier subtraction. In this dimension the incorporation might just be like the "as-if-not" religious stance that Paul talks about in the same first letter to the Corinthians.

> Each person should remain in the situation they were in when God called them. . . . I mean, brothers and sisters, is that the time is short. From now on those who have wives should live as if they do not; those who mourn, as if they did not; those who are happy, as if they were not; those who buy something, as if it were not theirs to keep; those who use the things of the world, as if not engrossed in them. For this world in its present form is passing away. (1 Cor. 7:20, 29–31 NIV)

Paul is here telling them that given the messianic time that remains they should participate in the world, but with an attitude of suspension. This stance does not legitimize the existing culture or power relations, only a refusal to be interpellated by the symbolic order. "I use the symbolic obligations, but I am not performatively bound by them."[12]

Giorgio Agamben, in his book *The Time That Remains*, argues that Paul's intention is not to abolish the law (symbolic order), but to render it "inoperative," though it is in force it loses signification.[13] The messianic vocation in this stance of "as though not" is "revocation of every vocation."[14] According to Agamben, Paul's "as if not" makes the law (symbolic order) "freely available for use."[15] He elucidates further: "Use: this is the definition Paul gives to messianic life in the form of the as not. To live messianically means 'to use' *klêsis* [vocation]; conversely, messianic klêsis is something to use, not to possess."[16] Agamben goes even further to argue that the law becoming an object of free use, the symbolic order deprived of signification, is based on Paul's understanding of the logic of grace. For Paul, "Grace cannot constitute a separate realm that is alongside that of obligation and law. Rather, grace entails nothing more than the ability to use the sphere of social determinations and services in its totality."[17]

Let us now turn to the third form of tongues-speech, the noninterpreted (uninterpretable) glossolalia. The uninterpretable tongues-speech is the Real (of the Spirit, the divine-human relation), which demands impossible commitment from Pentecostals. This Real resists their grasping or full understanding no matter how close the Pentecostals approach the Spirit. The tongues-speech is uttered with the full complement of the body and its senses, but it (or the Spirit) can never be "represented" in meaning. The Real transpires or shines through their reality or bodies, forever slipping through their fingers.

Uninterpretable tongues-speech is the enigma of God's desire, which is completely impenetrable and resists every attempt for the believer to understand it as it resists, eludes, symbolization. The speech opens up a gap of what is in the divine-human relation more than the divine-human relation, of the *thing* in the relation that resists symbolic identification. This kind of tongues-speech confronts the world with the impossible Real that is God, with the empty, pure formality of an injunction, "Speak up!," leaving the believer to translate it into something determinate. This is the void of an unconditional divine command, which compels the believer or the recipient to translate it into a concrete issue to address, preach, or evangelize about while offering no guarantee that the translation is right.

The speaker not only bears full responsibility for how she interprets and enacts this ethical obligation, but she cannot invoke any external circumstances or social constraints as an excuse for not interpreting, enacting, and obeying it. For this precise reason, like Žižek in a different context, "one is tempted to risk a parallel with Kant's *Critique of Judgement*: the concrete formulation of a determinate ethical obligation has the structure of an aesthetic judgment, that is, of a judgment by means of which, instead of simply applying a universal category to a particular object or subsuming this object under an already-given universal determination, [the] I as it were *invent* its universal-necessary-obligatory dimension, and thereby elevate this particular-contingent object (act) to the dignity of the ethical Thing."[18] The formal indeterminacy is at the core of what Kant means by ethical autonomy of the free enlightened subject. Pentecostals want and cherish freedom, freedom in the Spirit, and this is it and its responsibility in the sublime dimension. The free, believing God's subject is confronted with the necessary, unconditional authority of an untranslatable, uninterpreted speech. While the believer is "compelled" to speak because she can and must speak, the question of "What am I to say?" remains an open question. Herein lies the lure and terror of tongues-speech. The uninterpretative tongues-speech also has the character of the empty, formal demand of Kant's categorical imperative. The "Speak up," you "ought to speak," is like the abstract *Sollen* ("ought to be") of the categorical imperative in its formal indeterminacy.

This "ought to speak" has something else going for it. We can also interpret it as the openness of the Spirit-Pentecostal relations to new beginnings. Within the very unforeclosed character of the demand to speak up, in its very formal indeterminacy, the born-again believer is called up to reimagine the relationship. The openness of the relations, its incompleteness, leaves it up to each believer or community to live up to the impossible demand of the abstract "Speak up," to initiate something new, to decide his/her or the community's form of natality. The very formal indeterminacy undermines any enchainment of the believer to her inherited ethical substance, the given constraints of a particular (denominational, racial, national, ethnic) identity or tradition, for she has to posit a decision and without this contingent act of a free subject there is no translation of the "Speak up" and taking responsibility for it. There is no ethical act or listening to the voice (demand) of the Holy Spirit without breaking out of constraints. This is the "negative," the power of the uninterpretable tongues-speech that when it irrupts in us or in our community it stands as a reminder of the disruptive power of God's grace.

By way of reaching conclusion on this section, let me relate the language phenomenon to that of Babel (Genesis 11). It is often stated that Pentecost is the negation of Babel; instead of the confusion Babel signifies, the former signifies reconciliation and mediation. What if we turn this commonplace knowledge around and generate the thought and say Pentecost (in its broad meaning of the knot of three forms to tongues-speech) delivers humanity to the *Real*. Without renouncing symbolic understanding and articulation, Pentecost expresses (attempts to express) the inexpressible Real. Even if we can now "understand ourselves," language is pressured by the Real. This pressure is felt in at least two ways. The pure void of "Speak up" compels Pentecostals (if they really want to know the truth of their desires) to cut off symbolic discourse about God from the Real. Second, Pentecostals' daily (ritual) language now convicts them of guilt, already always guilty for not speaking out. This guilt splits the believer from within.

If Babel represents a displacement of human beings from one another and by implication from God, then Pentecost is a displacement of the subject, self from the self, limiting her identity with herself. The closeness of God is a traumatic kernel (intrusion) in the core of the person, a tiny bone caught in her throat that forces the believer to stutter or stammer in a presymbolic way when talking about the promptings of being-itself in her. In other words, Pentecost is in a sense the negation of the Babel negation but does not issue in a new, deeper synthesis. There is only a "formal" difference between it and Babel. In the world of Babel, language separated people by communication gap, whereas Pentecost is the gap itself. The untranslatable glossolalia is a kind of obstacle that makes it impossible for any two persons even within one language group to communicate or anyone to become identical with itself. Speaking in tongues represents an excess that cannot be fully incorporated into any synthesis.

Excess and Limit within Pentecost: Another Image of Splitting

If we examine the day of Pentecost from the perspectives of the 120 disciples and their audience, we will see a marvelous image of a split God. The bacchanalian revel the audience saw and simply labeled as drunkenness portrays a God of excess and extravagance. The gifts of the Spirit were poured out lavishly. Peter's speech framed this excess, defined its boundaries, and insisted that the behavior of the disciples was within limit (Acts 2:14–40). The speech performed an Apollonian observance of limits. These two dimensions or activities are the work of one God. The interplay of excess and control, contending and cooperating forces, is a characteristic feature of Pentecostalism. Even if for nothing, Pentecostals do not let us forget these two sides of God: form and formlessness, beauty and the sublime. The split in God occurs—as we can read it phenomenally through the lens of Pentecostalism—when the two sides are out of balance. The logic here is that the external opposition between the two forces may well gesture (if not, correspond) to the internal opposition in the "economic" work of God, that is, in the relations between God and humans in the process of human flourishing.

The move to go from pentecostal activities to the nature of God is based on pentecostal sensibility. Pentecostals attribute what they do or what happens in their lives to God, to what God is doing in their midst. Like the Psalmist who says this is the Lord's doing and it is marvelous in our eyes, Pentecostals sing, "Come and see-o; come and see. Come and see what the Lord has done; come and see what the Lord has done." Does what God is (presumably) doing reflect God's nature or not? If there is no correspondence between what God is doing and God's nature, there is a split between being and doing. If there is correspondence and what we observe in pentecostal life, event, and circumstance exhibits split tendencies, then we also need to turn to God to "ground" them. Of course, if what is happening to the Pentecostals or the Psalmist has nothing to do with God, this whole interconnection between my question and my answer collapses. And this collapse begs a different question: Does any religious claim or belief by any set of believers have anything to do with God? Can any vision, prophecy, or scriptural writing be attributed to God? If no, then religion, any religion, is a huge deception of man by man. Some may say the answer is yes, but there are internal criteria within any religion (or sect) to identify the true act of God. Such criteria will always be open to debate. More importantly, the principle of drawing a line of correspondence or correlation between events in pentecostal lives and God's acts is (should be) internal to Pentecostalism.

The logic here is the logic of "by-their-fruits-we-shall-know them." The reasoning here is that from the fruits we can decipher the kind of tree that produced them. Trees stand behind their fruits. The fruit is an epistemological shortcut to its mother-tree. Insofar as we consider Pentecostals' acts as divinely inspired (induced, led) or *theurgic*, then such acts are revelatory of (their) God, the God they serve. Their acts are in a sense the corporeal signatures of their God.

The behavior of observable divine presence (manifestation, power) is (points to) the immanent form of God. This kind of epistemological move is made all the time in science. The behavior of observable phenomena or objects is said to reveal the "truth" about the unobservables. Statements about entities, objects, particles, atoms, molecules, and so on, which are not open to direct observation, "can only be said to be verified by the behavior of certain characteristics of observable phenomena which are assumed to be 'symptoms' of variations in the unobservables."[19]

The connection I am making between God and pentecostal activities holds, as anthropologist Robin Horton (who is also an Oxford-trained chemist) similarly argues, "by virtue of an assumption that variations in the observable are symptoms of certain variations in the unobservable—an assumption which in both cases [that is, a modern scientific conception of unobservable theoretical entities and a Nuer/Kalabari conception of Spirit] can have no further justification."[20]

I do not want anybody to lose his or her temper over this methodology. It is only an axiom, a fundamental organizing assumption for old-fashioned speculative philosophy. It is nothing but a point of departure for a speculative-empirical study of the imbrication of God in a religious movement.

Freedom Implies a Radically Split Entity

The freedom inaugurated on the day of Pentecost that Pentecostals celebrate also harbors a splitting tension, which may be correlated with the divine also. The split is akin to the inevitable split between freedom and necessity (system). Any action or person in (submitted to) a system is ordered by the law, *arche*, the principle of the system. But freedom is essentially breaking up the chain of causality organized by a system's *arche*. The freedom ("general economy") cherished by Pentecostals is a liberation from the law, the "Name-of-the-Father" ("restricted economy," the extant network of causes and effects). There is a tension between these two forces or tendencies.

This tension, as F. W. J. Schelling taught us, starts in the divine as the tension between ground and existence, expansion and contraction—the rotary movement between natality and necessity within God. Schelling's audacious speculation of the existence of God begins with primordial "Freedom," a neutral "Will" that wants nothing.[21] This is only a potentiality, and in the process of conversion into actuality, in actualizing itself, the pure will (the primordial freedom) changes into a pure contraction, which translates to the annihilation of all determinate content. It actively wants nothing outside itself. In Schelling's reasoning the perfect freedom, that is, self-contented will (the mode of potentiality), is no different from a destructive fury (mode of actuality) that threatens to swallow everything. A parallax shift of perspective is needed to see that this conversion is purely a formal one; the indifferent will and the will that actively wants "nothing" are of the same being: "the same principle carries and holds us in its ineffectiveness which would consume and destroy us in its effectiveness."[22]

Note that the moment the primordial freedom attempts to actualize itself, the will is split into two: the will-to-contraction and the will-to-expansion. At the inception of this contraction (the fury of destruction), the will negates itself to become one that wants something, wants to expand. How is this tension within freedom going to be overcome? This positive will (expansion) cannot overcome the antagonism of the negative (contraction) and in this primordial tension the two wills frustratingly move in rotary form, the positive will not able to break out. The Godhead cannot withdraw completely into itself or open itself up, to admit Otherness. As Žižek puts it, "Every attempt at creation-expansion-externalization collapses back into itself. This God is not yet the Creator, since in creation the being (the contracted reality) of an Otherness is posited that possesses a minimal self-consistency and exists *outside* its Creator."[23] God did eventually create, expansion won. Schelling calls this progress the movement from freedom (impenetrable ground of existence, self-limitation, contraction, pure will, potentiality) to free act (subject, actuality of freedom). In Schelling's unorthodox view, God as free Subject, free Creator has to put a distance between God's ground and himself, and this was a primordial decision. There has to be a split between Ground (the contractive will) and Existence (will-to-expansion) in God. This split, which is atemporal, cannot be accounted for as it has to be retroactively posited.

Based on this reasoning about God, Schelling proceeded to aver that the act of human freedom also involves not only the atemporal gesture of differentiation of being and becoming and a passage from pure freedom to free subject, but also the atemporal decision has to be "repressed." "Freedom is for Schelling the moment of 'eternity in time,' the point of groundless decision by means of which a free creature (man) breaks up, suspends, the temporal chain of reasons and, as it were, directly connects with the *Ungrund* of the Absolute."²⁴ This is how Schelling links his concept of atemporal freedom to eternity, his "notion of freedom as the subject's free relating to the ground of her existence"²⁵ is to be a radically split entity.

> That primordial deed which makes a man genuinely himself precedes all individual actions; but immediately after it is put into exuberant freedom, this deed sinks into the night of unconsciousness. This is not a deed that could happen once and then stop; it is a permanent deed, a never-ending deed, and consequently it can never again be brought before consciousness. For man to know of this deed, consciousness itself would have to return to nothing, into boundless freedom, and would cease to be consciousness. The deed occurs once and then immediately sinks back into the unfathomable depths; and nature acquires permanence precisely thereby. Likewise that will, posited once at the beginning and then led to the outside, must immediately sink into unconsciousness. Only in this way is a beginning possible, a beginning that does not stop being a beginning, a truly eternal beginning. For here as well, it is true that the beginning cannot know itself. That deed once done, it is done for eternity. The decision that in some manner is truly to begin must not be brought back to consciousness; it must not be called back, because this would amount to being taken back. If, in making a decision, somebody retains the right to reexamine his choice, he will never make a beginning at all.²⁶

There is another crucial angle to this analysis of the connection between freedom and split identity, or ground and existence. Human beings, according to Schelling, also have split nature: material and spiritual entities. This split opens up the possibility of evil in them as the two sides, combined in one person, struggle for dominance. And for those whose spiritual side have been well elevated, evil could be raised to the power of the spirit, that is, "spiritualized." The woman is a split being, she is by nature split. She is a natural organism and, at the same time, a spiritual entity, part of nature and somewhat raised beyond nature. If she is merely a part of nature, she will live in harmony with (be at home in) nature or her environment as any other animal or plant. With the seamless inclusion in the circuit of nature she would not fundamentally be a threat to nature. If she were a spirit alone, she would not relate to nature as an object of exploitation "but maintain a relationship of contemplative comprehension with no need to intervene actively in it for the purpose of material exploitation."[27] The problem or possibility of evil arises from the combination of the two features in every human being and their difference posited as such. With their spiritual nature, the normal purpose of exploiting nature for survival becomes domination of the same and exacerbating it to the power of the spirit. Because the unity of two principles has been severed (weakened), they are internally split.[28] The more spirit cuts off its links with nature (and tries to dominate it) the more evil it generates.[29]

Day of Pentecost as Time of Divine Manifestations and Manifestation of Splits

Let us begin by restating the terms and frames of a pentecostal worldview. According to this viewpoint, there is phenomenal divine manifestation. It is observable, perceivable at the level of existence, human existence. This view also holds that the divine manifestation has its *ground*, that is, God. So we have existence and its ground when it comes to divine manifestation. Now Pentecostals also believe that some of their spiritual leaders can misuse divine manifestation, presence, or power. For the possibility of such misuse or the actual evil manipulation to occur, there has to be a crack, a gap, a split in the Absolute, a scission between God's actual existence and its impenetrable ground as put forward by Schelling.[30] This inherent gap, adapting Schelling's thought about the Absolute, forever prevents every divine presence from becoming "fully itself." The fact that there is this something about real presence means divine manifestation, miracle, anointing, potentially implies evil (manipulation, misappropriation, striving, longing or willing outside orthodox, orthopraxis bounds of commonly accepted divine commands) as its constitutive gap or openness. Is it not true then that the sacramental item, the bearer of (past or present) divine presence is marked with a gesture of withdrawal from such divine presence or with radical ambiguity, demonic opposition to the divine?

More thought provoking is the question: How is it that the divine presence or the Absolute splits itself from itself that such evil (misuse of divine presence) or ambiguity slips in? This problem is akin to what Slavoj Žižek calls the problem of "phenomenalization" of God.[31] How does it happen that the Absolute slips on bodies and objects and thereby "discloses" or appears to himself? Divine presence is not only an appearance for human beings, but it is also appearance for the omnivoyant God. Now the crucial question is not about the anointing that enables Pentecostals to see the noumenal itself beyond or behind the phenomenal veil, but "the true problem is how and why at all does this In-itself split from itself, how does it acquire a distance toward itself and thus clear a space in which it can appear (to itself)?"[32]

Let us return to our "evil pastor" or moral evil as a crack in divine manifestation. Following Immanuel Kant can we argue that the moment the divine presence cracks the phenomenal veil over reality it suffers a split that allows moral evil to penetrate it or the pentecostal subject? Kant argues that human beings can act morally, fulfill their duty only if their noumenal realm is not accessible to them. If a person were to go beyond the epistemic horizon and come directly with the *noumenal Thing*, he or she would lose his or her freedom, autonomy. He or she would have known the totality of the myriad causes and events in the universe and would be living in a totally deterministic world, a "causally closed cosmos." Kant writes:

> Instead of the conflict which now the moral disposition has to wage with inclination and in which, after some defeats, moral strength of mind may be gradually won, God and eternity in their awful majesty would stand unceasingly before our eyes. . . . Thus most actions conforming to the law would be done from fear, few would be done from hope, none from duty. The moral worth of actions, on which alone the worth of the person and even the world depends in the eyes of supreme wisdom, would not exist at all. The conduct of man, so long as his nature remained as it is now, would be changed into mere mechanism, where, as in a puppet show, everything would gesticulate well but no life would be found in the figures.[33]

Is Kant here not describing some pentecostal leaders who can do or perpetuate evil because they think they have direct access to the noumenal realm? They alone understand the whole network of causes and effects in all of existence and they are the only mere divine machines fighting to subdue free autonomous agents (of Satan). But this supreme stance hides something untoward. "G. K. Chesterton . . . views the causally closed cosmos of the deterministic/mechanistic materialist as 'about the smallest hole that man can hide his head in'—in other words, the notion of being as a fixed, predictable One-All, a seamless flow of causes and effects, is a seductively comforting image hiding something very unsettling."[34]

Day of Pentecost:
The Tension between Abstract and Concrete Elements in God

The divine manifestations on the day of Pentecost are not only instances of *real presence*, but also an exemplification of the inherent tension in divine-human relations or an inherent obstacle in the idea of God in all religions. There is the dialectics of the absolute (universal, abstract) and concrete (particular) elements in the idea of God. As Paul Tillich has argued, this is an inherent tension in the Christian trinitarian thinking about God.[35] The tension between the absolute and the concrete elements arises because human beings want concreteness in their ultimate concern, which drives them to polytheistic structures, but the reaction of the absolute element (ultimacy) initiates a movement toward monotheistic structures. The need for balance between the concrete and the absolute drives them toward trinitarian structures. The Christian triune God is concrete monotheism, the affirmation of the living God in whom the ultimate and the concrete are united.[36]

What is clear from Tillich is that these two drives are not only inherent in the trinitarian idea and nature of God, but are also in the very way human beings relate to God. What happened on the day of Pentecost when the abstract God manifested concretely, immanently, on the bodies of believers—as tongues of fire on their heads, their embodied voices as xenolalia, and as felt motion on their sensuous skin with the vibrations of wind around them—is nothing but the union of the abstract and concrete elements of God.

While the main part of "mainstream" Christianity is satisfied with the tension of the abstract and concrete elements in the idea of God as settled in the trinitarian conception of the divine: God is absolutely concrete and particular in Jesus Christ and yet he is absolutely universal (abstract) at the same time.[37] But for Pentecostals the theological frame of the trinity as it relates to the immanent God may heal the split (tension between the two elements), but not in the continuous, everyday outworking of the "economic" side of the God in the midst of God's children because human beings still want concreteness in their ultimate concern. The Holy

Spirit, the Spirit of Christ, in this pentecostal understanding is absolutely concrete and particular in real presences and community of believers, and yet he is absolutely universal (abstract) at the same time. Does the Acts 2 event of the day of Pentecost not exemplify this imaginary of today's Pentecostals and Charismatics?

The split between the abstractness and concreteness is extremely important for understanding Pentecostals' and Charismatics' practices and for getting a handle on their view of the divine realm. The split between the concrete and the abstract is what creates the phenomenal encounter with God or real presence; that is, God's abstractness establishes the concreteness (phenomenal, finite world and/or God's concreteness) as limit. Alternatively, the limit of the concrete is what gives abstractness, beyond-the-concreteness. As Clayton Crockett states, "the split between phenomena and noumena creates a noumenon; that is, the barrier that renders the 'thing-in-itself' unknowable is what provides certainty that there is a 'thing-in-itself.'"[38]

The Split between Power and Glory: Inoperativity of Pentecost

Jesus Christ told his disciples just before his ascension that they will receive power when the Holy Spirit comes upon them. Ten days after this promise the Acts 2 event occurred as its fulfillment. The power came, but the way of its materialization was split: power and glory, or power and three-pronged glory—the classical divide between being and acting. The power (*dunamis, dynamis*) of God is one, but the *oikonomia*, the concrete display of glory, the glory of power is threefold: wind (pneuma, "expansive will"), fire ("contracting will"), and word (*logos*, the pronouncement that breaks the deadlock between the two modes of the single will, as per Schelling).

This Schellingian preontological perspective should now yield to an Agambenian historical one that demonstrates the split between power and glory of the Pentecost event. First of all, Giorgio Agamben, in his book *The Kingdom and the Glory*, shows that power needs glory to accompany it in order to function.[39] He traced the root of this distinction or differentiation between power and glory to the fracture between being and praxis, God's immanent nature and God's government of creation, which the concept of *oikonomia* introduced into the Christian understanding of God, and this eventually led to the notion of being as praxis.

Power and glory, according to Agamben, are two modes of the same activity, but they can never come into full identity or coincidence. In their coincidence there is always a remainder.[40] This misalignment or gap is covered over or hidden by the glorification of power. That is, cracks between being and praxis are papered over by glory.[41] Power needs not only administration and execution (governance), but also glory (the liturgical, ceremonies, and acclamations) to function and sustain itself. Glory is not just an ornament of power, but it functions to correlate the two faces of the same machine of power. "It allows, that is, for us to bridge that fracture between theology and economy that the doctrine of the trinity has never been able to completely resolve and for which only the dazzling figure of glory is able to provide a possible reconciliation."[42]

From this insight, Agamben proceeds to demonstrate that the economy of trinity (*oikonomia*) and the economy of glory (*doxa*) are mutually constitutive.[43] They have a dialectical relationship. "Glory is the place where theology attempts to think the difficult conciliation between immanent trinity and economic trinity, *theologia* and *oikonomia*, being and praxis, God in himself and God for us. For this reason, the doxology, despite its apparent ceremonial fixity, is the most dialectical part of theology, in which what can only be thought of as separate must attain unity."[44]

So on the day of Pentecost when we see the effectivity of God's power demonstrated as baptism of the Spirit (accompanied by the whole July Fourth fireworks, the vortex of wind that belittles the suction power of a turbo engine, and the open acclamation for the brilliant, wonderful work of God) we also see being and praxis of God. There is the Holy Spirit who is administering the whole display, especially the release of power to speak in tongues and for boldness for evangelism. And we also see the accompanying glory. Peter's speech explaining what has just happened to the people of Jerusalem is a peculiarly long acclamation, which concerns Christ, the vindicated one, the person who united God's plan in heaven and earth, and his death and resurrection made him peerless among Israel's prophets and kings. This acclamation was constitutive of the Pentecost event. Peter's acclamation was integral to the emotionalism, the affect of the day. One is even tempted to view the whole Acts 2 event as a liturgical service that began in Acts 1 and somewhat analogous with a typical pentecostal service of today. The disciples had gathered in the upper room to pray and praise God with Peter and to spend time "sharing the word." Suddenly the anointing and gifts arrived. Then the pastor (Peter) spoke again, and the people themselves asked for an "altar call." After the service, disciples and converts retired to share bread and bond as church members. This liturgical service is in a certain sense the acclamation and paean that the efficacious action of Spirit baptism (the power of the Holy Spirit) wrapped itself in on the day of Pentecost. Here it appears divine reality (or *oikonomia*) and human praxis (*doxa*) communicate and "exchange clothes." The praises, acclamations, and doxology before, during, and after the move of the Holy Spirit is the tarrying in the gap, crack between being and praxis. This is part of the way power functions—because of the crack it must co-opt glorification. It appears that Pentecostals (cracked earthen vessels) understand this well, their intense praise and worship bears witness to this.

The overall point as it relates to the theme of this chapter is that the split is indispensable to the logic and dynamics of the inaugural Pentecost. And we have seen that the operations of that day (the "government" of the event by the Holy Spirit) consist in the articulation of economic trinity and immanent trinity in which each of the two aspects glorify one another. And of course, we also noted the disciples' glorification of God, which is an "echo" of God's glory. The day of Pentecost was, indeed, a "theo-doxological machine" that has its foundation in God's *kabhod* as created light, divine essence, and glorification.[45] "But the center of the machine is empty, and glory is nothing but the splendor that emanates from this emptiness, the inexhaustible *kabhod* that at once reveals and veils the central vacuity of the machine."[46]

This interpretation of Pentecost as a theo-doxological machine opens up a new space to understand or to ground worship practices of Pentecostals as *worship as pure means*, a prejudicial (pre-eschaton) *inoperativity* of divine-human relation.[47] A worship is revealed as worship as pure means (WPM) when it is an "ostensive [worship] whose functions are not executed but rather displayed" in their inoperative potentiality.[48] To put it differently, the typical, ordinary worship is "undone, rendered inoperative, liberated and suspended from its 'economy.' "[49] This is a noninstrumental worship "that displays the potentiality of its means as such without directing them towards teleological ends."[50]

To make (strengthen) the connection between our analyses of the day of Pentecost to worship as pure means we have to pass through the thought of Eric L. Mascall.[51] He argues that the supreme purpose of human beings cannot be in their acquisition of knowledge or their love of God. The acquisition of knowledge is not only egoistic and borders on the enjoyment of God, but it is also not ultimately useful in the postjudicial condition. It is psychologically impossible for human beings to love God without simultaneously thinking about their own happiness. Mascall states,

> The only thing that can define the first and essential element of our blessed state is neither the love nor the knowledge of God but only his *praise*. The only reason to love God is that he is worthy of praise. We do not praise him because it is good for us, although we find good in it. We do not praise him because it is good for him, because in fact our praise cannot benefit him.[52]

He goes on to add that praise (doxology and glorification) is indeed

> superior both to love and to knowledge, although it can include both and transform them, because praise does not concern itself with interest but only with glory [. . .] In the worship that on earth we bestow on God, the first place is due to praise as well [. . .] And what scripture allows us to glimpse of celestial worship always shows us praise. The vision of Isaiah in the temple, the song of the angels in Bethlehem, [and] the celestial liturgy of the fourth chapter of Revelation repeat the same thing: *Gloria in excelsior deo* [. . .] "Our Lord and God, you are worthy of receiving glory, honor, and power."[53]

We will take up more fully the scintillating theme of worship as pure means in chapter 6, but it is germane at this juncture to bring up the key insight of the discussions and analyses of worship as pure means in it. This will nicely lead us to another crucial area of the inaugural event of Pentecost that we have yet to explore: the inoperativity of the born-again life. Chapter 6 reveals that worship as pure means is purposeless, and in its "essence" neither the believer nor the Holy Spirit draw utility from it. Agamben in his analysis of the Christian theory of glory comes to the same conclusion.

> Here we discover all the elements of the theory of glory with which we have become familiar. The specific value of glory as the ultimate purpose of man lies, curiously, in the fact that ultimately neither God nor men need it or draw utility from it. And yet . . . praise is not extrinsic to God. "The archetype

of all praise can be found within the Trinity itself, within the eternal filial response of the word to God his Father." God is, in other words, literally composed of praise, and by glorifying him, men are admitted to participate in his most intimate existence. But if things stand thus, if the praise that men give God is intimate and consubstantial with him, then doxology is, perhaps, in some way a necessary part of the life of the divinity.[54]

The inoperativity of worship, as we have stated, flows from the doxological character of Pentecost. But to the extent that the Pentecost event points to the eternal life and the arrival of messianic time, it marks the life of the born-again with special inoperativity. This it does by splitting the life of the believer as her life can no longer coincide with itself: living with one leg in her ordinary (biographical) life and the other leg in the life in the messiah. Her life can no longer conform to a predetermined form as she is summoned to revoke and open her life (as *bios*) to the *new life* of Jesus (*zōē tou Iesou*).[55] "For we who are alive are always being given over to death for Jesus' sake, so that his life may be revealed in our mortal body" (2 Cor. 4:11 NIV). Paul's "as if not" (*hōs mē*) in 1 Cor. 7:29–31 shows clearly what it means to live this kind of life. Agamben, building on his *The Time That Remains*, beautifully summarizes the character of this life in *The Kingdom and the Glory* in this way: "To live in the Messiah means precisely to revoke and render inoperative at each instant every aspect of the life that we live, and to make the life for which we live, which Paul calls the 'life of Jesus' (*zōē tou Iesou*—*zōē* not *bios*!) appear within it. . . . And the inoperativity that takes place here is not mere inertia or rest; on the contrary, it is the messianic operation par excellence."[56]

Concluding Thoughts

Pentecostalism is nothing but an acknowledgment or affirmation of the radical splits in the founding moments of Christianity. The split image of God in Pentecostalism is not a negation of the "traditional" view of a harmonious, tension-free God, which is a healing of the split within a theological frame. Pentecostalism breaks the frame so radically that it undermines any fundamentalism on the nature and work of God. The logic of the break is both discerned in its social practices and how it organizes the practices. If Pentecostals believe that reality is unfinished, incomplete, then their God has to be correlative to a reality that is ontologically open.[57]

The next six chapters present a pentecostal lifeworld structured around the splits, gaps, and voids, and desires for splits and slits. In addition, the chapters demonstrate how Pentecostals' everyday habits and practices exercise "reciprocal action" on the theological base (belief in splits in God and reality). This is not to say Pentecostals fully identify with this belief or theological base. Like any other subjects in society, Pentecostals relate to this belief with some degree of distance. There is always a noninterpellated "leftover."[58] Chapter 2 shows that what seems to be an "opening" to information at the level of knowledge (epistemology) is actually an opening, a slit, a crack in the object of knowledge (reality)—an ontological split in reality. This might be a problem, right? The problem is not that Pentecostals' claim to gain insights into reality or the noumenal—the real problem is that reality is already cracked, a nonharmonious, inconsistent whole, a non-All. The most important insight of our next chapter is that the belief in the split God is found at the level of pentecostal everyday practices of spirituality, and not their conscious systematized knowledge.

2

Spiritual Discernment

Bathroom Mirror as Metaphor

Introduction

On the morning of July 11, 2014, I went into the bathroom, walked over to the sink, picked up my toothbrush, put paste on it, and then raised my head to the mirror over the sink to look at my face, but my face was not there. Gone! In shock, I wondered what had happened. Had my face been ripped off in the night as I slept? Instead of my face I saw a white, lily-white sheet, an impenetrable, blank, white background staring monstrously back at me. For a moment I thought the skin of reality had been torn off and I was confronted with the horror, the raw flesh of reality, which was inert and irreal. In a split second I realized what had happened. The mirror had been removed from the face of the cabinet. I could not discern my face because the mirror that cracks reality and splits me into two persons was not in its place; only a white metal frame that formerly held it in place remained.

We know that a mirror does not just reflect appearances and return images. A mirror, as Jean-Pierre Vernant argues, "opens a breach in the backdrop of 'phenomena,' displays the invisible . . . and lets it be seen in the brilliance of a mysterious epiphany."[1] Given this specular connection between reality and discernment, we will be well served to adopt a method of inquiry that can deal with mirroring and invisibility. In a sense, the art and practice of discernment is holding up a mirror to reality, helping us to figure out the cracks that enable us to see more clearly, to see the not-yet (or more precisely the invisible, that which is not visible or sensible as of now).

Discernment as a religious art presupposes two dimensions of reality. First there is the first-order reality, the phenomenal realm. Then, there is an unfathomable X (abyss) to it, an impenetrable core that is mysterious and elusive. This second part lurks behind the surface, and I can presumably get to it through the deployment of my spiritual (religious) sense and sensibility, acumen, training or practices, or "looking glass." On the summer morning after the mirror fell off the wall in the night and my wife heard it, woke up, and cleaned up the broken pieces without telling me until the horror of my encounter, I was denied the apparatus for discernment. Discernment of my face was frustrated, impossible, because reality was a complete whole without fissures, and I was not split.

Our relationship with mirrors, whether physical or supernatural, is a complicated one. The apparatus, which enables us to see the breach in the phenomena of reality, is also a veil over the very reality (or the Real) that it attempts to reveal. The mirror, a veil of appearance, serves as a protective wall against the monster of the noumenal dimension of reality. That is, when the mirror was gone I was directly exposed to the unfathomable X (abyss) of my face or the white pre-face of the wall as an other. This is the nature and contradiction of discernment in Pentecostalism: discernment reveals secrets that hide secrets and drives the discerning person to seek after the ultimate mystery and impenetrable core of reality or creation. A mirror cracks space and light in order for me to see the appearance of my face. The mirror itself cracks. My composure cracks in the crack of the morning. Where do I crank up the energy to deal with all the cracks in a broken world? Discernment is about acknowledging cracks in reality and in our selves and creating the capability to live in the crack of life, the gap that cannot be closed or foreclosed. The goal of discernment is improvements in levels of protection, prosperity, faith, and obedience.

In another sense, discernment is the art of investigating three different kinds of bodies as foundations of knowledge. The first kind deals with natural bodies, the body with its general features, specific social practices, and with the knowledge of lived experience. The second kind deals with spiritual bodies, in particular invisible, intangible beings, their actions, passions, and reasons, and interactions with visible, tangible beings. And the third kind is with artificial bodies; that is, the rhizomatic networks of relationships between natural bodies, spiritual bodies, and between natural bodies and spiritual bodies. Often the energies of these relationships can connect, summon, or activate the inner energetic forces and inner processes that presumably lie behind the concrete forms or representations of the natural and spiritual bodies.[2] These relationships that emerge from the natural and spiritual bodies mediate their encounters in ways that tie the relations between truth and meaning to a particular theologico-ethical constellation.

This tripartite structure engenders a triadic conception of reality and foundation of knowledge. There is the man, his image in the mirror, and the relationship between the man, his reflection in the mirror, and his grooming habits. This triadic reality is always marred by cracks, the gaps between the Real and experience as always mediated. The art of living or keeping sane concerns "covering up" the constitutive cracks in reality, even as we allow or summon or indwell the cracks as gateways for the creation of new things, emergence of new possibilities, the exploration of new dimensions, and for securing specific insights and guidance for interpreting life. Discernment as part of the art of living is directed at addressing the cracks.

I have laid out in very simple and homely style a general understanding (concept, if you like) of discernment at its deepest level. What specific form does discernment then take in communities with different key characteristics? In other words, what is the nature of discernment, say, in African Pentecostalism? To answer this question, we need to first lay out some key features of African traditional religions as the common font of inheritance or the environmental air that African Pentecostals breathe and thus inform their theory and practices of spiritual discernment.

Relevant Features of African Traditional Religions

There are several ways to list the key characteristics of African traditional religions (ATR), but here I want to list those attributes that will shed relevant light on the subject of our discussion. First is what I will call split or crack. The basic belief is that reality is cracked or split: phenomena and noumenal, the thing and the thing-itself. Then with the appropriate training, the equipment of "seeing eyes," and sensibility, a person (or the diviner, native doctor, priest) can "know" the Real, the thing-in-itself. Simply, all human beings are not under the universal limitation of phenomenality. We should be careful not to think this is a peculiarity of ATR. Religions in general make some claim to piercing the phenomenal veil insomuch as they claim to give access to nonmaterial spirits, angels, demons, and gods.

Second, in addition to the claim of split reality or thing, there is also a split in the self. The self can be split as a person can be possessed or imbued by spirits (good or bad) or by power from outside him- or herself. There are also parts of the person that venture into witchcraft, act in different places, when the person is asleep. Another way the self is split is in the Pauline (Romans 7) sense. The self wars against itself as spirit and flesh. There is a duality in the core of personhood, and the person who harbors this duality is quite capable of dealing with each of the agonistic parts of the self. The flesh (the body) can be "mortified," "crucified," during various disciplines or technology of the self in order to elevate the spirit.

Third, though discernment often occurs in consultation with religious specialists, it can occur anywhere and at any time. In fact, it often occurs at the busy intersections of life, not in the quiet grooves, serene shrines, and appointed offices of priests. A split in a "decision tree" provokes the quest for discernment. For instance, a man who is faced with a crucial decision when there is more than one path to the solution has to discern the best course of action. Discernment may take the form of deciphering the probabilities of occurrence of various states of nature or allowing for only the two extreme points in probability distribution. Like the four lepers in 2 Kings 7:3–4, African Pentecostals can discern a future course of action based on a decision tree that shows relevant distribution of probabilities between zero and one. But there are times when the probability distribution is limited to either stark zero or one and nothing in between. For instance, if a bird flies across a fisherman's canoe from the right to the left while the fisherman is on his way to his fishing ground and he subsequently suffers a poor catch, he will attribute the poor catch to the bird's flight. He will say that a medicine man or an angry competitor sent the bird. He will not think of coincidence or the probability of an event happening. In his conceptual scheme (or the discerning mindset based on cracked reality in which the phenomenal is in the grip of the noumenal, the unseen realm) an event either happens or it does not. The probabilities of events are either zero or one. The fisherman does not ponder or accept the chances of anything happening. Similarly, there is no concept of randomness, meaning an event is completely unpredictable, or that the event cannot be explained. He does not believe that there are events his spiritualistic theoretical model cannot explain. Not to have an explanation for the religious person, who works with a two-point probability distribution, means there is no causality.

Fourth, one major effect of split reality on the nature of religion is that religion in such an environment tends to gravitate more toward the dimension of explanation, prediction, and control than communion with gods.[3] According to anthropologist Robin Horton, the Kalabari (Niger Delta, Nigeria) use the idea of an unobservable underlying reality of gods to make sense of the contingencies of everyday existence. They interpret the vast diversity of everyday experience in terms of a scheme of three forces: ancestors, founding heroes, and water-spirits. They use this interpretative scheme of these three forces to transcend the limited vision of cause and effect relationships provided by common sense, reaching to causal explanation of events. Thus, Horton argues, Kalabari religion is more about explanation, prediction, and control (hereafter, EPC).

EPC cannot be separated from the way the Kalabari interpret the world, which is to see inner processes of forms with their inner sense (mind's eye) and understand them to have meaning and significance through their relations with other things present or absent. As Horton himself argues, explanation kicks in when a thing appears to have more to it than ordinarily meets the pure sensory organs, when it appears *as* a form *of* something.[4] Kalabari say *jenso ani bio emi*, meaning, "There is something else in the matter." The immediate case points beyond itself; it is something other than itself. To understand this "something else," to extend their vision, to re-present to themselves causes that are not present in the commonsense world, they create theoretical models: they trace an analogy between the structure of certain observations they want to explain and the structure of certain phenomena whose regularities of behavior are familiar to them.

Fifth, this "something else" or more to reality is keyed to or underpinned by the concept of the sacred in African religion. The concept of the sacred is captured by *So* in Kalabari. The concept of the uppercase *So* directs the people to both note their limitations, the set of possibilities opened to them or excluded from them, liberatory potentials for the transformation of selves and structures of society, and the sum of possibilities conceivable given their level of social, technological, and economic development. *So* also refers to the infinite possibilities in the sacred.[5] The Kalabari *So* relates not only to the people as a whole, but also to individuals, institutions, lineages, and communities.

In addition to the uppercase *So*, we have the lowercase *so*. The lowercase *so* are the possibilities available to an individual, cultural institutions, and social structures. The uppercase *So* are the possibilities excluded from them. More precisely, it is the universe of possibilities from which some are defined as available to persons and institutions and others remain either unfulfilled or the set of possibilities excluded from them at any given time. It should be noted that the uppercase *So* and lowercase *so* are not opposites. Thus what is not part of the lowercase *so* is not confined to extinction. The uppercase *So* is the ground of lowercase *so*. The lowercase *so* is only a set of appropriated or available possibilities at any given time. For instance, a person may have the *so* to be a good teacher from all the possibilities that are available to members of the community and even beyond. If she dislikes being a teacher, she can go to a diviner and ask for her occupation to be changed and thus draw another career from that unlimited urn of possibilities that the uppercase *So* can give, and it is a pool that can never be completely realized. Though a person can literally ask for any possibilities, *So* (the sacred) has the right to defer or "project into the future whatever may be too much for any community or society [or the individual] to fully experience or acknowledge in the present."[6] Because an individual can only be given or allotted a part of the set of all possibilities available to the community at any given historical moment, what she has "always points beyond itself to the full range of possibilities for either salvation or destruction."[7]

So in contemplating a person's *so*, the Kalabari are going beyond the appearance of a quotidian life to what lies beyond it. Thus there is always more to a person, more from where a person can draw strength, power, and direction for life or initiate the new. There is more to a person than what other human beings can comprehend with the naked or inner eyes. What enables this comprehension beyond the physical eyes, the *krokro* eyes? It is the faculty of imagination. This faculty plays a very crucial role in discernment. It is what allows the Kalabari people to go beyond the merely physical and apparent to the *something else*. The Kalabari cannot engage in explanation, prediction, and control without imagination. This imagination is not only the precursor of EPC, but also the capping segment of the process or connections of EPC, its principle of finality. When a diviner is consulted and goes through the entire process of EPC, the process inevitably involves the act of forming a particular narrative—sequence of events, noisy data of experience, past and anticipated—into a particular shape. Imagination (productive and reproductive) figures in the form, forming, and thinking/reflecting in the narrative logic that engenders comprehensible patterns of experience. It is impossible to also separate EPC from imagination as an element in motivating people to engage in it.

Before Kalabari persons can explain, predict, and control their environment, they must understand it. At the minimum, understanding requires that they apply categories, concepts, and laws to nature. They are able to impose these concepts on their experience of phenomena through the image-forming power of imagination. In explaining, predicting, and controlling events, Kalabari people are not just applying specific culture-brewed concepts to nature and social systems, and directing their thoughts to some regulative telos; they are also applying specific rules or concepts to particular situations, or they are moving from the particular to the universal (*je'ne bu pakaye*). In this latter case they are deriving or inventing a rule or concept that the particular points out to them. For example, someone might frame a new principle to account for a particular situation instead of forcing it to fit under an established principle. This is the search for pattern (a pattern internal to it), a frame within which the observed facts, events, abnormality can fit, by assuming a kind of finality of nature, a design (principle of finality). This mode of reflection, this form of assumption, is driven by imagination, the challenge to find an order within a chaotic situation—this is the task of bringing an event or object under understanding. If a particular event falls outside of established rules, representing a temporary form of chaos, then creative, productive, and appreciative imagination enables people to find a rule that it exemplifies. Every budding forth of EPC presupposes understanding and imagination.

The movement from phenomenality to noumenality that is facilitated by imagination is fraught with danger. (Discernment as a spiritual practice is always problematic.) The passage from the symbolic world of phenomenal reality to the noumenal universe of spiritual contact might demand tarrying with the negative. This negativity may well point to the nocturnal abyss of subjectivity that is glimpsed with the cracking of phenomenality. Here imagination in a Hegelian fashion ("night of the world") discomposes, dissects, and dissolves reality before harmonizing and synthesizing it in the faculties of intuition and understanding (in a Kantian fashion) to give us the content of revelation. Hegel expresses, in these terms, the monstrous character of understanding, and, hence, the frightful nature of tarrying with the negative.

> Man is that night, that empty Nothingness, which contains everything in its undivided simplicity: the wealth of an infinite

number of representations, of images, not one of which comes precisely to mind, or which [moreover] are not [there] insofar as they are really present. It is the night, the interiority—or—the intimacy of Nature which exists here: [the] pure-Ego. In phantasmagorical representations it is night on all sides: here suddenly surges up a blood-spattered head; there, another, white apparition; and they disappear just as abruptly. That is the night that one perceives if one looks a man in the eyes; then one is delving into a night which becomes terrible; it is night of the world which then presents itself to us.[8]

Imagination thus constitutes the sixth attribute of ATR that we want to highlight for the purpose of this chapter. The seventh and final feature is forms of knowing. All things have two dimensions: physical (material) and spiritual (immaterial). To know is to understand one dimension by way of common sense or physical laws, the other is by spiritual (metaphysical) laws. The primary way of knowing is pragmatic common sense or physical laws, and the Kalabari resort to spiritual explanation as a second-order reflection when there is a (an inexplicable) pattern to events, sufferings, or misfortunes. In order to reach for this second-order level of understanding, one needs certain non (meta)-physical apparatuses such as "seeing eyes," "hearing ears," or other sensory organs that can penetrate the object or pattern of events, just as scientific instruments penetrate objects to reveal their inner contents. While the scientist reaches deep down into the physical domain, the spiritual tool penetrates the ontological level.

The immaterial penetration is principally not intended as invasive or violent but moves toward intimacy. The knower engages the object (his or her partner in the unveiling of truth) with care and affection. Sometimes, this involves knowing the needs, logic, and dynamics of the partner and taking care of them. The production of esoteric knowledge requires penetrative and receptive intimacy as in sexual intercourse. The intimacy is penetrative because the seeker attempts to enter into the inner dimensions, functions, and processes of the object to ferret out wisdom. This can also involve the knower penetrating him- or herself through interior intuitive means. The intimacy is said to be receptive when the being or object being investigated "possesses" the seeker or knower and reveals its inner workings through him or her. The affinity between the penetrative and receptive intimacy of knowledge production that evokes sexual intimacy is suggested by the Kalabari word *nimi*, "to know." *Nimi*, which also means knowledge, wisdom, recognition, or awareness, is used to also refer to sexual intercourse, just as the word *yada* does in Hebrew.

A part of knowing a person or object is to place her or it in her or its webs of social, symbolic, cosmic, and temporal relationships, and lawful possibilities (*so* in Kalabari). It is in this situatedness and embeddedness that reality, which starts off dyadically divided between noumenal and phenomenal, becomes triadic. Phenomena and noumena are related to the evolutionary processes and rhythms of human characters, habits, and actions (which are both physical and spiritual, always vacillating between regularity and irregularity) in history, and together they either elicit or divert final cause (destiny). The praxis or methodology of knowledge production that interrelates the two dimensions of reality creates a supervening, emergent dimension of connectedness (a force field of presence and interactions) that places truths in their teleological setting. The perspective or third dimension of situatedness enables the seeker to understand that there is a kind of final cause that draws persons to their destiny (temporal trajectory).

This final cause, however, is neither mechanistic nor random. It is more like a tendency toward an end state, such that with proper discernment and appropriate actions, persons can exploit their open-ended nature to allow for the emergence of novelty and benefits of deliverance and prosperity. This is why individual character, habits, and social relations take on a huge significance in African traditional divination-diagnostic practices.

This dimension of relationality may become under certain scenarios the most important part of the triadic metaphysical system that undergirds and informs discernment in African traditional religions. Take, for instance, the Kalabari philosophy of religion, which holds that it is human attention and relationship with certain material beings or objects that generate the noumenal dimensions of existence. The gods or spirits (except the Supreme Being) who are the products of such phenomenal relationships could be disempowered and dethroned if they overstep their bounds in the relationship or become too demanding. The mechanism for such a radical rejection and annulment of the power of any god is the collective withdrawal of worship, sacrifice, and attention by the members of the community.[9]

We have here a complex metaphysical dynamic at work. The triadic structure can collapse to a monistic one, and a monistic structure can transition into a dyadic one and eventually a triadic one. In this logic, discernment examines not only the body (matter) alone, but also the spirit (soul) and the myriad relationships between matter and spirit, matter and matter, and spirit and spirit.

Ethos of Discernment:
From African Traditional Religion to African Pentecostalism

The seven features that we have laid out are important in understanding the character and nature of and interest in discernment in African Pentecostalism.[10] By and large, African Pentecostalism has appropriated these features, and the key difference between discernment in ATR and in Pentecostalism is in the (claimed) categories of gods as the main sources of the power of discernment. Pentecostals hold that they focus on or work only with the Holy Spirit and that adherents of the ATR do not. Never mind that this claim presupposes a capacity to distinguish the Holy Spirit, who is present and active in the world, from other spirits who are (might be) similarly functioning in the world.

Pentecostals in Africa, like their ATR brethren, are invested in the search and creation of knowledge by fissuring phenomenal reality, by tarrying with the negative, the crack.[11] For African Pentecostals this epistemological quest, this form of spiritual discernment, is indicative of what it means to live in the Spirit. They will ask, when a person is set free by the Spirit, is she not supposed to go beyond her phenomenal capacity, which is part of the causal chain, to reach her noumenal capacity (the actual place of freedom) to interrupt the automatism of her causal enchainment and begin something new? African Pentecostals contest any watertight distinction between the noumenal and the phenomenal realms. For them life in the Spirit involves the divine gifts and capabilities to live, move, and have their beings in both realms.

Life in the Spirit is not *merely* a heightened execution of the techniques of the self on the self. It is to "crucify" the sinful, heavy flesh so that the flesh is "resurrected" as a *transformed* body, a "transphysical" body, whose still-corporeal sensory organs are able also to "transcend bodily normal limitations."[12] African Pentecostals believe that life in the Spirit, as far as embodiment is concerned, can asymptotically approach Jesus's resurrected body (John 20:19, 24–28; Luke 24:30). If this view interprets the new physicality of life in the "life in the Spirit," then how is the Spirit interpreted in the same phrase? Spirit is the experience of new creation by the transphysical body, its transforming encounter with new possibilities from the sacred infinite set of possibilities that characterize the Holy Spirit. The "in" in "life in the Spirit" connotes involvement in and an enveloping by the work and grace of the Spirit as on the day of Pentecost. On this day, the Spirit was felt as a surrounding presence, physical-transphysical touch on the human flesh as the tongues of fire, and as an empowered voice that declared and proclaimed newly acquired transforming truths.[13] In sum, life in the Spirit is a life (body) that is increasingly revealing its pneumatic elements as it approaches the finer, thinner nature of the Spirit.

African Pentecostals are phenomenalizing the noumenal, to put it crudely. They are also noumenalizing the phenomenal: everything becomes the thing-in-itself; the mundane becomes miraculous; the ordinary becomes magical and extraordinary; everything, every event, is receptive to divine interpellation. In short, they "supernaturalize" the natural. Their thinking is that the significance of the phenomenal cannot be equal to itself, such that there is always a quest for the new in order to understand what has already taken place and what is about to be retroactively ignited. God is present and acts in the phenomenal, and that is why the significance of what we do, say, or hear is infinitely richer than what is encoded and immediately readable in the phenomenal register, the hard, concrete situation of action. On the whole, knowing goes beyond the level of epistemology and reaches into ontological issues. The possibility of knowing is concerned with the possibility of human existence, which means the possibilities written in our actions, temporality, finitude, embodiment, and destiny. We have described the character of discernment in African Pentecostalism, and now how do we interpret it?

Discernment as Tarrying with the Negative

To theologize or theorize discernment is to determine how access is given to discernment. How does a people or religious community get the access through which discernment occurs? This is a tricky question or endeavor to undertake. Indeed, there is no point outside this access on which we can stand to assess this access. We can only find the split within the access, the fracture within discernment, to understand discernment. "As a result, it is only a presentation of presentation [a discernment of discernment], a vision of vision, but also the originary fragmentation that all vision is in itself, in its always being outside itself, exposed to the gaze of the other."[14]

Discourse of discernment is the advent of discernment as an other. The discourse is an expression or representation of the mirror, with its split dimension and depth, holding a meta-image. Discernment is always a discernment of discernment, splits within splits, and like the mirror, it ultimately hides the reality it purports to reveal. Finding the access is akin to finding the ultimate elephant on which the earth stands. First, there is a crack, a gap in the human will that makes discernment possible. The fact that the will can be divided against itself makes it possible for us to get periodic flashes of insights. We lose the reflective capacity to deliberate or think on our tendencies to action if there is a unified will. A will that is perfect, undivided, and thus clearly sees the right, good, and truthful path to take does not need discernment, the cultivation of sensitivity necessary to decide when temporal turns of events challenge embedded traditions or demand new thinking. A perfect will has foreordained closure and completeness. It only "imposes" on the world. But in an existential world of becoming, division or incompleteness is a sign of livingness.

A will with a single orientation or inclination does not work well with discernment, which is an immanent process that grows from the unfolding intersection of embodied thinking and situation. It is because the will, the self, is divided against itself as Paul points out in Romans 7—because the self cannot comprehensively know its situations or cannot always do what is right—that it looks toward the aid of discernment. As we have seen, this split self sees or wills a split reality to both decipher and paper over the splits in social relations.

Second, discernment has a much wider semantic range in African Pentecostalism than it does in Catholic or Protestant mainstream theologies. It includes, for example, four categories: social, technological, textual, and the Real. The social category of discernment involves believers consulting pastors or anointed ministers to figure out fractures and fissures in social relations as causes of problems and crises and ultimately to heal or proffer solutions for them. A typical pastoral diagnosis (which makes use of experience, reflection, attentiveness to the Holy Spirit, meaning-making, and spiritual exercises) determines that a person's life course is not going on well because of fractures in social relations. There is a neighbor, relation, in-law, or coworker who is fouling the person's chances for a good life. Such an interferer is declared demonic, and therefore appropriate ritual and deliverance exercises are prescribed to help the troubled person repair the relationship, effect healing, or protect him- or herself.

The technological category of discernment refers to the everydayness of the noumenal as spiritual antennae. The feel or orientation to the numinous antennae, which is *ready-to-hand* in everyday ordinary life activities, grounds the worldhood of daily human and nonhuman interactions. This form of discernment enables Pentecostals to relate to the visible and invisible realms as a coherent and smoothly functioning single world. Once in a while there is a breakdown of the equipment, the antennae, and a disruption of the world occurs as when my bathroom mirror fell down and broke. Forced to step back from the everydayness of existence, the believer merely sees disparate objects, hopes, accidents, and gaps in life. The world is discerned as an other. It is time then to summon the anointed pastor to help cover the gaps and restore the specific *aroundness* of the momentarily broken-down world! The bestirred believers now head for the "consulting clinics" of the expert for either social or textual "prescriptions."

What I call the textual category involves discernments that create fantasies to cover and support the social relations and the gaps in the world. These fantasies enable people to live and survive, to manage and manipulate the gaps between the recalcitrant social circumstances they must endure and those alternative situations they deserve or desire. Pastors and deliverance ministers weave certain narratives with yarns of prophecies, scriptural interpretations, and visions to discern acceptable, sound future states of the people, which enable individual persons to confront tough situations and go on with the act of living with hope. Many Pentecostals recognize the ritualistic nature of such discernments and their associated expressions. Ministers who make such prognoses are not often held accountable for their words.

The last category is the Real, the invisible realm. It is ontological in its orientation. Discernment is not so much the path to good decision, but rather it engenders the ontological context within which decisions and actions ultimately make sense. In other words, it supplies the *contexture* within which dilemmas and challenges are related to ultimate reality. This form of discernment accents the impossibility of a person or thing being completely itself. The invisible is always part of what is visible; it is like Alain Badiou's null set that is part of every situation. There is always something else, something more to a situation, and that something extra is the fount of possibility, but yet it appears constitutively absent from it without the equipment of "seeing eyes."

The quest for this something more, the pursuit of which can lead to the grotesque mazes of ontological existence, is an indication that hermeneutics (interpretation) has not replaced visionary experiences (prophetism) in African Pentecostalism as it has generally happened in the larger Christian world.[15] These four categories of discernment indicate that to properly interpret the discernment practices of African Pentecostals we must always decipher the character of each of the categories and understand how access to them is theologically (biblically) justified. The scholar must not only work to understand their discernment practices, but she also has to know how the discerners ground or distinguish their practices.

Third, discernment is always a fracture within discernment, requiring a split within the very access it grants. The African Pentecostal quest for noumenal knowledge within the framework of Christianity appears to split the very framework that grounds it and denies Christian theology a separate place to assess African Pentecostals' access to discernment. Their epistemological quest tracks the way things are divided internally within Christianity or Christian theology. The life in the Spirit (an invitation and participation in the fullness of life) that African Pentecostals celebrate is grounded in Christianity and eros toward God, and they distinguish it from other forms of life by their fervent commitment to the Holy Spirit. They claim to be God's subjects. Yet in this very strength of commitment lies a weakness. The African Pentecostals' penchant for the noumenal, the thing as such, thing-in-itself, actually reverses the Christian notion of the subject: the subjectivity as structured by the Word, the Logos. Christian subjectivity is not a *Hegelian phantasmagorical representation*; according to the New Testament, the pure self is not surrounded by night; rather, it has been clarified by the Word, by the true light, which enlightens everyone that cometh into the world. Here is the paradox of pentecostal epistemology: the African Pentecostals' effort to access the noumenal, nontransparent stuff of existence is saying to us that the Word fails to shine enough light on the "night of the world." It fails to give spiritual shape to the shapelessness of subjectivity (and of existence). But then, is their epistemological quest, their practices of spiritual discernment, not what it means to live the life of the Spirit? Are all visionary experiences or prophetism dead in Christianity? Indeed, there is no point outside this very Christian access on which to stand and assess the African Pentecostal access to discernment. By faith and experience African Pentecostals believe that the world was framed by the word of God, so that what is seen is not made out of things that are visible; they also believe that the

Spirit will disclose to believers what is to come, show them all things (Heb. 11:3; John 16:13).

The access to this promise, they argue, is kept open by a life in the Spirit, risking one's life, being exposed to the chaos and possibility of death in the night of the world. This is how access to discernment is given. Spiritual powers enable believers to pierce the phenomenal veil, gaze at the face of death, and in Hegelian terminology, the anointing strengthens them to not shrink from death or devastation but to endure and defeat them. In their lights, to discern is to open things up. Discernment is the un-closing, dis-enclosing, of theology. Discernment in African Pentecostalism works to retrieve truths that modern liberal theology and even some segments of pentecostal theology in academe have barred.

Finally, discernment is also an access to market or serves as a context for commodity exchange. *Discerned truths* or advisory products founded on the mystique of the invisible world are produced and consumed along the lines of the economic logic of the market, along the lines of values that approximate market ethos as the health-and-wealth gospel gains ascendancy in African Pentecostal circles. There is now a shared community of production and consumption of discerned truths as Pentecostals increasingly look for ways to improve their well-being with an increasing propensity to truck, barter, and exchange information. The ethic of production demands a morality that emphasizes a this-worldly asceticism, fasting, long prayers, and self-denial. This ethic promotes the production of spiritual insights, information, analyses, and knowledges. There must be people who are motivated to consume these spiritual products in the form of advisory services. So there is a real market or shadow market for discernments. There are now contractor-prayer warriors and "fasters" who undertake deep spiritual exercises on behalf of paying clients. Financial payments are the mirror reflecting the value of the visions and information extracted from the noumenal realm, a measure of the confidence in the spiritual representation of the phenomenal reality. In the language of Plato's allegory of the cave, discernment in this shadow religious system is a measure of the collective trust of consumers in the "seeing eyes" of the producers to interpret the shadows on the noumenal walls. The producers of discernment mirror (mediate, represent) the numinous shadows, the market in turn mirrors them, and the market price further reflects the desires and expectations of consumers, situated in concrete phenomenal settings, for *revelation knowledge* offered in the market. Indeed and ultimately, the phenomenal lives of the consumers show themselves as shadows on the noumenal (cave) walls. Spiritual information is trapped in a self-reflexive cycle whereby discernment is a mirror unto itself. Are philosophy or psychoanalysis correct to insist that there is no direct access to the Real?

The Face, the Mirror, and the Real of Discernment

All this brings us back to my bathroom mirror, which was procured from the market and not from Venus, *babalawo* (master of secrets), or anointed Pentecostal pastor. And as you now know, it broke into pieces on July 11, 2014, and the discovery of this awful mundane fact sent me meandering in an ontological void.

The shock of July 11, 2014, demands further thought as we begin to bring this chapter to a close. My face was taken from me. How could this be? The mouth that uttered, "Where is my face?" that fateful morning and the brain that organized the thought were parts of my head or face. Technically, it was the reflection of my face, that image produced by the play of light and the opaque background of the mirror that disappeared. It was the discernment, the appearance of my face that was absent, while the face was still there. Was it really there? How did I ever know that I had a face? The mirror produced and informed me that I had one. It was the mirror as glass, water, human glances, and human faces that assured me that I had one. I assumed that since other human beings had faces, I too must have one. My eyes could not see themselves, could not see my face *sui generis*. Alas, the eyes could only see through constructed lenses. The objects the eyes see through the constructed lens begin their lives outside the eyes but become integral parts of them. The pupils always take in the objects standing in front of them. Next time you stand close to a person, look into his or her eyes and you will see yourself standing in them, you will make an appearance in them. You will see yourself *in them* looking at yourself. The eyes that see their world through the pentecostal constructed lens see a Pentecostal. But is this not what discernment is all about? Believing is seeing! And believing-is-seeing easily slides into seeing-is-believing. Discernment is the image of the reality of the connection between the discerner and the form of her world or the inner processes of her world, of knowledge and its mutuality.[16] The Spirit makes an appearance inside our constructed lens. Or rather, the Spirit lets the image of time or a cut of possibilities stand in our lens.

My face makes its appearance every morning in the light of the bathroom mirror. Before July 11, every morning the mirror cracked the space between my eyes and the infinite depth of space before them to show me my face. The mirror was the means through which my face, an other to my body, was seen, recognized, and greeted every day. Over time, the mirror morphed from being a piece of equipment that permitted the appearance of my face into a preternatural figure. My fervent commitment to it every morning, standing in front of it with the offering of toothpaste, over and over again, gave me access to a "noumenal" world. The mirror is a god, household god, spirit of light-and-space religion that enabled me to read my invisible face every morning. It creates light and darkness. It creates my face, as an object outside myself, after my own image. In the revelation of my invisible face it hides or cannot reach the back of my head and what is inside my head. The capacity to reveal that which is hidden or to make visible the invisible is at the same time an incapability to reveal. It gives and denies access through images.

The physical eye limits itself to the constructed mirror in order to see the invisible. The eye of the scientist limits itself to the microscope or telescope to tell the truth. But the spiritual eyes of the Pentecostal, aided by splendid imagination, want to see within and behind the mirror, telescope, or microscope. They always want to go beyond. The very refusal of Pentecostals to accept the impossibility of direct access to the Real ("the beyond") inaugurates their entire order of prayer language, the symbolic, and self-world correlation, which ties truth and meaning in a particular theologico-ethical constellation.

But when the mirror removed itself in my bathroom for my pentecostal eyes to see what was behind it, *the beyond of the mirror*, the eyes recoiled in horror instead of experiencing perfect jouissance. Consequently, I, the owner of the eyes with toothpaste-laden toothbrush in one hand, screamed: "Woe is me, for I am undone! Because I am a man of physical mind, and I dwell in the midst of Pentecostals with transphysical minds; for my eyes have seen the Real, the ~~black~~ white hole where light does not escape. The Real is a white metal panel of my bathroom cabinet door." And the white metal panel calmly responded: "No access today."

Concluding Thoughts

"No access today"—is this not, perhaps, what the angel with the flaming sword said to Adam and Eve after God had driven them out of the garden of Eden and they wanted to go back in? They transgressed God's commandment by knowing how to discern good and evil on their own, and for this disobedience they were rendered nude and sent out of their home. Just before they left, God graciously clothed them with animal skin.

When Adam and Eve transgressed God's commandment, for the first time their eyes were opened and they noticed their nudity, saw their appearance as a privation of clothing. Before this occasion, even though they were without clothing (presumably covered by the "clothing of grace" or supernatural grace), they were not considered naked. Sin makes their bodies visible, so to speak. God eventually covers them with animal skins; grace ("grace with skin") covers them again, conceals their naked, pure corporeality. Grace is a garment.[17]

But grace operates differently in the pentecostal quest for invisibility; grace (gift of spiritual eyes) is nudity. The pentecostal understanding of the divine gift to lift the phenomenal veil is aptly rendered as "opening of the eyes" or "opening the spiritual eyes." The eyes that are open can lift the "clothing" over the phenomenal to denude it because seeing the invisible is linked to nudity and gaining knowledge is connected with nakedness. Pentecostals often direct this gift of lifting of the clothing over the phenomenal to their neighbors or "enemies." They aspire to render their neighbors (unbelievers) and their innermost secrets visible but prefer that they themselves remain invisible to the neighbors; the Holy Spirit will protect them from the penetrating gaze of neighbors or the "enemies." Here we see the quest for visibility of the other and invisibility of the self. This combination of visibility and invisibility takes my mind to the myth of Gyges. According to this myth as related by Plato in the *Republic* (359d–360b), after an earthquake one of the shepherds of the king of Gyges found a ring in a tomb, and this ring could make him invisible to others by turning it toward himself. While he remains invisible to them, they are visible to him. When the ring is turned away from him, he becomes visible to them and he continues to see. Having this power of invisibility at will, he seduces the queen, kills the king, and becomes the new king. Emmanuel Levinas interprets the myth in this way: "The myth of Gyges is the very myth of the I . . . which exist[s] non-recognized. . . . [When one sees] without being seen . . . [it is] a determination of the other by the same, without the same being determined by the other."[18]

So one way grace is deployed in Pentecostalism is to use it to uncover that which is concealed. The quest for invisibility is the becoming visibility of nature's (reality's) nudity. Grace in the name of anointing exposes the inner, secret nature of the unbelieving neighbor and renders him legible—and possibly suitable for voyeuristic enjoyment. The neighbor in the moment of "revelation," in that moment of denudation, becomes obscene *homo sacer*—impure, killable by Holy Ghost fire—and is not considered sacred (saved).

This turning of the biblical relationship between grace as represented by clothing and nature as represented by nudity into grace as nudity and nature as clothing forces us to rethink the Genesis writer's presupposition of grace. For the writer, grace always already presupposes a naked nature. Erik Peterson makes this point clear.

> Finally, we also reach this ultimate truth: that just as clothes veil the body, so in Adam supernatural grace covers a nature abandoned by God's glory and left to itself. This is presented as the possibility of human nature degenerating into what the Scriptures call "flesh," the becoming visible of man's nudity in its corruption and putrefaction. There is therefore a profound significance to the fact that the Catholic tradition calls "clothing" the gift of grace that man receives in Paradise. Man can begin to be interpreted only through such clothing of glory that, from a certain point of view, belongs to him only exteriorly, just like any piece of clothing. Something very important is expressed in this exteriority of mere clothing: that grace presupposes created nature, its "absence of clothing," as well as the possibility of it being denuded.[19]

Pentecostals (as the seers in the Bible) presuppose that created nature is clothed (there is the fabric of unknowability over it) as well as the possibility that this nature can be denuded. This slight shift of emphasis is important for understanding the way Pentecostals see the world. The shift represents a desire to see reality or nature in all its transparency. What is this pentecostal gaze that can only be satiated by nudity, that can better understand or interpret reality only when the phenomenal piece of clothing is laid aside?

It seems Pentecostals have rendered grace *inoperative*, taken it out of its original relation with reality and directed it to new needs and desires. The exercise and inoperativity of grace come together in their quest for invisibility. The "old," "original" use of grace as clothing for nature or reality's nudity is not abolished, but the new use displaces it toward a new direction even as "it persists in it and exhibits it."[20] All this presents to us for meditation a higher "technological paradigm" of grace. What does it mean that Pentecostals are making a slight adjustment to grace's relation with nature or phenomena so it works according to their desires or cultural inclination? The next chapter will attempt to respond to this question.

3

The Beauty, Skin, and Monstrosity of Grace

Introduction

What is grace at the pentecostal street level, not at the pentecostal theological academy? Let me respond with a story. When I became born-again, that is, when I became a Pentecostal in 1993, I worshiped in a pentecostal church (Zoe Ministries) that was on Victoria Island, the lush, upper-class area of Lagos, Nigeria. This part of Lagos was also adjacent to a very poor neighborhood, Maroko. So the church was a mixture of the upper echelon and the lowest rung of Nigeria. The poor were in the majority. I experienced grace as an irruption of God among people who were perpetually vulnerable to death because of poverty and the excess weight of suffering. Yet worship among the poor was a form of play, an explosion of joy, a pure means. Grace was an excess, surplus power beyond the obligations of the law and the constricted possibilities of life in Maroko.

Before I came to study theology in a seminary, the congregation at Maroko had schooled me in the pentecostal notion of grace. I learned from the actions, practices, and words of the people who worshiped with me that God's grace is not only about the beneficial actions of God toward God's creation, transforming human beings into God's subjects or into obedient subjects of the state, but also about providing an alternative vision to the existing order of things. Grace is both constructive and disruptive. Pentecostals consider the born-again experience as an *event* of grace, which compels them to proclaim themselves as the subjects of God who are open to divine surprises, to alternative visions. Grace initiates and sustains them in the *Pentecostal principle*, which is the capacity to begin, the capacity to initiate something new amid ongoing social automatism. Grace opens up what the law tends to close off. In every society there are three sets of possibilities: one that is open to all individuals, another that is available to only a few with the rest excluded, and the universe of possibilities that are yet to be fulfilled or not available to all persons and institutions. The law acts to bring the range of possibilities to a manageable proportion and then to distribute them into the three sets.

This is what "street-seminary" taught me about grace. According to the popular pentecostal mindset, grace is an event, a disruptive one. God's grace radically challenges and unsettles our human presumptions of self-sufficiency and self-complacency and warmly embraces and settles us in salvation, service, identification with Christ, and as beings indwelled by the Holy Spirit. Grace is the appearance of something new into creation, human life, the human condition—it breaks into the order of things. Grace as the *evental* movement of God, the Holy Spirit, is full of novelty, possibilities, and potentials. In the pentecostal way of thinking, the "big," "serious" purpose of grace is the freedom to play in salvation for freedom. Grace is characterized by play, having no purpose at all. It is to exuberantly embrace the Holy Spirit as the spirit of play. Under grace, Pentecostals believe they have a playful relation to the law, and this opens up a space where they can fulfill the demands of the law under the figure of love. How does grace open up a playful relation to the law? The logic of grace is the logic of play. In its nature of purposelessness, play transcends the instrumental demands and constraints of the present given world in the direction of possibilities and not-yet-defined potentialities.

Let us unpack the phrase "playful relation to the law." To begin with, play *deactivates* the law and radicalizes saving grace. Under grace, the law is not abolished, but "deactivated," rendered inoperative. Under the power of God's grace, the law is separated from its end of condemning us to eternal damnation, and it is also delinked from its power to induce the desire for transgression in us. Remember Paul's language in Romans 7: the law is not gone, but grace opens it to a new possible use. We learn that it is no longer for condemnation and guilt, but for common love. The law shows us how to live and live well in our common existence; it is severed from its original instrumentality or purpose. It is in this nature of losing its purpose and by moving us to realize the moral imperative of our lives—the demand to become what God wants us to be—that it becomes like play. This is what I mean by grace opening up a space for a playful relation to the law. In the language of salvation, play is the freedom of grace within the constraints of law as redefined.

When asked what does this lived experience of such a playful relation to the law feel like, Pentecostals would answer that, on a daily basis, there is a feeling of joy and freedom and expectation of surprises from the Holy Spirit. There is the realization that grace does not require a counter (reciprocal) service or work obligation. First, by rendering the law inoperative and yet empowering them to live the life-in-the-Spirit, they believe that they can fulfill the expectations of love of God, love of fellow human beings, and love of all God's creation. They now respond to God or God's law not out of fear of condemnation, but out of love. Second, the active reception of God's grace means that one takes work seriously (but not as salvific) as supported by an inclination to play. Grace frees and transforms work. He who does not know how to play will find it difficult to appreciate God's grace and work of existence, which is Being at play.

The Beauty of Grace and Work

It is my contention that the interrelation of grace and play constitutes the "essence" of work. Grace is not opposed to work. Grace is disruption of boundaries so a new beginning can be made. It is in this sense like work, expansion of possibilities or a goal-oriented act. Work, broadly understood, is the unfurling of humanity toward a wholeness in which all selves and others are inextricably linked.[1] (The whole refers to both the social whole and to the whole that points to the cosmic order: God, persons, not-yet born, nature, and society.) Work is the daily means (involving body, mind, and spirit) of humanity to begin, to cut open (*be-ginnan*) the iterative dynamic of becoming itself that is human existence. Work fulfills our need to make a fresh beginning in the fluid dynamics of transcending our current humanity. Working is fundamentally the communication and exchange of that by which a human being is in dynamism of positing a new possible world.[2] The *that* that is communicated is the set of possibilities (potentials) for forward movement. Work is that by which human beings "stand in" and "stand out" of actualization of potentialities, the processive openness toward the not-yet. This is also like the logic of play: the desire to transcend the instrumental demands and constraints of the present given world in the direction of possibilities and not-yet-defined potentialities. This is also the logic of grace. God gives God's grace freely to humanity to repair, reconstruct, and re-create social existence, relationships, character, health, and so on. Grace, the giving of salvation, is linked to divine workmanship (Eph. 2:8–10).

Let us further explore the relationship among grace, work, and play. First, they all contribute to eudaimonia, the well-lived human life. Second, they are forces behind the freedom to begin anew, what Hannah Arendt calls the concept of natality. I recognize them as gesturing to the power (divine, divine-human, human) to re-create and replenish both inner life and social existence. There is a deep dance going on between grace, work, and play all the time. God's grace (which by definition is free) is received and appropriated by the free self when it "allows for play and allows itself to play." Work is the transformation of grace and play into new spaces for freedoms, overcoming unfreedoms. Grace imbues work with the sense that there is redemption and hope for failures or after failures. This can then transform the attitude toward work from that of instrumentality to that of pleasure, intrinsic finality. Work becomes play and can then really become the play of the creative potentials of humanity. Grace in this interplay can be construed as working-sans-works. God's grace exemplifies play and work. Put differently, *being-with* is exemplified by grace, play, work, and the relations among them.

What makes play play is neither the absence of an instrumental orientation to outcome nor "purposiveness without a purpose." Surely, it is all that, but much more. *Being-with* constitutes the *essence* of play. This is what displaces, dislocates, or dissolves every substantial essence. Play displaces or discloses the being-in-common, being-with one another. This *with* denuded of instrumentality is not external to play, is not an extrinsic addition to the players, and is not interior to each of the players. The play is the *with*, the *cum* that puts the players together. Play is the celebration of being-with.

Work, as I defined it in my 2008 book, *The Depth and Destiny of Work*, is the expansion, preservation, repair, and innovation of the being-with of existence. So at a fundamental level it shares the bare essence of play. Grace is the dynamic, the hope of rupture and event of the being-with. It is not a dimension added on to a primitive being-with even if it were to occur as "masculine kairos," an in-breaking force. It is simply the immanent and intrinsic condition of the being-with that is coexistence, that is play, and that is the work of threading and rethreading the fabric of existence, the copresence of human beings. There is no appearing of grace to itself except as appearing to work and play or as appearing of work and play to one another. Grace is the very presence of the Spirit of God in the being-with, which in an endless way disrupts persons, groups, and institutions and disposes such to a better level of flourishing. Grace is repetitive, as it is affirmative of the being-with. It is the condition of affirmation of being-with, with one another and with God. This repetition is not the repetition of the same or of origins, but of continuity and discontinuity and re-creation of connections. This repetition is a form of plasticity. In some crude sense, grace is the power of the plasticity in being-with.

The Skin of Grace

To get a fuller understanding of the working of grace in Pentecostalism, we have to consider it under the extended framework of anointing. In everyday theology, grace is primarily used when talking about salvation ("For it is by grace you have been saved, through faith . . . not by works" Eph. 2:8–9 NIV), to invoke God's approval of a planned action ("by grace we shall do this or that . . ."), or to hide an intention or deeds under the banner of God. But grace is also used in a broad sense—and this tends to have more resonance with actual lived experiences of Pentecostals. Grace in its broadened usage incorporates anointing, the divine empowerment or enablement to accomplish something. Operating or luxuriating under the rubric of anointing, grace becomes the tangible, pragmatic effects of God's presence in human bodies and objects (such as olive oil, handkerchiefs, chairs, floor, or voice—glossolalia). Grace is real presence. Real presence is grace in tangible things, the manifestation of the Holy Spirit in material forms. Often when Pentecostals in worship services say, "I feel the anointing in here," they follow up with, "I feel the Spirit of God in this place." Anointing is the materiality of grace, *appearance qua appearance* of the Holy Spirit.

The question now is how do we understand grace in and through its manifest presence in objects, physical stuff or through sensual and material practices? How do Pentecostals sense grace through their bodily senses? What are the mediated, sensational forms of grace in pentecostal gatherings? Simply put, how is the discourse of grace born as a discourse of anointed bodies and religious objects? In this way of approaching grace, it becomes easy to see how Pentecostals perceive and create their worlds through the movements of grace on bodies and group of bodies. Pentecostal worship services make the subtle point that it is no longer adequate to talk about grace without paying attention to aesthetics (in its full sense as sensory perception, form, beauty, and senses and sensorimotor skills) of religion. It is no longer adequate to talk about operations of grace without paying attention to how the gospel message of grace is danced, gestured, seen, tasted, smelled, drummed, heard, and embodied by ordinary folks.

Sociologist Annalisa Butticci, pursuing the study of the politics of real presence among Catholics and Pentecostals in Italy, reveals how poor African migrants deploy the empowerment that comes from "seeing" the Holy Spirit pour herself into their bodies and religious objects to produce a space for their flourishing.[3] Her book, *African Pentecostals in Catholic Europe*, is about, among other things, different religious worlds in interlocking sacred settings that are not divorced from the mundane, everyday environment of human existence. At one level the book shows us the encounter of Catholicism and African Pentecostalism in Italy; at another level it portrays the rituals, interactions, and the drama of this encounter in very vivid constructions of aesthetic sacred spaces. Bodies and senses, arts and rhetoric, and sights and sounds define, differentiate, produce, and expand sacred and social spaces. In this work of expansion we discern grace as "approaching withdrawal and withdrawal approach";[4] it reveals and conceals itself at the same time, inspiring new visions of the self but never allowing itself to be grasped. And in this way, embodied and bodying grace is key to the aesthetics of human-divine encounter.

Butticci's skills in excavating the depths of pentecostal aesthetics of worship help her readers to identify the underlying structural principle of sensuality of the human-divine encounter. I identified this principle using Jacques Lacan's triad of the Imaginary-Symbolic-Real. There is an idealized self-image of what African Pentecostals want to be (*imaginary*). And it is based on their reception of God's grace. There is the gracious God (the *Big Other*) whom they want to impress through impassioned prayers, dance, and gifts and who implores them to give the best of themselves to God and to the world (*symbolic*). African Pentecostals have a symbolic identification with God. The Real is the same God for whom they try the "impossible possibility," demanding of themselves a crucifixion of the flesh in order to experience the jouissance of heaven on earth, to enjoy the expanded possibilities of life in Italy. This Real that is God resists their grasping or full understanding no matter how close the Pentecostals approach him. He is approached with the full complement of the body and its senses, but they can never "represent" him. The Real transpires or shines through their reality, forever slipping through their fingers, as Slavoj Žižek might put it. What we can discern as the Real in the divine-human encounter are "traces" left behind on the body surfaces or in the psyche.

Such traces include the fragile moments of smiles, laughter, radiant faces, sweaty bodies, pleasures, feelings of elevation and empowerment, emotions, sense of new possibilities, and so on. These traces at best remind us of the leftover glory of Jehovah that shone on Moses's face after he only saw the backside of God. Despite their strong belief in the transimmanence of the divine, the Spirit of God cannot be fully mediated, represented, or captured. The Spirit remains enigmatic and untouchable. The Real in our Lacanian-pentecostal triad can be likened to the unstable temporal presence, the imperceptible, ungraspable gap between the past and the future. And the real presences that Butticci analyzes in her book are constructed or constituted by human beings throwing their bodies and their objects into this clearing or gap in order to sustain, expand, and exploit it.

Through Butticci's examination of the belief in and the role of anointing in producing real presences among Pentecostals, one can infer that the event of grace in migrants' lifeworld produces subjectivity brought about by subjects faithful to its consequences. It is within the logic and dynamics of the triad that she locates pentecostal subjectivity. She portrays the subjectivity of African Pentecostals as located within a system of senses that is in dialogue with the hard, real world and the immaterial divine realm. Butticci describes pentecostal subjectivity as nitty-gritty materiality that disturbs, disrupts, and subverts power relations through artful deployment of senses and sensibilities. Her book shows us how fidelity to the event (grace-anointing) is primarily worked out and sustained on a daily basis through the interaction ritual chains of senses and the "distribution of the sensible" by the *parts of no-part* in Italian society who are relying on grace to see them through from one day to another.

The Monstrosity of Pentecostal Grace

We will illustrate the monstrosity of the pentecostal notion of grace with three examples or discussions: grace in lived experience, the effectivity of grace in form of worship as pure means, and grace as limit of salvation. The grace that we encounter as lived experience has two sides to it: internal and external. The internal is the recognition by a person that God has accepted her, believing that she is saved. The external part is the material practice of saving grace. We observe grace from the outside as practices of faith, belief in the saving God. From the inside, it is confidence. We work as we believe and we believe as we work. We enact in our work, in our external behavior the internal measure of grace inside of us and our internal belief expresses itself as work. Work inhabits grace. In Pentecostalism there is an added tension in this relationship between grace and work. *I know very well that I am not saved by grace, but I nonetheless believe that work works.*

Why must grace here be supplemented by belief in work? The commonplace thing to say is that in a type of Pentecostalism, with its focus on prosperity message, belief in work is a way to "coerce" grace or the divine to unleash material wealth. The real situation is to note that there is an immanent gap, a split within the subject's experience of grace, a split within grace. And it appears Pentecostals feel this immanent gap more acutely. Grace is not articulated around a purpose, a quality, or a predicate of its receiver. It articulates around its own void. So the believer cannot subjectively assume it. Belief in work supplements this gap or void. So in a sense the Pentecostal follows the work, keeps the belief in work, and savors the manifestations of the power of the Holy Spirit and then grace as inner belief comes.

Why is the immanent gap within grace felt more acutely by the average Pentecostal than, for example, the Calvinist? The typical passage of a person, such as a non-Christian African, to born-again life in Pentecostalism is often violent. There is often a cutting of previous symbolic links, connections to the person's natural environment and tradition for the light of the Holy Spirit, the power of grace, to come into one's life. The person somewhat descends into a Hegelian "night of the world" before a new symbolic universe is constructed for her. How does the person climb back from the chaos and madness created by the radical withdrawal from her inherited symbolic texture and coordinates? She emerges through narratives. She retells her daily life activities, triumphs, and defeats (awaiting transformation into victories) as acts of faith, as works that give shape to her everyday grace. Through these narratives, testimonies, she incrementally and subjectively transforms herself into a true born-again. The truly new emerges neither when grace is imperceptibly received nor when the believer acts but when a declaration, a performative retelling of the act, is made.[5]

In sum the pentecostal *nonetheless I believe that work works* gestures to something akin to Alain Badiou's concept of the emergence of revolutionary subject. The new only becomes an event when it restructures a person's symbolic texture and makes her a believer in it. It is the fidelity to the contingent event that actually makes it happen, enacts its necessity. The *nonetheless I believe that work works* is the necessary "fall" into belief in work that opens up the passage into the Christian life proper. Note this fall is set off by an encounter with grace, and eventually grace completes a totality. But this movement toward completion is not before the encounter with the eventual "I act because I believe," a crack in the ring of grace that encompasses the life of the new believer.

Let us add another perspective to this discussion. This is the idea that the full realization of grace—without a crack in its totality—will lead to its self-destruction or self-profanation. We can only receive grace with reference to non-grace situations. But when the background itself is universal grace, then grace becomes particular. (Grace by definition becomes "grace is grace.") This is like the universal encountering itself in its specific elements. The particular is a species inside the universal genus. This is a particularity that embodies the universality of the whole while at the same time is its negation. Grace is grace is an identity that contradicts itself. If the first "grace is" the grace that encompasses all the good things, predicates, and particulars we associate with grace, then the second one excludes all of them. It becomes its opposite, the absence of its predicates and particular contents. The returning first "grace is" does not meet itself exactly as it began its journey, but meets an empty collectivity.

The next point to note is that grace always arrives at its destination. Grace, like a letter from elsewhere, must reach its addressee, and it is only her recognition or acceptance of it that makes it a letter to her. Grace can only be asserted after the unfolding of its consequences, even if it engenders these very consequences. But once grace is addressed to itself, it falls into a vortex of drive, not dissimilar from what Schelling describes as the pre-creation rotary movement of drives in the Godhead.

As Slavoj Žižek argues, "The universal is the opposite of itself insofar as it refers to itself as a particular, insofar as it attains its being-for-itself in the form of its opposite."[6] The key point to note here is that this paradoxical particularity is always already part of grace, the totality, ensemble of elements. As a totality, a universal has an element in it that functions as an exception. The different elements (types) of grace begin to acquire their universality once we have excluded work as an embodiment (or enabler) of salvation in general. If grace is not the unique foundation of salvation or existence, then work is grace pretending to be the expression of the unique principle. Grace as a universal constitutes itself through subtraction of work that embodies it (or its functions) as such. So the scission is immanent in grace and not in work, the particular. The immanent inconsistency of grace prevents it from fully realizing itself irrespective of the presence or absence of external obstacles. So we have a perpetual postponement of the arrival of heaven on earth.

The "monstrosity" of pentecostal grace is also discernible in its worship or the idea of worship as pure mediality (medium), not as something instrumental, as the free selfless offering to God. Worship as pure means is free, which is to say it is ultimately grounded in itself, and we cannot attribute to it any purpose or a network of causal instrumentality or scheme. There is a discontinuity in the texture of purpose. This thus implies a hole in the fabric of social relations or divine-human relation, an incompleteness in the texture of the phenomenal reality of religion. Worship as pure means in Pentecostalism somewhat approximates the Kantian notion of freedom. Is this not what grace is all about? Is grace not ultimately grounded in itself and apart from the natural or social causes? We receive it not because of the causal chain of our preceding actions. It is an intervention into our phenomenal reality—the chain of our natural and social causes does not cover all of our religious reality. There is a gap in our phenomenal reality through which grace pours in, suspending or violating socionatural laws.

More importantly, the very gap (limitation, impossibility) that separates human beings from "saving" themselves, the humans' failure to grasp their salvation, the gulf between human beings and God, simultaneously indicates grace. What is regarded as grace separating human work from salvation should be simultaneously seen as the gap immanent to human work itself or phenomenal reality. All this means that the human agents of worship, freedom, or the (supremely free) divine agent of grace cannot be "reduced to phenomenal reality. Phenomenal reality is thus incomplete, non-All."[7]

Worship as pure means also enacts a certain reversal of the subject-object dichotomy. At the moment of worship as pure means, the Holy Spirit or rather grace becomes the subject. Grace not only mediates between God and human beings and between the human beings in the worship as a general equivalent of all interaction chains but it is also the active agent of the interaction. The result is that the entire movement of the worship service becomes the self-movement of grace or rather the Holy Spirit. Is this precisely not the "self-alienation" of the work that is worship? Is it not that what emerges as grace—that which structures the whole divine-human relation—is through the alienation of work? And yet we have no direct access to grace except through the error and failure of work. Is grace not something that is retroactively posited once we notice the failure of work to save us? Take the notion of predestination as an exemplar of this purposeless grace, of grace that is unrelated to human work. When a person comes to Christ, begins to sense that she, the unacceptable, is now accepted by God, then the whole eternal past (predestiny) is written by this sense or act to accept salvation. Predestination does not mean some persons are eternally sealed in advance to live in heaven, but that a temporal decision is capable of retroactively changing destiny, erasing the *virtual eternal past* of sins and setting them free. As Friedrich Wilhelm Schelling would put it, as if the decision had been made before even the person is conscious of it, as if it occurred outside of time. The free act becomes a necessity. The act that never took place in reality is presupposed for the believer in order to make sense of her contingent action.[8] It does appear then that the decision chose its maker before she makes it. (This is the impossibility around which the divine-human relationship structures itself.) As if the person were born to embody their salvation, born to come to God through Christ. This does not mean that an actual decision merely actualizes an atemporal divine decision but retroactively (re)constitutes the past (decision) itself, so that persons "become what they are," to use Hegel's words.[9] A Christian is "the retroactive result of his own choice," a paradox of forced choice.[10] This perhaps explains why Pentecostals are not enamored by the classical doctrine of predestination and as such put so much emphasis on evangelization, making altar calls, and asking not-yet Christians to make decision to accept Christ.

The idea of grace as self-propelling and self-enhancing means that the ultimate limit of salvation is grace itself. Apocalypse understood as unveiling, or, crudely, the end of the world, is an attempt of grace to escape its unconditional spiral. The revolutionizing and unconditional dynamic of grace—the sun shines on the good and the bad; the bad and the good are touched by grace—underlie the development of civilizations, both good and bad. Grace that is born at the same time as the impossibility of atemporal work attempts to escape its material conditions by consuming all temporal human work (in the language of Peter, the earth and work therein will be burnt up). This is what is expected at the end of the world, according to a reading of the book of Revelation. There is another way to interpret the end of the world. The free circulation of grace—God's refusal to kill off unbelievers in Christ as some Pentecostals want, but rather allowing them to prosper and create obscene works of arts—is the "condition of impossibility" for realizing the full "positive effect" of grace itself. What such Pentecostals fail to understand is that the condition of impossibility is also the condition of possibility of grace. To remove the unbelievers as obstacles to realize the fundamentalist utopian vision of a perfect world is to simultaneously remove the dynamic of grace, the very thing that makes it what it is. It is purposeless and nonselective. The "obstacle" is not external to grace; it is inherent in it. The world as we know it ends when God answers the prayer of those who want grace to end.

Real Presence and Split Holy Spirit

The grounding of grace in the sensing of body or objects conveys a message not only about the pentecostal worldview, but also its notion of the Holy Spirit. The manifestation of God in real objects or bodies—the real presence—presupposes a two-world metaphysics. There is an interaction between the realm of phenomenal objects as appearance and the realm of noumenal things-in-themselves, the realm of the Spirit. The objective phenomenal object, which appears to observers in the real world, not only manifests or discloses its objective being, but also doubles as the appearance of non-manifest supersensible entity or noumenon. The Holy Spirit, the supersensible person comes into being from the world of real presence that mediates her. The divine as real presence "comes from the world of appearance which has mediated it; in other words, appearance is its essence. The supersensible is the sensuous and the perceived posited as it is *in truth*, but the *truth* of the sensuous and the perceived is to be *appearance*. The supersensible is therefore appearance qua appearance."[11]

The preceding Hegelian quotation reveals that there are at least two possible interpretations of the real presence of the Holy Spirit—suggesting a split in the notion of God. One way is to interpret the Holy Spirit as the primary cause of the real presence—the supersensible, inner world causing the sensible, phenomenal manifestation. But Hegel suggests that the supersensible world, contrary to the tenets of the two-world metaphysics, "*comes* from the world of appearance." The inner world, which does the appearing and is perceived as objective interiority, is nothing but a subjective interiority. A positing of an inner world beyond phenomena and treatment of physical objects as representations of an underlying world precede the understanding of real presence as appearances of noumena. So what lies behind the veil, the non-appearing underlying "what" that precipitates the real presence, is consciousness; consciousness is subjective interiority as supersensible inner world. Does the divine manifest in objects or do we perceive the objects as such, and to whom does this manifestation belong? How can we grasp the relationship between objects of real presence and the Holy Spirit? Perhaps, instead of asking what the Holy Spirit is for the objects and bodies, and how we can grasp her in this respect, we should ask the obverse question: What is (the exuberant rise of the) real presence for the Holy Spirit?

The point before us is that objective real presence, "the palpable anointing," on a person or object does not settle the question as to whether the Holy Spirit "is a secondary effect rather than a primary cause" or is the effectivity of real presence "generated specifically through the deployment of intentional consciousness of the category of appearance" or not.[12] The answer relies on our personal decision of faith. There is no clean logical way to infer one way or the other. So the politics of real presence falls into the class of *truth procedure*.

There are other vexing issues about real presence, such as, how do we interpret what the Holy Spirit is doing in manifesting in religious objects or bodies? The Holy Spirit in manifesting as real presence appears to herself. Another issue is how and why the Holy Spirit doubles herself by appearing as real presence, manifesting as appearance from its invisible, indivisible oneness (or trinitarian substantial self). With the manifestation of the divine in any object there emerges now a distinction, a gap introduced into the notion of the Holy Spirit: distinction between appearance and essence. This distinction can be inscribed into appearance itself as essence appears within appearance.[13] Thus, the question is no longer about sifting through real presences that are false appearances or how to see authentic underlying reality, but the question is how and why the Holy Spirit appears to herself. The real presence of the Holy Spirit is the Holy Spirit's self-reflection. In addition, the difference between the object of manifestation (phenomenon) and noumenon, between the Holy Spirit and real presence, is transposed back into the Holy Spirit.

This is precisely what the pentecostal inclination toward the real presence does to its notion of the Holy Spirit. The Spirit is not reduced to appearance, but we are nudged to conceive the very process of appearance from the standpoint of the Holy Spirit and this changes the questions we ask about appearance and real presence. The split that separates physical objects from the noumenal spirit is fully admitted, or the split in the Holy Spirit is fully admitted, but "this very split is transposed back into [the Spirit] as [her] kenotic self-emptying."[14]

Are the antagonisms, inconsistencies, and gaps due only to the underlying notion of split Holy Spirit in pentecostal thought? Could it be that the contradictions and conflicts concerning real presence or false appearances are part of the Holy Spirit? What are the conditions for the Holy Spirit appearing in objects? What are the conditions for appearance of the Holy Spirit arising in a gathering of worshipers? What are the conditions for the Holy Spirit appearing to himself?

The Economy of Real Presence and Grace

If the Pauline doctrine of grace as outlined in Romans 3:20–25, 28, disavows exchange and social obligations, then the logic of real presence inserts the "impossible gift" of grace into the economy of exchange. Whether the manifestation of divine power in objects or bodies is represented as God's acts to awe unbelievers (1 Cor. 15:22), or as recompense for a life of holiness, or indeed as the reward of intense desire and prayers for God's intervention, grace is reinserted into an economy of exchange, desire, and gratification. Grace as evidenced by the multiplicity of real presence in the circular economy is a *machine* for miracles, a machine that is *in*, *with*, and *under* the matrix of life and the lifeworld.

The pentecostal understanding of grace implies a view of life as miraculous. All of life and the lifeworld are potentially miracle-textured. The personal lives of believers can display outward and visible signs of an irruption of grace. If bread and wine can be characterized by the phrase *finitum capax infiniti* (the finite can contain the infinite), then so can the rest of creation. Pentecostals go further to posit that the infinite, eternal presence of the Holy Spirit (or the risen Christ) can extend the logic of this impossible possibility to improbable events in the lives of believers. The notion that the finite contains the infinite suggests that "supernatural" forces operating in nature are not always from outside; they are already present within nature. (As we shall demonstrate in the next chapter, this pentecostal view of divine intervention gestures to the idea of God that is both within and outside nature, which founds the sacred.)

The sign of the active presence of the "supernatural" forces in a believer's life, which is also the sign of grace, is indexed by personal miracles. Put differently, grace takes the form of miracle; grace becomes miraculous grace and miracle becomes both its sign and its ground.[15]

Conclusion: Blended Impossibility and Possibility

By way of reaching conclusion and as a precursor to the discussion of the notion of the sacred in the next chapter, I need to quickly state that the pentecostal emphasis on the miraculous life is not tantamount to a rejection or downplaying of phenomenal life. As Ruth Marshall has rightly reported, there might have been in early years of Pentecostalism when personal work and dedication were suspended upon (because of) the grace of God, but now there is a well-developed discourse and practice of techniques of the self on the self, self-improvement and self-governance, work, and refashioning and control of desires, and a powerful tilt toward this-worldly life. Religious scholar Afe Adogame's ethnography work on African migrants in Europe well illustrates this shift.[16] He demonstrates that the African Christian or immigrant Christian focuses on the visible and invisible realms. What is most important to migrant believers is that these two realms are in constant communication and supernatural and human beings "travel" between them. Adogame records these words of a prospective African immigrant to Europe: "Since the visa officials have become slaves to paper documentation, we will continue to exploit their ignorance. Even if they request for signatures from God before they approve visa, we will get them. It is only a matter of time and money."[17]

There is not only the notion of possibility that echoes through the informant's statement, but also a traditional African sensibility. In it I hear the wisdom of Eneke the bird in Achebe's *Things Fall Apart*: "Since men have learned to shoot without missing, he [Eneke] has learned to fly without perching."[18] There are more echoes. Consider the informant's assertion that "it is only a matter of time and money." What do you hear or sense? I can hear the rustle of forged papers. I can also sense the sensibilities of African traditional religions filtering through it. Willingness to make sacrifices, as Yoruba Ifa's *Odu* relentlessly states, is key to realizing one's request before God. So the *matter of time and money* might mean time spent in prayer and fasting and money spent in offerings, tithes, and gifts to anointed preachers. *Time and money*, aided by a little imagination, faith, and faithfulness to the cause, will nudge the invisible God to "sign" his signatures on visible tangible papers. Imagination, faith, and faithfulness of this magnitude are a form of resistance to bureaucratic rationality and formality that reduce humans to slaves of paper documentation.

The prospective migrant's statement draws from a theology that emphasizes possibility in the face of all impossibility, even as it highlights the commingling of the visible and invisible realms. The pentecostal everyday form of theology is a theology of possibility and the scent and accent of possibilities sustain the grit and energy of rejected, oppressed, and marginalized people. The people who espouse it are always demanding in their words and deeds: Is there a creative alternative to the current regime of obstacles, to the forces that thwart human flourishing? Their answer is always yes and soon there will be an opening, a space for miracle. They believe that they only need to deploy their imagination and show fidelity to their cause and course of enhancement of life to succeed or grasp a miracle.

Any analysis of grace in everyday theology of Pentecostals and its twists and distortions must pay attention to Pentecostals' understanding of miracle. Their everyday form of theology is firmly anchored to a non-Humean concept of miracle. Theirs is not so much a contravention of known laws in the physical world as the work of a parallel realm, which is always tangent to the physical and capable of activating dormant possibilities or inserting new possibilities into it without overturning its physical laws. Their view of miracle is keyed to a worldview that accents the unfinishedness of all existence, which is rooted in God's productive will. This is just one (an ontological) way of looking at matter.

Miracle is also acclaimed when an unknown (unrecognized, underappreciated) physical or statistical law operates in believers' favor. What surprises in the sense of going against the normal run of things generates the feeling of an encounter with the numinous or miraculous. This sense of surprise is given verbal expression in the form of "Na God" ("It is God") in West Africa, which indexes an encounter with the miraculous.[19]

What Pentecostals interpret as miraculous is not fully captured or translated by the word *miracle*. When an event or story inspires awe and wonder, it is a miracle. But the word in different contexts could be used to designate an extraordinary demonstration of human intellect, obedience, and dedication. That which is miraculous is always unexpected, against the extant order of beings or things, out of place. If what is desired is out of harmony with the ongoing run of things and it happens, it is a miracle, and when that which is not desired positively happens, it is also a miracle. Because what Pentecostals mean by miracle varies so much it is really a description of their world, how such a world is experienced, and their expectation to build new structures and norms in society's assemblage of social relations. The word is thus well suited to investigate the relationship between lived experiences and such theological constructs (e.g., grace and the sacred) as can be revealed in an everyday form of theology. Pentecostal understanding of the sacred not only provides a good example of how to investigate the relationship between lived experiences and religious-theological constructs, but also helps us to further our investigation of the sites of blended impossibility and possibility as environs of a split God.

4

The Sacred as Im/possibility

Expect a Miracle!

Introduction

Pentecostals are noted, good or ill, for their love of miracles. They expect and talk about miracles without qualms, even in so-called respectable, enlightened, rational-intellectual circles. Those intellectuals subjected to the pain of listening to their "babbles" often think that by miracles Pentecostals mean a transcendent God (Power) regulating or intervening in the empirical reality to enact favors for believers. They berate them for their "precritical minds" that strive to gain direct insight into things-in-themselves or for a naïve, even childlike dependence on an omnipotent father figure. This criticism is only based on a limited or distorted view of what Pentecostals understand as miracles. The pentecostal notion of miracle is much subtler than the common view of transcendence, eternity, or spirit breaking into history or nature. While Pentecostals contest the limitation of human knowledge to the domain of phenomenal representations, the majority of their miracles arise from the density and intensity of the phenomenal realm. Pentecostals more often expect and talk of what I will call "immanent miracles" than direct intervention of a faraway God in an existing causal network.

In the Pentecostal movement there is an understanding that encompasses both views of miracles: as an external, inbreaking power or an immanent-temporal irruption in becoming. Miracle is an impossible possibility in a world of enspirited matter. Miracle represents an impossibility (excluded, prohibited, or deferred possibility) that has been anticipated or has emerged but is transcended such that new possibilities are revealed, and this critical transformation is endowed with a sense of the momentous or produces a feeling of wonder.[1] The miraculous is part of the mundane and everyday life and is not necessarily transcendent. Miracles are events, occurrences, and manifestations that induce wonder and awe in a given context. The miraculous is in the ordinary or extraordinary, regular or irregular, explained or unexplained, utilitarian or holy, personal or social, and even in the quotidian practices of rationally relating means to ends. Each of these is an embodiment of surplus possibilities. Simply put, miracle is an event or occurrence that cannot be fitted into the existing causal network or fully accounted for by preexisting conditions. This "inability" to bring an event into a covering causal network or its preexisting conditions may be due to epistemology (the limitation of knowledge), ontology (an understanding that reality is always incomplete and subject to the chaotic power of becoming), spirituality (we can not always understand the mysterious working of God), or everyday mysticism (an intense passionate attachment to the phenomenal that shatters its coordinates).

From whence came this broad and labile notion of miracle? The only way to come to grips with the pentecostal notion of miracle is to reexamine the notion of the sacred. As we shall show, a proper understanding of the sacred will enable even the cultured despisers to make sense of why Pentecostals see miracles everywhere. The pentecostal understanding of the sacred is a bricolage; it is complex, robust, and innovative. I will try to delineate its vast contours by passing through an African concept of the sacred, engaging in conversations with a sociologist of religion (Richard Fenn), a theologian (Catherine Keller), and spicing the engagements with these scholars with philosophical insights from continental philosophers (Slavoj Žižek and Quentin Meillassoux) and a religious scholar (Mark C. Taylor). The summary of these engagements and conversations is that for Pentecostals the sacred is always at hand and it is primarily conceived in terms of possibilities and potentialities. Some of these preexist their manifestations and others happen without a place in any preexisting set, only retroactively creating their conditions of possibility. We are however getting ahead of my plan to carefully lead you to a deep insight into a robust understanding of the sacred. I begin the unfolding of this plan with a personal reflection (infused with some African energies) on the sacred. These energies will not only shed light on the sacred, but will interrupt the narrowly Americanized readings of Pentecostalism and the liberal disdain they fuel.

The Sacred as Sets of Possibilities

The sacred is near all human beings at all times. We encounter its omnipresence in our everyday possibilities and we are always trying to shape it even as it shapes us. In fact, the sacred emerges from how we understand, relate, treat, and divine im/possibilities of our everyday life. In every society there are three sets of possibilities: one that is open to all individuals, another that is available to only a few and the rest of society is excluded, and the universe of possibilities that are yet to be fulfilled or not yet available to all persons and institutions. The latter is actually the *horizon of unfulfilled possibilities*.

And there is the law (as acts of legislature, *nomos* and *ethos*, symbolic structures that regulate practices and representations, or specific regimes of interpretations of the [oral or written] scripture/faith, and so on). The law acts to bring the range of possibilities to manageable proportion and distribute them into the three sets. There are included and excluded possibilities in every existing state of affairs. It is the law that defines the boundaries of these three sets, what is possible and what is impossible. The law is the power that regulates possibilities and access to them. It is the law that tells members of a community what works within a given framework of relations.

There is also grace or its equivalent in every society. Grace has the power of the exception (to use Carl Schmitt's language), which can act to stop, suspend, reopen, or open the enjoyment of certain possibilities. Sometimes, grace can transcend laws or boundaries from within them, such that potentialities are actualized not in spite of the restrictions of the law but through them. This is like a player mastering the rules of a game and then initiating new skills to overcome obstacles. Every invention, every innovation, every revolution, and every scientific breakthrough has always been about extending the boundaries of the possible, making what was once impossible to become possible.

How does this knowledge of the three sets of possibilities lead to a conceptualization of the sacred? The person-to-person encounters of our daily lives constitute a ground for the "holy" to emerge. These encounters are often parts of social practices, overlapping social practices, and generative of social practices. While a particular social practice fulfills a finite set of possibilities, the originative space of the encounter of person to person that engenders the social practice is a horizon of unfulfilled possibilities. The excluded or the unfulfilled is a primordial soup out of which can crawl the religious, the sacred. This originative site is the sphere that social practices try to exclude from view or reckoning. What is excluded and unfulfilled is believed to transcend the passage of time, and this makes it sacred. What is sacred in any society is believed to always have a purchase on eternity. As sociologist Fenn has recently argued, the sacred is the embodiment of unfulfilled possibilities.

> Because the sacred embodies only *unfulfilled* possibilities, it always points beyond itself to the full range of possibilities for either salvation or destruction. This set of all possibilities, both actual and hypothetical, I call the Sacred, and it is to the sociology of religion what dark matter is to astrophysicists, or "the god above the god of theism" is to theologians.[2]

This realm of unfulfilled possibilities haunts the realm of realized possibilities and pushes it toward the not-yet. In every human-to-human encounter that both limits and enhances the power of being in each self, something develops that lies beyond such an encounter. No matter how innovative a social practice or law is, it always defines the limits of aspirations and "institutionalizes" the set of possibilities of human interaction that the system of society is willing to allow at a given moment or deems practicable. Yet the law or social practice is haunted by the unfulfilled possibilities. Over time, this brooding sense of the haunted will give rise to some kind of resistance; something brings the awareness of such unfulfilled possibilities into popular consciousness for a more abundant life.

The idea that the holy emerges from social practice has long been something that many in traditional African cultures take for granted. Among the Kalabari of the Niger Delta in Nigeria, the holy, or a god's power, is an emergent phenomenon of human worship; like social systems, it realizes itself through practices. The holy emerges and is ensconced in the social practice of worship. The gods arise from such practice insofar as their power of being is in it. The gods are conceived as a source of tremendous power. But the power that the gods possess is believed to depend on the social practice of human worship. Their powers derive from human worship and as such humans can reduce or completely efface the power of any god by withdrawing worship.[3]

Most believe that spirits and gods do not have intrinsic powers of their own such that the withdrawal of worship from or worshipful dependence on a god deprives it of power and authority to act on humans or control human activities. Kalabari insist that a god that is not worshiped loses its power. So if a god becomes too furious or demanding, they will tell it from which tree it was carved (*agu-nsi owi baka kuma en ke o kara sin en dugo o piriba*).[4] This means that a community can unanimously annul the power of a god by refusing to worship it.[5] Robin Horton interprets the aphorism this way:

> Literally, if a spirit's demands become too burdensome, the whole congregation can join together to destroy its cult objects, and by this unanimous act of rejection render it powerless to trouble them further. . . . Broadly, then, the more people lavish offerings, invocations, and festivals upon any spirit, the more powerful it becomes both to reward and punish them. And conversely, the less they attend to it the less powerful it becomes—up to the point at which unanimous rejection results in the complete loss of power. Generally, of course, a single man cannot reject a spirit at will; for while he is only one among a congregation of many, it will have the power to punish him.[6]

This way of thinking is not at all surprising once one grasps the importance of relations as constitutive of both society and personhood in Kalabari communities. Worship is not just reverence, obeisance, praise and exaltation, or appropriate response to deity, but the dynamic maintenance of deep, thick relations, social bond with a deity. All forms of power, be it political or spiritual, are always predicated on the strength of social bonds among persons and the fracture or rupture of the bond or the displacement of harmony in the bond means erosion of power and authority.

In the Western tradition, Émile Durkheim long ago pointed out to us that individuals generate some sort of divinity when they come together. In the collective occasion, they discover their connectedness with each other, deem themselves transformed and transfigured, and discern a set of possibilities that lie beyond the community. The sacred emerges in this setting of corporate identity as "collective effervescence" and claims for itself the capacity to transcend the ravages and passage of time. The *numen* is generated when the individual sense of identity is merged with that of the group or collective. Under these conditions the sense of possibilities soars to new heights, repressed elements jostle to float to the surface, and the *numen* emerges. The crowd or the collective comes to embody—however temporally—the impulse of the *numen*. To experience the *numen* "is to find oneself in the grip of a passion or presence that seems to come from beyond oneself."[7] But often this feeling of being affected by a presence that seems physically absent or distant is also the experience of ecstasy, "of being beside oneself, or being captivated by the presence of another soul who seems to take precedence over one's own."[8]

> To experience the primitive (numen) one may feel that it is God, a distant and invisible being, who is present and at work beneath the forms of everyday life. Alternatively, one may settle for the unseen but palpable presences of angels and saints.[9]

The Structure of the Sacred

In the Kalabari (Niger Delta, Nigeria) worldview and philosophy, the notion of the sacred as a set of possibilities is encapsulated in one of the words for God, that is, *So*.[10] The word *So* refers to both destiny or directing-destiny and the sum of possibilities available to the people. In a sense, the two meanings of the word are not different. Destiny in Kalabari understanding refers to the set of life possibilities allotted to a person before his or her own birth. *So* in the sense of destiny refers to the dialectical outworking of the *telos* of individuals, communities, and the world. It is an unfolding world process that is not confined to follow a fixed groove. The shaping of destiny is done by or rather understood via the possibilities that *So* makes available to each person, group, or institution. (*So* when applied to individuals is called *so*, to households is *wariteme-so*, and to communities is *amateme-so*. We will refer to this application of the notion to particulars—the matter of destiny—as lowercase *so*.) The directing concept of *So* is not just about working out of preassigned telos. The concept of *So* directs the people to both note their limitations, the set of possibilities opened to them or excluded from them, liberatory potentials for the transformation of selves and structures of society, and the sum of possibilities conceivable given their level of social, technological, and economic development. Let us call *So* as applied to the sum of possibilities as uppercase *So*. The uppercase *So* is the set of possibilities excluded to individuals, cultural institutions, and social structures. More precisely, it is the universe of possibilities from which some are defined as available to persons and institutions and others remain either unfulfilled or simply the set of possibilities excluded to them at any given time.

When lowercase *so* and uppercase *So* are taken together, we get the sense that *So* is the ultimate source of possibilities, and the principle of limitation or selection. This combination of infinity and limit defines the structure of the sacred as lived experience in the Kalabari worldview, shedding important light on our idea of the three sets of possibilities that mark the sacred.[11]

I would like to note that the uppercase *So* and lowercase *so* are not opposites in Kalabari. Thus what is not part of uppercase *So* is not confined to extinction. The uppercase *So* is the ground of lowercase *so*. The lowercase *so* is only a set of appropriated or available possibilities at any given time. For instance, a person may have the *so* to be a good dancer from all the possibilities that are available to members of the community and even beyond. If the person dislikes being an artist, he or she can go to a diviner and ask for it to be changed and thus draw another career from that unlimited urn of possibilities that the uppercase *So* can give, and it is a pool that can never be completely realized. A person can literally ask for any set of possibilities, but *So* has the right to defer or "project into the future whatever may be too much for any community or society [or the individual] fully to experience or acknowledge in the present."[12] Because an individual can only be given or allotted only a part of the set of all possibilities available to the community at any given historical moment, what he or she has "always points beyond itself to the full range of possibilities for either salvation or destruction."[13] As Richard Fenn puts it,

> At some level, societies know that they are based on the foreclosure and postponed fulfillment of possibilities for both life and death. Every social system . . . creates an index or prohibited satisfactions. . . . The sacred always offers only a very limited embodiment of unfulfilled possibility.[14]

The individual may encode within her the possibilities allotted to her by the social system (or the gods), but she always stands to look upon the uppercase *So* as the embodiment of unfulfilled possibilities. Humans can imagine alternatives not currently available to them and can take steps to attain what is denied them. In fact, this is the whole impetus and impulse behind *bibibari*, recanting of destiny.[15]

What does the Kalabari notion of *So* tells us about the nature of the sacred as an im/possibility, the impossible possibility? There are three principles or forms of relationship in what the Kalabari call *So*, and they will help us to address the question. First, within what the Kalabari named as *So* there is an uppercase *So* as a kind of creative force, the inexhaustible ground of (impossible) possibilities that overflows into human activities. *So* in this sense is considered as *Tamuno*, the Supreme Being. Second, there is *So* as the principle of limitation—the part that gives meaning and structure to the infinite possibilities and results in modification and concretion so that there is no chaos. Third, there is a feedback mechanism that works to properly align the interaction of the first two principles in the context of a particular person's or group's life. This mechanism is called *bibibari*. This is the continuous process of retooling the actualization of potentialities, the appropriation of possibilities and their reshaping.

Bibibari is the process through which past possibilities that determine a person, institution, or group are themselves retroactively changed. The past in this process becomes something like Deleuze's pure virtual past. The Kalabari believe that a person is created to embody a certain destiny: there is a virtual self that follows her, and in this sense her concrete deeds do not add to her virtual past as they only unfold what she is, as she only becomes what she is. The fact that *bibibari* is part of this process means that ultimately the Kalabari do not take a literal teleological reading of a person's destiny. Destiny as a necessity is an outcome of a contingent process. A person's deed is not a mere acting out of her atemporal encased set of possibilities as any of her numerous acts can retroactively reconstitute her past. She can change her eternal past, the transcendental coordinates of her existence. "We have thus a kind of reflexive 'folding back of the condition onto the given it was the condition for': while the pure past is the transcendental condition for [her] acts, [her] acts do not only create new actual reality, they also retroactively change this very condition."[16] This change in the condition for her acts now gives her life a new necessity (destiny), but it is only a necessity she contingently created. In this process of *bibibari*, there is unfolding, folding, and enfolding of possibilities that are reversing necessity into contingency and in turn contingency into necessity.

The overall lesson the Kalabari notion of the sacred teaches us is that the realm of the im/possibility, the impossible possibility, is the sacred. Put differently, it teaches that how a society understands, treats, and manages its possibilities or sense of possibilities defines its notion of the sacred. The sacred is not understood only as a site where a society constructs and deconstructs its notion of impossibility; it is also the site where, in the open sight of everybody, the people perform the trick of making what they regard as "transcendence" (beyond, impossible, not-yet possible) to be internal to the world, integral to the process of unfolding possibilities, to work in immanental ways. It appears that without these sleights of hand in society, in social life, civilization itself becomes impossible. If there are no impossible possibilities in the sacred, everything is impossible. The founding order of the sacred is that the forbidden acts or jouissance are already impossible. If the sphere of the impossible does not exist in the sacred and by extension in the society it encompasses, then one finds oneself at any moment trespassing the limit of the possible, breaking arbitrary or nonexistent boundaries. In this scenario any act or movement is already forbidden, a transgression of a nonexistent impossibility. The constant transgression of a nonexistent impossibility means anything one does is impossible. Thus every possibility is forbidden.[17] We need the limits set by the sphere of the impossible to know that our actions are within the sphere of the possible, within the acceptable bounds of our community. If we do not know where the limits of the impossible begin, then it means they begin anywhere and everywhere, are within the realm of the possible, and thus members of society would appear to be trespassing the limits of the possible all the time.

The basic paradox of impossibility is that it is both possible and unavoidable. It is never fully eliminated, always there, but, simultaneously, overcome. Every conversion of impossibility into possibility generates a possible impossibility; every conquering of impossibility generates a new horizon of impossibility, limitation, and so on. Possibility creates the impossibility it tries to subdue. So if we eliminate impossibility, we also remove possibility. This reversal provides the definition of the realm of impossibility. It is the result of itself or the outcome of possibility, which all mean the same thing. All this suggests that the sacred plays some functions in social existence. Its invention, discovery, or imposition serve to oversee aspirations, hopes, and expectations of the members of its community. It encourages the search for alternative possibilities. The sacred becomes corrupted or works against itself and society when it discourages the search and implementation of alternative possibilities. Sooner or later it will be replaced or displaced by another (new) form or version of what members of the society consider sacred.

Purpose of the Sacred

With mindful ignorance, let me say that the purposeless purpose of impossibility is to make possibility possible.[18] The sacred forbids an act because it is trying to impose a rational order onto prerational chaos of the universe of possibilities. The perverse core of the sacred is to encourage or nudge us toward an abyssal act of freedom, to act outside the enchainment of possibilities open at any given moment in order to impose a novel rational necessity on uppercase *So*, the universe of possibilities. As if through the act of freedom, the fecund void of numinous impossibility directly transforms itself into phenomenal possibility. The act momentarily tears the veil that separates possibility from impossibility, forcing all obstacles into the past. The act happens *in the present* but changes *the past itself*. For without such freedom (as per Kant or Schelling) a society and its sacred cease to promote human flourishing. In the case of *bibibari*, this kind of act can reach deep into the eternal past to re-create a person's terrestrial destiny. This is not dissimilar from the temporal event of conversion in Christianity, which rewrites the eternal past of predestination. Connecting this view of conversion to Kant's notion of freedom, Slavoj Žižek has this to say:

> The later Kant articulated the notion of the noumenal act of choice by means of which an individual chooses his eternal character and which, therefore, prior to his temporal existence, delineates in advance the contours of his terrestrial destiny. Without Divine act of Grace, our destiny would remain immovable, forever fixed by this eternal act of choice; and the "good news" of Christianity, however, is that, in a genuine Conversion, one can "recreate" oneself, that is *repeat* this act, and thus *change (undo the effects of) eternity itself.*[19]

So what does all this tell us about the so-called realm of impossibility? The sacred stands for the paradox of impossibility that maintains its status of impossibility precisely by its stubborn attachment to the dimension of possibility that serves as its unacknowledged vitality. Without impossible possibilities, then impossibility ends up as an empty, lifeless, self-identical void. The fare or the implicit claim of the sacred is that its declaration of impossibility is none other than the assertion of not-yet possibilities, possibilities waiting for the act that will transform them from the numinous to the phenomenal.

I can almost hear you, the reader, turning in your chair. If impossibility is only not-yet possibility waiting to materialize, then there is really no true impossibility, only psychic (or "false") impossibility. This line of thinking misunderstands the sacred; it is irrelevant whether the realm of impossibility exists or not, as long as it is effective in constructing the way our deeds, insights, or breakthroughs pass from myth to existence, serving as a reference point to make sense of the improbable character of our accomplishments. "By definition, there is something so improbable about all [*novum*] that one is in effect questioning oneself about its reality."[20]

One more point before I drop this topic. For two reasons, the distinction between psychic and true impossibility is unnecessary. First, the impossible is impossible because it does not exist, but nonetheless we attribute properties such as being excessive to it and forbidding intercourse with it. This is why a couple of pages ago we stated that the founding order of the sacred is that the forbidden acts or jouissance are already impossible. This nonexistent thing presides over people's actual striving and, if its effects on actual persons are to disappear, then the texture of the sacred as we know it will dissolve. The sphere of the impossible is the *Real* around which the sacred as a system operates.

Second, the sacred, according to the Kalabari who can tell a god from which wood it was carved, is neither some kind of a transcendental spirit who controls human history, nor does it ossify possibilities. It is none other than the human process of dealing with life's possibilities—reflexively shaping and reshaping potentialities amid obstacles—through which the process of knowing *So* takes place and human consciousness of mega-Spirit thus arises. Out of the foaming ferment of human creativity in dealing with the entangled possibilities of coexistence, *So* arises fragrantly, as Hegel might be tempted to put it. (Let us not forget that the very emergence of the sacred is in itself mysterious or adds to the "sacredness" of social intercourse. An "objective order" emerges out of the interactions of individuals, and once it appears it cannot be reduced to the interactions and it stands above or is viewed by them as a substantial agency that now determines, controls, or conditions their lives. This is what Slavoj Žižek calls "the ultimate mystery of the so-called human or social sciences."[21])

Once this *So*, the sacred, arises among the people, it is not a just a blind "mental" process of fears and hopes that regulates social life or the interactions between possibility and impossibility. There are persons, practices, rituals, dances, utterances, and institutions that proclaim its status as sacred and it thus appears to develop self-consciousness, a life of its own.[22] Here I am using self-consciousness in the sense Hegel applied it to the state, as "the self-consciousness of a people."

> The self-consciousness of the state has nothing mental about it, if by "mental" we understand the sorts of occurrences and qualities that are relevant to *our own* minds. What self-consciousness amounts to, in the state's case, is the existence of reflective practices, such as, but not limited to, educational ones. Parades displaying the state's military strength would be practices of this kind, and so would statements of principle by the legislature, or sentences by the Supreme Court—and they would be that *even* if all individual (human) participants in a parade, all members of the legislature or of the Supreme Court were personally motivated to play whatever role they play in this affair by greed, inertia, or fear, *and* even if such participants or members were thoroughly uninterested and bored through the whole event, and totally lacking in any understanding of its significance.[23]

Impossibility as the Sacred

The way and manner we have conceptualized the sacred—the set of possibilities cast against the background of impossibility and that which imposes itself over the collective life of a community as a "being"—differs from that of religious scholar Jeffrey Kripal, who talks about impossibility as the sacred. Whereas we have focused on possibilities and im/possibility in social existence, Kripal takes the possibilities of the paranormal as the sacred. He argues that what rational thinking, modern science, and materialism consider as impossible, enchanted events (psychical phenomena) happen in the physical, objective, material world and it is this paranormal impossible possibility—the weird and wonderful—that is the sacred. The sacred is the reality of the paranormal within a materialistic, disenchanted worldview. Kripal maintains the psychical is "the sacred in transit from the traditional religious register into the modern scientific one."[24] The sacred proper, he adds, is "a particular structure of human consciousness that corresponds to the palpable presence, energy, or power encountered in the environment," which modern science rules out as impossible.[25]

Another important difference between my conceptualization of the sacred as the im/possibility and Kripal's view of the sacred as the impossible is that he keys his notion of the impossibility to an underlying metaphysical reality, which a disenchanted, established modern scientific method cannot access. For us the sacred is not necessarily the supernatural or metaphysical but the social structure ("the hypertext") that arranges, distributes, blocks, and invents possibilities over time in the lived world.

Mark C. Taylor's view of the sacred also disagrees with the onto-theological stance of Kripal. To Taylor, the sacred is neither being nor nonbeing; it is "the condition of possibility and impossibility of both being and non-being. If the sacred were a ground, which it is not, it might be understood as the ground of the ground of being, which otherwise is 'known' as God."[26] In simple language, he views the sacred as *interstitiality*, a relation of neither/nor rather than binary opposition. It is relation "as such." The sacred as interstitiality does not mean the sacred is an instantiation of the interstitial. Taylor argues that "the site or more precisely, the *para-site* of the sacred is the interstitial. I would not use the term 'instantiation' in the context because it suggests too much stability or fixity. Rather, the interstitial is the domain of alternation (one of the nuances of altarity) where the sacred oscillates in an approaching withdrawal and withdrawing approach. The interstitial is neither here nor there; it is not present and yet not absent."[27] In other words, the sacred is fragile, fleeting, and slippery.

Catherine Keller, in her recent book *Cloud of the Impossible*, represents an alternative theological position to the stance of both Taylor and Kripal.[28] While Taylor insists that the neither/nor of his a/theology is not mysticism à la negative theology, Keller takes the position that the im/possibility of existence is elucidated (but not grasped) by a mysticism-hugging negative theology. Her negative theology, she holds, is not a mere opposite of theology or a simple absence of metaphysics of being, but a "denegation" of the attributes of God and contestation of the knowability of God. She, unlike Kripal, does not decipher the fleeting presence of concretions caught in the interstices of being and nonbeing or in the trail of the cloud of impossibility as the sacred. Her negative theology does not take a stance opposite that of the established scientific worldview. It is rather about the struggle over time by theologians and physicists to say the unsayable with language that is recalcitrant to the logic of neither/nor. This neither/nor, which she situates in the density of relation that constitutes the fabric of existence and creativity, holds the key to deciphering the sacred, the site of the im-possibility. Amid the noise and nonteleological entanglements of relations in and impossibility of revelation from the infinite density of our micro and macro worlds, there emerges signification—an overture, at least, to the production of a sacred order. But there is no necessity to its emergence from the network of relations. What she calls "the cloud of the impossible" and what she leaves unthought in her book hold tantalizing clues to her thinking about the sacred.

The Trails of the Cloud of the Impossible

Though Keller does not directly theorize the sacred, there are hints that she understands the sacred as the set of all possibilities. Let me lay out the logic that warrants this assertion, a position based on my interpretation of her book and the implications of her line of arguments. (And this position is also a condensation and clarification of what I have already said about the sacred, now filtered through the lens of the *Cloud of the Impossible*.) The position is inherent in Keller's thought, but Keller did not comprehend its implications deeply enough; she felt she was dealing with negative theology rather than a theory of sacrality. Keller explains that existence is a network of evolving relationships. Possibilities or potentialities are nothing but aspects of relationships. Relationships define possibilities and potentialities.[29] We live in an expanding universe of relationships. Some of the possibilities are background independent and others are background dependent. (Being background independent means, inter alia, that an event emerges that was not in the cards by retroactively positing its conditions of possibility.) Time seems to "evolve" with the event; time and event appear to be codependent. The sacred, the floating site of im/possibility is where the pressure and tension of the relationships coincide, where they simultaneously push apart (pressure) and pull together (tension). Religion names the *coincidentia oppositorum* as deity and the pressure and tension as wrath and grace, respectively. Religion is articulated around the belief that something (agency, deity) external to the universe of relationships and possibles not only imposes order on it, but also ultimately makes the choice of possibilities and potentialities for us. If a religion does not admit to an outside agency, it posits that the agency is the power of the universe of relationships as a whole. Religion helps human beings to organize and conceptualize their experience of the sacred.

Let me now take the reader through some of Keller's suggestive statements on the sacred, even as I endeavor to unearth their creative impulses. My initial reading is that the closest she comes to conceptualizing the sacred is what she calls "the primordial locus of possibilities," which at the same time urges the actualization of possibilities.[30] This primordial locus is another name for the impossible that engenders the possibility itself, which is endlessly made and undone. At the core of this never-ending process there is a lure of planetary creativity and disregard for congealed hierarchy. More precisely, the sacred is our infinite entanglement that invokes, invites, and sustains care for its finitudes. She argues that the entanglement and creativity that sustain it are theopoetic, that is, God-making or the bodying of God. But this God, in keeping with her negative theology and expansive process theology, cannot be positively determined or known. This God is not some kind of positive agent that guarantees or underlies creativity itself. The "divine element in the universe" is not a "congealed God-entity," not an idol.[31] We do not really know this God or what we designate as God. At best God, whom she argues is an outcome of creativity itself, is the lure of all other creatures. This unknowing of God, she holds, should energize an alter-knowing of the relation between God and world or at least a rejection of the inherited classical view of the God-world relationship. Over and over again she rejects the idea of a discreet, unentangled God (subject) acting on God's world or human bodies (object). She maintains that God is entangled in the relations of all creation and is part of non-ex-nihilo creation that unfolds, folds, and enfolds within the primordial locus of possibilities, the site of im/possibility.[32]

The divine boundlessness that enfolds and unfolds within the im/possibility of relations is not only marked by the Cusan logic of the *coincidentia oppositorum*, but also by reversal of classical verticalism. Not only transcendence and immanence coincide in relationalism, in non-absolute Absolute, but also the experience of the Absolute is *evental*, manifesting in vulnerable flashes. The Absolute in Keller's thought is eventual, mediating creativity in a process in which the temporal, the creatable, is everlastingly *infini*.[33] And this Absolute (*Resolute*) itself is a fragile, changing concretion, the "Most-Moved Mover."[34] The logic here is that the eternal in the classical sense is unstable, changing, and the non-eternal (created, creativity) is what is everlasting. Between the ultimate category of creativity and becoming nature (becomings in process), the Absolute (Resolute) shines forth, entangling each actual occasion in new possibilities.

Keller's book invites the reader to meditate on the "possible impossibility." This is to say the reader is mindfully to ponder how what is now considered impossible can generate new possibilities. Impossibility birthing new possibilities! This is an inversion of commonsense logic. In this vein the vertical relation between the eternal (above, spirit, "uncreated") and the temporal (here and now, the flesh, created) is inverted, not in the sense of transcendence demoted to immanence but in the sense of the flesh being more lasting and continuous than the spirit.

To reiterate, for Keller the impossible is the sacred—at least according to this reading. This is not because the impossible is God or God is the impossible, but because the sacred is the traces of the possible impossibility woven through all the processes of life, or it is the cracks in the network of relationships that turn up possibility that had appeared as the impossible. The cracks or traces are not engendered or bolstered by an inaccessible transcendence, outside power, external entity, or independent substance but by the energy of the relation itself, the cloudy radiance and resonance of the effervescence of life that form and deform existence.

I need to quickly point out the methodology of my engagement with or critique of Keller's work. I do not here present an orthodox engagement with Keller's thought in the *Cloud of the Impossible*. I am only attempting to follow a trail of the clouds of her original thinking as it folds, enfolds, and unfolds implicitly through the book. I invite the reader to join me to regain or uncover the creative impulse that Keller missed in the actualization of her thought, to walk with me to connect to "what was already in ['Keller] more than [Keller] herself,' more than [her] explicit system, its excessive core."[35] This is to say, reading Keller to isolate the key breakthrough of her thought in this book as it relates to the notion of the sacred as a set of possibilities and impossibilities, im/possibility, then show how she necessarily missed this key dimension of her own discovery, and "finally, showing how, in order to do justice to [her] key breakthrough, one has to move beyond [Keller]."[36] This going beyond means betraying the "letter" (actual) of her thought in order to grasp its "spirit" (virtual). So precisely what is the dimension of the sacred that shines through in the explosion of thought on the clouds of impossibility and negative theology and its concrete actualization in her book but slipped into the virtual state and haunts any close reading of the book? What is the proper embodiment of this excess betrayed by Keller's book?

Let us begin this exercise with her description of negative theology. She dwells brilliantly on the nature of negative theology, arguing it is about lack or contrariness. It is all about excess that escapes speech.[37] Contrariness designates a form of difference within classical theism or authorized space of talking about God, while the excess that escapes speech designates ways of talking about the divine that gesture to a breakdown of the preapproved linguistic and "rational" space for talking about the divine element in the universe. Here it appears she has unknowingly stumbled onto two types of lack: there is the *lack proper* and *hole*.[38] There is a constitutive lack that does not threaten the system of knowledge or order of being per se. A hole designates a gap in the system or order of being. In this sense the contrariness or lack she mentions—to use Žižek's words—is only "a *void within a space*, while a hole is more radical, it designates the point at which this spatial order itself breaks down (as in the 'black hole' in physics)."[39] Her book did not explicitly name the hole, which would appear to provide the aim and goal of her brand of apophatic theology. Its goal is to circulate around the concept of God within the theological space without reifying God, claiming a certainty of knowledge, or providing a contemplative sanctuary in the face of uncertainty, and its true aim is endless circulation around its goal-object. Perhaps, its satisfaction is its repeated failure to pin down God or the impossible possibility that ever eludes the human reach.

She conveyed the sense of the second type of lack, the hole in the ontotheological knowledge space, with her brilliant discussions of entangled particles with their mutuality characterized by "faster-than-light relationality."[40] She was able to transmit the apophatic affect of the quantum world of particles and waves in her discussions. Their world of unbroken wholeness "actually appears as the discontinuous quantum jumps and jitters."[41] Here the very lack seems to be holes in the system, entangled particles that dance and operate in unanalyzable, indeterminate ways. Their apophatic entanglement appears to demand that we drop the whole mechanistic order that informs scientific imagination in order to analyze it. Quantum entanglement is an impossible possibility. She missed the key dimension of hole as a form of lack in her work.

Keller's focus on ontological relationality robbed her of the idea of another hole, "black hole," in social reality or sociality, the play of impossibility in reality. This hole gestures to the im-possible and to the terminally difficult term God and God's existence or inexistence. Following the creative impulse of her thoughts, one could reach the conclusion that the new emerges, an impossibility becomes a possibility, because there is no power in social existence that controls the preconstituted totality as possibilities. The im/possibility is the inherent immanent power of creativity in human communities that can retroactively create the condition of possibility of the novum. She may or may not agree on what the existence of black holes in the fabric of social reality (cracks in the fixity of potentialities) represents. Perhaps for Keller the "black holes" in social reality express the One of Creativity (Becoming) or there is no underlying Oneness (created or creatable).[42] Nothing or Something? The notion of the sacred does not rule out one or the other. The answer depends on the community.

Žižek argues that the existence of "black holes," an impossible possibility in reality, means that God does not exist. But for Pentecostals their presence confirms the existence of God; there is a God, transcendent or immanent, that springs surprises on the extant configuration of things. It appears both Žižek and Pentecostals share the same sense of the sacred—at least in the sense we have interpreted it in this chapter, as a common field of potentialities and possibilities without omega point. But Žižek and Pentecostals differ on where to place God in (*en*) the oceanic plenum of the sacred.[43] Pentecostals place God in (*en*) it and nominate same as its anchor and guarantee.[44] Žižek rejects all these, preferring a simple sacred without father or mother and without site of privilege or reification within it.

Let no one think that Žižek's rejection puts his position absolutely at loggerheads with Pentecostalism. Pentecostalism's two-pronged position on the sacred (godly and special mundane events or "potentiality" and "virtuality") is always mediated by the playful character of the pentecostal spirit. Pentecostalism "profanes" the sacred without abolishing the sphere of the sacred. It *deactivates* the aura that attends to the rites and stories (myths) of the sacred sphere.[45] Pentecostalism demystifies the sacred and shows the profane as inherent to the sacred.[46] This is not done in disbelief and indifference toward the divine, but as "a behavior that is free and 'distracted' . . . released from *religio* of norms before things and their use."[47] For Pentecostals the sacred is dispersed into multiple sites of encounter (space is cut so that the "trans" of transcendence is not a "cross over or going beyond" but a tracing of "being-with"). Pentecostalism is the sacred in a *playful* mode.

We have gone too far ahead of ourselves in our plan to discuss the missed opportunity in Keller's second type of lack (negative). Let us now return to it by unveiling what French philosopher Quentin Meillassoux understands by potentialities and possibilities. His conceptualization of these terms will help to shed light on what we have come to consider as the set of possibilities, the play of im/possibility in reality. Meillassoux makes the distinction between virtuality and potentiality.

> *Potentialities* are the non-actualized cases of an indexed set of possibilities under the condition of a given law (whether aleatory or not). *Chance* is every actualization of a potentiality for which there is no univocal instance of determination on the basis of the initial given conditions. Therefore I will call *contingency* the property of an indexed set of cases (not of a case belonging to an indexed set) of not itself being a case of sets of cases; and *virtuality* the property of every set of cases emerging within a becoming which is not dominated by any pre-constituted totality of possible.[48]

Meillassoux's definition gives us a new language to conceptualize the sacred or to reexplain what Kalabari or the Pentecostals understand by the sacred as a set of possibilities. He shows that events can happen because of their potentiality, something comes out of a preexisting set of possibilities. If we roll a single die and any of the numbers (1–6) come up, then that is a possibility becoming actualized. But if we throw the die and number seven comes up, then virtually something new has come up. Number seven has no place on the die, in the set of preexisting possibles, but the emergence of the new retroactively creates its own condition of possibility. As Meillassoux put it, "Time creates the possible at the very moment it makes it come to pass, it brings forth the possible as it does the real, it inserts itself in the very throw of the die, to bring forth a seventh case, in principle unforeseeable, which breaks the fixity of potentialities."[49] As if in a gesture ahead of its time, Meillassoux throws a view of the emergence of phenomena *ex nihilo* before Keller's *creatio ex profundis*, not as a denial that events draw from their *situation* but the assertion of radical contingency based on an ontology of *non-All* or radical becoming. He continues, "If we maintain that becoming is not only capable of bringing forth cases on the basis of a pre-given universe of cases, we must understand that it follows that such cases [the New] irrupt, properly speaking, *from nothing*, since no structure contains them as eternal potentialities before their emergence: *we thus make irruption ex nihilo the very concept of a temporality delivered to its pure immanence.*"[50]

Here we are seeing in different registers what the Kalabari and Pentecostals consider as the operations of the sacred. The virtuality, the emergence of the new that is not mere actualization of preexisting possibility, that Meillassoux is describing here resembles the entangled particles of the micro-quantum world that Keller describes. Meillassoux—and Žižek following him—clearly sees the potential theological or religious use of his argument of ex-nihilo emergence of the new and quickly proceeds to block it by giving a materialist interpretation of them. Meillassoux states, "Every 'miracle' thus becomes the manifestation of the inexistence of God, insofar as every radical rupture of the present in relation to the past becomes the manifestation of the absence of any order capable of overseeing the chaotic power of becoming."[51] Žižek then concurs.

> This emergence of a phenomenon *ex nihilo*, not fully covered by the sufficient chain of reasons, is thus no longer—as in traditional metaphysics—a sign of the direct intervention of some super-natural power (God) into nature, but, on the contrary, a sign of the inexistence of God, that is, a proof that nature is not-All, not "covered" by any transcendent Order or Power which regulates it. A "miracle" (whose formal definition is the emergence of something not covered by the existing causal network) is thus converted into a materialist concept.[52]

This play of potentialities, possibilities, and virtuality in social existence is what I mean by the sacred. Materialist scholars like Žižek and Meillassoux obviously call it another name and religious people like Pentecostals view it differently. For some it is strictly profane, for others it is strictly holy and religious, and for Pentecostals and Kalabari, as we have seen, it is in *coincidentia oppositorum* with the profane.

The kind of a new discourse of the sacred that is in some radical *coincidentia oppositorum* with the profane has been extracted from a trail of the clouds of Keller's original thinking as it folds, enfolds, and unfolds implicitly through the *Cloud of the Impossible*. We have attempted to uncover the creative impulse that Keller missed in the actualization of her thought, to walk in the trail of the clouds to connect what was already in Keller more than Keller herself. We will continue to isolate the key breakthrough of her thought in the *Cloud of the Impossible* as it relates to the notion of the sacred. As stated earlier, in this kind of exercise we will betray the "letter" (actual) of her thought in order to grasp its "spirit" (virtual).

In reading Keller in light of our theory of the sacred, it is important to bear in mind how her implicit view on the sacred differs from the argument in this chapter. This difference enables us to search for the proper embodiment of the "excessive core" in her thought betrayed or neglected by *Cloud of the Impossible*. One source of this difference relates to the orientation of her book. She focuses more on ontological relationalism than on the regulative force of sociality.[53] As a result we have to think her thought after her to show, for instance, that the sacred is constructed out of the feelings of possibilities at the level of language, culture, and materialist affectivity. What does the fold between our unknowing of the divine and planetary nonseparability mean for bodies in interactional/intra-active ritual chains? If one enfolds and unfolds her idea of the body of God, the enfleshing of infinite entanglements, and dehierarchization of the typical divine-human relation, the thought arises: Is sacred, the lure of something, not the fleeting event over the density of entanglements of bodies? Her work, which examines the entanglement of the divine and unknowing in many facets of human and beyond-human lives, does not explore how entangled human bodies generate the sacred or the sense of the sacred. She fails to explore how her own conceptualization of the relation between unknowing and relationality itself moves her reader to ask, how do entangled bodies become surfaces for the fleeting appearances of the unknowable God? Or how does God temporarily construct Godself (or God's flesh) from and in relations of entangled bodies as *real presence*?

For a scholar intensely focused on entangled bodies and relationalism and interested in the discourse of the sacred in some radical *coincidentia oppositorum* with the profane, the neglect of real presence as a locus of the divine is somewhat surprising. In my opinion, real presence, which is experienced across (almost) all religions, provides us with an important perspective to develop a planetary ecumenical and doctrine-resistant sense of the sacred. If Keller has applied her analysis of im/possibility to how the divine manifests in the forms of affectivity of bodies, words and voices, relics and arts—that is, to real presence—she would have given body to some lines of argument that now haunt her text.[54] This is an opportunity that what was already in the *Cloud of the Impossible* more than in Keller's conscious articulation of her ideas. There are lines of argument in the book of which Keller herself is unaware, arguments that will help us understand a dimension of the sacred as experience or enacted in co-affective worship services.

Now, in order to understand the pentecostal logic and practice of the sacred as revealed in co-affective worship services, we turn not directly to her explicit arguments, but to her logic. For some time I have been mulling over the pentecostal logic of sense, trying to understand how Pentecostals invert the eternal-temporal order to "construct" God on their bodies and senses. This skill of inversion is something they share with Keller. She is patently good at inverting any transcendence-immanence schema in constructive theologies. How does one ferret out this hidden line of similarity in *Cloud of the Impossible*? Before my active contemplation of the pentecostal practico-ethical and enkinaesthetic theology and Keller's constructive-theoretical theology, Gilles Deleuze's *The Logic of Sense* had indirectly taught me how inversion takes place in worship services. Deleuze, following the Stoics before him, inverted Plato's dualism between the eternal ideas and material things, which are only fleeting appearances of the eternal in the empirical, sensuous world. For Deleuze this view shows that material bodies are the "substance and cause," and the fleeting becoming of Sense located at the interstices of Being and non-Being is the immaterial virtual effect.[55] In his words:

> The Stoics are the first to reverse Platonism and to bring about a radical inversion. For if bodies with their states, qualities, and quantities, assume all the characteristics of substance and cause, conversely, the characteristics of the Idea are relegated to the other side, that is to the impassive extra-Being which is sterile, inefficacious, and the surface of things of things: *the ideational or the incorporeal can no longer be anything other than an "effect."*[56]

Keller missed the opportunity to examine how bodies entangled in worship display and play the sacred or how immanent sensing bodies engrossed in affective reciprocity also invert Plato's dualism in the fashion of the Stoics and Deleuze. This is so because she does not connect or extend her notion of planetary entanglements, clouds of the impossible, and im/possibility to worship services, where literally bodies and their sweat, breath, and agitated dust create clouds of their own, folding, enfolding, and unfolding the divine. Careful observations of pentecostal worship services after thinking hard about Keller's book, Deleuze's logic, and Žižek's notion of fragile Absolute lead this scholar to discover the *pentecostal logic of sense*. Pentecostals in their worship services appear to invert the dualism of eternal and fragile material reality into the dualism of sensuous material bodies and such bodies generating the eternal or the Absolute as fleeting experiences, moments, or waves of divine presence, which in turn serves as their opposite. So instead of the human body being the extremely fragile, fleeting reality, it becomes the hard particle and the Absolute appears fragile, as flashes or bursts of energies in the matrix of bodies.

Pentecostalism gives us a deep sense of how the sacred is constructed and, as Annalisa Butticci's work on the concern for the *real presence* among African Pentecostals in Italy shows, how the poor and marginalized migrants deal with what we called impossible possibility.[57] Catholic and Pentecostal aesthetics of *real presence* encounter each other in agonistic contact zones. African migrants, *parts of no-part* in the Italian society, are attempting to invert the powers relating to the generation and control of real presence. Butticci narrates the story of the encounter between African Pentecostalism and Roman Catholicism in Italy, the story of the weak and the powerful sharing a common space, from the lens of the powerless. In doing this she exhibits the sensitivity and acumen of James Scott and Michel de Certeau in highlighting the everyday practices and weapons of the weak that African Pentecostals are using to subvert overbearing authority in the Catholic stronghold of Italy. She clearly shows how the subjugated, marginalized, and racially degraded Africans are struggling to carve out a space to worship God, earn basic human dignity amid the Italian Catholic ordering of space and privileges, and create possibilities for their own human flourishing.

At the very sophisticated theoretical level that Keller performed her thought, *Cloud of the Impossible* could not shed light on the sacred as an entanglement of the bodies pushing the boundaries of the senses and social spaces or as a concrete struggle for the distribution of the im/possibility. More importantly, the nonexamination of the "cloud" of impossibility as it might relate to the sacramentality of the (im)possible, a nonexistent thing, shows that to do justice to her book one has to move beyond her thought in order to grasp its spirit. The impossibility, impossible possibility, is not only the nonexistent thing that has properties and exercises effectivity, but also it is the Real around which society or religion operates. I wish Keller worked out the way in which "false" impossibility operates as the reference point around which the system of possibilities deduces its truth and the *sine qua non* of the way systems in general operate. It is around our belief in the realm of impossibility that our phantasy about possibility and alternatives is articulated. And, Hegel has taught us, this belief is "objective" as it materializes in the way a system or society functions.

Keller's brilliant analysis of the non-knowing (unknowable) cloud of impossibility operates mainly in a very different epistemological register to Pentecostal thinking, like most of the mainline theologians and philosophers of religion, and she thus missed a key dimension of applying her thought to charismatic and spiritual movements, which mark the public resurgence of religion in the twenty-first century. The mystery of impossibility that she focuses on is the mystery and mystique of unknowing, suffering, uncertainties, ecological catastrophe, and the religious other. It is not the intense, passionate attachment of an everyday mystic who struggles to inhabit the perceived tiny crack or gap between noumenal and phenomenal so he can erotically approach things-in-themselves. What would it mean for Keller's understanding of the mysticism of the impossible possibility if she were to consider an intensity of eros toward the mystery of God so strong that it shatters (however briefly) the very transcendental coordinates of knowing and unknowing, it releases our perceptions from their human coordinates, pushes them outside human reality (as per Deleuze)?

All these insights bring us to the pentecostal notion of the noumenal, things-in-themselves. Often modern theologians see the noumenal in Kantian terms, opposition between phenomenal and noumenal. But this is only a limited way of interpreting what Pentecostals understand as the noumenal. The noumenal also refers to impossible phenomena, things that are excluded from taking place in the extant order of being/things. The noumenal is the impossible whose happening shatters the coordinates of our symbolically constituted common reality. "The gap that separates us from noumenal is thus primarily not epistemological, but practico-ethical and libidinal: there is no 'true reality' behind or beneath phenomena; noumenal are phenomenal things which are 'too strong,' too intense or intensive, for our perceptual apparatus, attuned as it is to constituted reality."[58]

Keller's missed opportunity is this: having rejected a transcendent, classical godly dimension to human reality, she was unable to reverse or transcend the Kantian logic of opposition between noumenal and phenomenal, of the inaccessibility of things-in-themselves.[59] What she needed to do in a Hegelian fashion was to transpose the split between noumenal and phenomenal unto a split within the phenomenal itself, as the split between normal "gentrified" phenomenon within usual human coordinates and "impossible" phenomenon outside symbolically constituted human reality.[60] (Though the "impossible" phenomenon is outside human coordinates, it is still part of the human reality, nothing but a *fragment of the sacred*.)

This distinction between "gentrified" phenomenon and "impossible" phenomenon helps us to get a better conceptual grip on Pentecostals' understanding of miracles. The commonest, everyday meaning of miracles in pentecostal circles is akin to what Alain Badiou calls *event*. Like event, what composes a miracle or "impossible" phenomenon "is always extracted from a situation, always related back to a singular multiplicity, to its state, to the language that is connected to it, etc."[61]

Concluding Thoughts

The key idea of this chapter is this: the sacred could be considered the set of possibilities, opened, closed, hypothetical, or unimagined to a society. But the sacred is not a set of all sets; it is not an absolute totality of all possibilities in a given society. There cannot be a set or entity that is a collection of all possibilities, sets of possibilities, and all there is. French philosopher Alain Badiou in *Being and Event* used the mathematical theories of Georg Cantor (1845–1918) to show that such an entity cannot exist; no set can belong to itself. The number of parts or subset of elements in a set is larger than the elements themselves—there is an irremediable excess of subsets over elements such that there cannot exist a set of all sets.[62] The sacred is infinite, but it cannot be the largest, the last infinite.

We do not want to miss the opportunity of stating that the sacred in one crucial sense is about how a society understands "the concept of the new." How does the new emerge? How does it come forth as causality constrained by historical life, amid preconditions, and yet in the new is "underivable" from its conditions? The sacred is the most constitutive and determinative modality for liberating or chaining the "virtualizing power of time" or for creating the new.

The sacred in this sense of possibilities and the emergence of the new is common to all societies (secular, profane or neither) across time. Where societies differ is with the name they give to the sacred. They also differ on the basis of whether or not they conceive it entitatively or non-entitatively, or some combination of both. In the past the deity is referred to as the Sacred Itself, no distinction between god(s) and the sacred. Religion is only one of the institutions deployed by societies to manage human interactions with the infinity of possibilities. Priests tell people how to approach the deity in small doses of possibilities, never presupposing that members of their societies can face the full ply of possibilities in any one moment. And once in a while an apocalyptic prophet comes around to slightly lift up the veil on the sacred and we see in staggering detail the "monstrosity" of the sacred.[63] The veil is often so lifted to "spell" the "end of history" to those the prophet wants to see come to ruin. Richard Fenn puts it well.

> Direct exposure to all the possibilities contained in the Sacred would of course stagger the mind and the imagination. Who can stand in the presence of the deity, the Sacred itself? That is why the deity is best approached in the form of lower-case sacred, since it is crucial that the entire range of possibilities for both life and death itself remains unfulfilled if even limited access to them is to be granted. Otherwise, as the apocalyptic imagination has long known, were these possibilities for salvation or destruction to be fulfilled, the end would have come.[64]

Today, in the postmodern, postindustrial society, religion no longer has a monopoly of overseeing access to the sacred, and many people no longer equate the sacred with the god(s) or deity. But there is a lingering attitude toward the sacred that is a carryover from the premodern time into our secular or postsecular society. Actually, making a distinction between past and present society on the basis of secular/profane and nonsecular is not an adequate way to understand attitudes toward the sacred. The correct approach is to investigate whether the predominate worldview about reality is an *All* or *non-All*. Belief in *All* (One or Being) means the world is governed by law: there is "a determinate set, finite or infinite of possible cases—a law, deterministic or aleatory, always comes down to the specific set of indexable cases."[65] Time is what enables the actualization of these cases or eternal possibles. But belief in a non-All reality means that reality is always incomplete, and time is not subordinated to the role of effectuating the universe of possible cases and it has the power to modify the set of possibles. Insofar as postmodern society or traditional societies of the past always find a way to circumvent the "pure power of chaos of becoming," the argument about secularity and sacredness of societies as keyed to historical periods is not very convincing.[66] Let me here quote Meillassoux, on whose work I have relied to make my arguments on the periodization of secularity.

> In the guise of a radical evolution, it seems that since the Greeks, one conception, and one only, of becoming, has always imposed itself upon us: time is only the actualization of an eternal set of possibles, the actualization of Ideal Cases, themselves inaccessible to becoming—this latter's only "power" (or rather "impotence") being that of distributing them in a disordered manner. If modernity is traditionally envisaged . . . as the passage from the closed world to the infinite universe, it remains no less true that modernity does not break with Greek metaphysics on one essential point: finite or infinite, the world remains governed by the law—that is, by the All, whose essential signification consists in the subordination of time to a set of possibles which it can only effectuate, but not modify.[67]

In this regard, whether it is religion or other institutions, the conception of the sacred has been "reduced" to the effective practices and procedures directed by a society to enable the cosmos and nomos to maintain themselves against the threat of chaos by strengthening and renewing the ethos. One of the primary roles of religious imagination and the habits of other organs overseeing the forbidden aspirations of people is to explain, control, and predict the pattern of appropriate responses to the passages, damages, and surprises of time. Religion, political systems, the economy, and others often function to assure society of its mastery over passage of time. The sacred (in this constricted viewpoint or shortened as religion) is how a society oversees life with regard to continuity between the past and the present and the future. The key goal of the practices and procedures of the sacred-as-religion is to control the passage of time over life and society's institutions by subordinating the "virtualizing power of time" to a superior power or set of powers.[68] The aim of the controlling intent is to ensure that novelties, radical (or unauthorized) ruptures, do not emerge to defeat all continuity between the past and the present and the future. For such novelties or "miracles," to paraphrase Meillassoux, will become a manifestation of the inexistence of order, of any power capable of overseeing the chaotic power of becoming and the aspirations of the people.

One result of these attempts to subordinate time to a set of possibilities as preset by the law of an All-reality is that the sacred comes to be primarily seen not only as a community's energy brought to deal with the passage of time and change, but also as how a community experiences, understands, interprets, and strives to transcend time. Instead of thinking and doing something to overcome the subordination of time to an eternal set of possibles, scholars focus their scarce energies on theorizing sacred and profane times, temporal orientations, rate of time preference, and so on. The key question about the sacred today is how to liberate the sacred or the virtualizing power of time from religion or from oversight of so-called superior power(s).

Our earlier descriptions of Pentecostals' understanding of the sacred and their penchant for miracles suggest that they are unconsciously rooting to overcome the subordination of time to an eternal set of possibles; their effective practices and habits appear to be beckoning for the "virtualizing power of time" in the twenty-first century.[69] This is one good way to interpret the orientation of the Pentecostal movement toward miracles, radical ruptures in the continuity between the past and the present. There are also at least three problems with their understanding and approach to the sacred. The critical irony of the pentecostal appetite for miracles is that if their wishes are fully realized, we will be delivered to the world of pure power of becoming that no power or order can control. And as both Meillassoux and Badiou suggested, every miracle would then become a manifestation of the inexistence of God. Finally, can pentecostal theologians think the kind of sacred that is beyond religion and the profane, or beyond good and evil, without philosophizing about becoming, possibility, and potentiality—ideas not always celebrated by classical theism or by pentecostal preachers? For everyday Pentecostals, at least in part, the sacred is an affectivity of space and time. It is a manifestation or interstitiality of the space of possibilities and the virtualizing power of time. There is a certain impossible possibility of theologizing the sacred in the Pentecostal movement.

5

The Impossible Possibility, Capitalism, and the Pentecostal Subject

Introduction

In chapter 4 we examined how the pentecostal theory of sacrality pivots around im/possibility, impossible possibility. This chapter examines how the Pentecostals' relationship with the sacred conditions their subjectivity. Pentecostal Christians believe they have special access to God or the transcendental thing-in-itself and part of the sphere of impossibility, which will allow them through the grace of God to always carve spaces of possibility from within for their own flourishing. It would not take long for a visitor to a pentecostal church to hear these verses sung or declared: "I can do all things through Christ who strengthens me" (Phil. 4:13 NIV). Luke 18:27 also says, "What is impossible with man is possible with God." In my Nigerian pentecostal church on Victoria Island we used to sing: "He makes impossibility possible (twice). Jehovah Nissi (or Jireh), he makes impossibility possibility."

The pentecostal subject emerges only through the recognition and acceptance of the realm of impossibility, of the part of the sacred seemingly barred to phenomenal reality. Knowing how to navigate or truck and barter in the realm of impossibility is not an objective knowledge as the acknowledgment of its existence requires the subjective position of being a pentecostal subject; "[the subject] is in this sense self-referential, included in its own object of knowledge."[1] When the pentecostal subject gets behind the phenomenal veil to look at the noumenal, what he discovers is not some hidden substance or something that was there waiting to be discovered, but the form that the realm of impossibility takes as an object of knowledge or phenomenal gaze.[2] When he gets behind to look, "he is bringing with him the very thing he will find."[3] He sees what is always already there. So the line between possibility and impossibility in the sacred, instead of being a scission that permanently separates the two opposing realms or subject and substance, is actually what unites them. The scission sutures the cut. The solution is in the problem. The pentecostal subject, therefore, does not view the scission as out there, but inside of him and it is something he must discipline himself to overcome. Internal impossibility marks the pentecostal subject. His impossibility does not preexist him. The reversal in perspective that this simple analysis of pentecostal subjectivity provides enables us to better understand the pentecostal quest for wringing possibility out of impossibility.

In order to compel im/possibility to release possibilities to them, Pentecostals engage in techniques of the self on the self. This exercise of forcing the hands of the sacred, so to speak, involves touching two deep, and apparently contradictory, dimensions within the human psyche. The self is ascetically governed even as the body is prepared as a machine of jouissance. Pain and pleasure are worked out together in the mode of self-governance. The body is seen as an end in itself and yet it is directed as only a means to please. Now there is no contradiction in this. The Pentecostal believer who takes this combined task seriously and disciplines her body to obey divine laws, to live in God's symbolic order, is the same person who follows the law to maximize the pleasures of the body that supposedly good relationships with the divine provide. Is pentecostal service itself not this coincidence of apparent opposites? There is a tender, warm, intense embrace of the Holy Spirit (the divine other) and the objectification of one's body for the juices of jouissance.

We could call this self-objectification of the body the gaming of the body or the self in religious practices. The freedom to treat the body as only a means, as a "thing," as complement of religious jouissance transforms Pentecostalism as joyful, playful relations between believers themselves and between God and believers from an I-Thou into relationships between things (It-It or I-It). The play (gaming) of the self is the opposite itself of Pentecostalism as a religion of play because through the gaming of self (treated as a means and not as an end in itself) a person is not free or is not a person in the full meaning of the word because her activity is not play.[4] The treatment of a person as a means in religious services indicates that such a religion is no longer promoting human flourishing in its broadest meaning. Such a religion is following the logic of purpose, instrumentality. Bodies are valued for their products or labor, which can be exchanged for divine or human favors. The gaming of self is the opposite of play, because when it begins religion loses its playful character. The effective result or content of this gaming is the subjugation of religion to social suffering, and the truth of social relations of domination and oppression irrupts in it. We will start first investigating how Pentecostalism forms subjectivity by *embalming* suffering; that is, preserving systems that generate social suffering or give pleasant fragrance to excessive social suffering. Second, we show that Pentecostalism's attitude to the sacred and the miraculous produces subjects whose mantra in life is "I can do it" amid virulent capitalism that has rendered increasingly most aspects of economic life fragile; subjects who are making a common cause with late capitalism without realizing that their souls have been captured and reformatted by late capitalism for its profit.

Excessive Social Suffering and Pentecostalism

Social suffering is not the only thing that precedes Pentecostalism as religion *as* play and its embrace of the logic of exchange. As a religion that started with the poor in the late industrial age, excess social suffering operates both as a *desire* and *drive* in the global Pentecostal movement. In the beginning it aimed to ameliorate the suffering and racism faced by its members even as they were prepared for heaven or the eschaton, the period when the rich and the powerful would be brought down from their thrones and be sent away (into existential hell) empty. From the beginning there was joy, enjoyment, rejoicing, and expectation of a good future, which contributed to building up the playful character of pentecostal worship. The body was thrown fully into this adventure of jouissance. This is the founding division, duality (concern for excess weight of suffering and passion for play, enjoyment), that brought Pentecostalism (as a social practice) into being. This duality, which, as we shall learn later, is tearing Pentecostalism apart, is the same set of forces or dynamics that brought the movement into being as a universalist mass religion in the first place.

The prosperity gospel, which focuses on narrow egoism and private welfare, now indicates the gap that separates Pentecostalism from its founding goal. Let us not forget that in Lacan's terms desire represents the gap between the subject and its object—the person lacks the object.

By contrast, drive "takes the lack itself as an object, finding satisfaction in circular movement of the missing satisfaction itself."[5] Prosperity gospel preachers, by the milking of their followers, the fleecing of parishioners to buy multimillion-dollar jets, and the cavorting with anti-poor governments and the rich and powerful, appear to enjoy moving the problem of excessive suffering without solving it. The saintly pastors use the suffering of believers to bring about their own narcissistic satisfaction through their purported mediation of anointing, as the seventeenth/eighteenth-century Nicolas Malebranche would bluntly put the matter if he were alive today. The weight of excessive social suffering is a screen on which they project quick divine help to poverty in order to lure their followers to part with their hard-earned incomes. They say to the poor—*Okay, now come to the screen (altar) and exchange your money for prayers and anointing that zap poverty away!*

The rise of virulent prosperity gospel is one indication that Pentecostalism has been subjugated to the logic of capitalism. The utopia of Pentecostalism is precisely the belief in a world in which religion as play and as logic of exchange are universalized as we tarry with the negative that is the weight of excessive social suffering. A wise man has said that one might divide Pentecostalism (the religion as play par excellence) into play, exchange, and weight. This remark is profound and it is hard to devise a better classification. The third element (weight of social suffering) disturbs the harmonious relationship between the two. It (particular, contextualized social suffering) disturbs the "perfection" or innocence of universalist pentecostal play and directly gives body to the inconsistent whole of the harmonious couple. It embodies the nonrelationship between them, play and exchange. As if social suffering manages to intrude into the room when the two are making or about to make love.

The weight of social suffering is the "part of no part" in the tripartite whole. This "part of no part" is the highest signifier of Pentecostalism (particularly in its wealth-and-health variant). Pentecostalism wants to see a totally *repaired* world. It is also Pentecostalism's lowest signifier. Social suffering is like the embarrassing old demented church founders that preachers hide in the attics of the sanctuaries, hoping they will not come down unexpectedly to ruin the Bacchanalian revel or the mad rush of Jerusalem temple-type *bureau de change* going on in the nave. In its location as the coincidence of opposites, the weight of social suffering, the "part of no part," stands for the whole. This is not because it occupies a neutral space between the two, but represents their constitutive antagonism. It represents their difference as such. The third element unsettles the other two and opens them for endless reassessment.

It is a disaster of thought or practice when believers think that the body and its products are actually a means in the network of relationships between the profit-seeking priestly hierarchy and the ordinary subjects. The body (gaming of the self) in this sense thwarts Pentecostalism from within and makes it inconsistent. In the very failure of Pentecostalism to bear witness to the body (to human beings) as an end in itself it becomes a form of subjugation of the body to the capital, which treats everything as a pure means. The very deficiencies of Pentecostalism in dealing with the weight of social suffering or the unreliability of the pentecostal subjectivity in bearing witness to the truthfulness of the trauma of social suffering in late capitalism signals its truthfulness (not factual truth): religion takes the form of social suffering, and not necessarily a projection of the inner turmoil of the masses or social suffering disguising itself in a religious way. Pentecostalism, or religion for that matter, is not just about believers coping with social suffering in society or with alienation from society. It is simultaneously the story of society telling itself about itself. In a limited sense, religion is the active relationship of society to itself. There is only self-reference. Pentecostalism came around as revolt against society—so it appears at the beginning. But then the Master (society, the "Big Other," late capitalism) appropriated it as its form or one of its new material forms. This reminds me of Kafka's wit: "revolt is not a cage in search of a bird, but a bird in search of a cage."[6] In the next section, we discuss the kind of story many Pentecostals are telling themselves about capitalism amid the story capitalist society is telling itself about itself.

Fragility of Economic Life and Pentecostal Subjectivity

Late capitalism exacerbates fragilities, delivering shocks and disruptions that unsettle ethos and institutions, and imposing excess sufferings, sacrifices, and burdens on the most vulnerable in society as well as the middle class. The well-being of ordinary citizens is tensively poised, an uncertain and fragile balance, always leaning toward disintegration and vulnerable to an excess of suffering. The market and finance capital have rendered life and livelihood of ordinary citizens fragile, while they (market and finance capital) thrive beyond-robustness. The "antifragility" of late capitalism (new economy) comes at the expense of the fragility of ethical citizens.[7] In the words of political theorist William Connolly, "Today we inhabit a world in which the fragility of things—from the perspective of the endurance and quality of life available to the human estate in its entanglements with other force fields—becomes apparent."[8]

The response of the Pentecostal, like most of her fellow American citizens, to the fragility of social existence is to do more and do more, and then do more, plunging into more activities as a way of protecting the self and its flourishing against the massive forces of fragility unleashed on society by late capitalism, when the appropriate response should be to do less. As capitalism limits the ability of the Pentecostal to control her life, exacerbates its entanglements in her world, or constrains her courses of action, she strives to be less and less defined by her human limitations. She works more, buys more smart technology, and seeks out miracle medicines so that she will be less bound by limitations. She wants to be seen as capable, more capable than ever, the perfect American with an impeccable "I can do it" attitude. A profound similarity exists between a Pentecostal's permanent self-revolutionizing, the endless struggle to be flexible and amenable to the inexorable demands of the market as articulated by the formal, enunciated "I can do it," and the inherent self-propelling power of capitalism to exceed its limits. The echoes of "I can do it" from the *objectified speaking mouth* of the Pentecostal (American citizen) is the form in which this capitalist *something* that is in her more than herself survives, sustains itself, and haunts her. This something is like a *superego* agency generating unbearable guilt within her for not doing enough or not being nimbly adaptive amid the changes and demands around her.

So there is always a pseudo-urgency to *act now*. She does not step back to perceive the violence inherent in this state of affairs. The urgency to act is often coming from a body and its desires that have been invaded and disciplined by capitalism and its forces. "At the immediate level of addressing individuals, capitalism, of course, interpellates them as consumers, as subjects of desire, soliciting in them ever new perverse and excessive desires (for which it offers products to satisfy them); furthermore, it obviously also manipulates the 'desire to desire,' celebrating the very desire to desire ever new objects and modes of pleasure."[9]

With this interpellation there is always an urgent injunction to act out her freedom of choice, which ultimately amounts to playing by the rules of the system or self-destruction of her "impotentiality."[10] As Slavoj Žižek puts it, "At its most elementary, freedom is not the freedom to do as you like (that is, to follow your inclinations without any externally imposed constraints), but to do what you do not want to do, to thwart the 'spontaneous' realization of an impetus."[11]

The overall result of this inclination to do more and more is that Pentecostals seem to have severed themselves from the ability not to be or not to do in the market. Pentecostals appear to enjoy the destruction of their impotentiality as "an aesthetic pleasure of the first order." Giorgio Agamben laments this outcome of modern democracies and market systems.

> Separated from his impotentiality, deprived of the experience of what he can not do, today's man believes himself capable of everything, and so he repeats his jovial "no problem," and his irresponsible "I can do it," precisely when he should instead realize that he has been consigned in unheard of measure to forces and processes over which he has lost all control. He has become blind not to his capacities but to his incapacities, not to what he can do but what he cannot, or can not, do. . . . Nothing makes us more impoverished and less free than this estrangement from impotentiality.[12]

To accomplish our task in this chapter, I will proceed by discussing the fragility of life or social existence in the new economy, late capitalism. Next, I will elaborate on the problematic nature of the irresponsible "I can do it" of Pentecostal Citizens in the face of the relentless onslaught of the forces of late capitalism.

The Fragility of Social Existence in the New Economy

From a purely religious point of view, one of the great impacts of late capitalism or new economy on society is the rupture between meaning and truth. Religion strives within the horizon of meaning, to ground truths within a framework of global meaning. But late capitalism and its globalization enact truths outside meaning. What matters for capitalism is its self-revolutionizing movement. The global market mechanism detotalizes meaning insofar as capitalism is at home in different cultures and resists efforts to enframe it within a system of shared values or common "cognitive mapping." There is no global common substance or worldview that we can say characterizes all communities in which capitalist globalization has penetrated. The truth of capitalism is its self-revolutionizing power (which is under the aegis of global market mechanism) and it operates as truth-without-meaning. Capitalism adapts itself well to all local situations, local and foreign values, and civilizations as a "neutral economic-symbolic machine." Global capitalism directly posits any cultures, values, and representational frames it encounters as its driving force.[13] (One of its faces in America is what William Connolly calls the "evangelical-capitalist resonance machine."[14]) Among some religious scholars or believers this character of capitalism engenders a sense of fragility of meaning—meaning is now only about diverse and unstable interplay of multiple meanings—that threatens to completely marginalize the dimension of (noncapitalist/market) truth in public discourse or common social life.

Karl Marx writes about the desacralization of all sacred bonds in capitalism in its self-engendering movement. In the analysis of this self-propelling movement it is easy to make a mistake by insisting on the distinction between the abstraction (the movement of capital) and the real people and things behind the movement, the distinction between the "real" and the "reality" (which "truly exists"). One of such distinctions is financial circulation of money and the industrial circulation of money and thinking that what really matters is the industrial circulation of money that concerns the production and distribution of concrete goods. The endless (speculative) financial circulation of money is seen as an epiphenomenon, a foaming ferment of finite hard transactions, and believing that we can grasp the reality of industrial production (real people and their products) in the economy without comprehending the financial circulation of money, the so-called mad dance of Wall Street. This way of approaching the analysis of capitalism is flawed, as it ignores the effectivity of the *Real* and, more importantly, downplays the fact that the functions of financial circulation of money must be presupposed if we are to make sense of the dynamics or reality of capitalism as they are.[15] The dynamics of the monetary system and finance capital determine the structure of real-life processes. When in 2008 the so-called abstract, speculative, financial movement of stocks, bonds, and futures irrupted into crisis, it adversely affected material social processes.[16] Herein is the power of finance capital to impose fragility and excess suffering on average citizens and beyond. The violent convulsions of the financial systems from time to time render all other systems in the socioeconomy vulnerable to loss and instability. And in their destabilized state they exacerbate the fragility of citizens' lifeworld. Ordinary persons experience the irruptions of the financial system as a negativity. Maurizio Lazzarato noted in his book, *The Making of the Indebted Man*:

The series of financial crises has violently revealed a subjective figure that, while already present, now occupies the entirety of public space: the "indebted man." The subjective achievements neoliberalism had promised ("everyone a shareholder, everyone an owner, everyone an entrepreneur") have plunged us into existential condition of the indebted man, at once responsible and guilty for his particular fate.[17]

Amid all this excess suffering, destabilization, and variability, finance capital is growing stronger and stronger by the day or, at least, its hold on daily economic life is getting firmer and firmer. Finance capital thrives by endlessly reinventing itself, taking advantage of randomness and variability. Finance capital and by extension the market system of late capitalism have created the environment in which citizens pursue their everyday activities of production and reproduction. While finance capital benefits from randomness (that is, it is antifragile), most citizens avoid or endure the randomness created by it, while some are nonrandom in their ethical practice. The market and finance capital have rendered the life and livelihood of ordinary citizens fragile while they thrive beyond-robustness. The antifragility of late capitalism (finance capital) comes at the expense of the fragility of ethical citizens.

Against the antifragility (*creative destruction*) of capitalism and against the flood of fragilities unleashed against the socioeconomic fabric, the average Western citizen has only lifted the banner or standard of freedom, the freedom to-do. But the problem is that the freedom that is often celebrated in Western-democratic-market societies amounts to a doctrine of freedom as the democratic citizen's impotence in the face of threats to his or her well-being, the social fabric, and the commons and its good. According to Giorgio Agamben, modern democratic powers and state structures increasingly prefer to act on the im-potentiality (potential to not-do) of its citizens.

The Citizen's Boast of "I Can Do It"

In the United States—in the competitive ambience of the new economy—there is a strong attachment to abilities, potentials, and this is taken as a positive and powerful character trait. The majority of American Pentecostals are interested in the potential to-do, but there is also the potential to not-do, what is called impotentiality. There comes a time in life when in order to resist an unjust system or to keep our soul we need to focus on this potential to not-do. Modern democracies or late capitalism separate citizens not only from what they can do, but also, and more importantly, from the power to not do, from what they can not do. Everyone is seduced, cajoled, and driven to offer the flexibility that the market demands. Most of them have lost the capacity *not* to be flexible, forgotten how not to give their participation to the system to reproduce itself. The eager readiness of today's woman or Pentecostal to repeat "I can do it" indicates that she has actually been commandeered by the fierce free market system, which does not allow her to preserve any freedom that can undo the prevailing order in her incessant acts of selling her labor power, buying stuff with the proceeds, and guarding her ever-slipping economic security. Today, man's boastful "I can do it," that is, his potential to-do in late capitalism, has become an echo chamber of the freedom to do what he pleases with his property in the marketplace, and it resonates with the freedom to recklessly use the earth's resources for profit. This hubris is the pathetic arrogance of a man whose soul has been captured and reformatted by late capitalism for its profit.

We identify this as hubris because the response is pseudo-activity; the response to take actions, to intervene, is mistakenly considered as courage, as the character of a person who is a captain of his soul or fate, as a conquering spirit charging at his world with the powerful technology of the twenty-first century, when it is actually none of these. The effort is all empty theater, the impotence of man trapped under an unbearable weight of frustration and marked by a deep indifference to the Real and reality of late capitalism. While the all-powerful American (Pentecostal) consumer is boldly declaring, "I can do it," capital is saying back to him in a harsh voice, "I can do whatever I want with you!" Instead of his kind of pseudo-actions, as Žižek advises, it is

> better to do nothing than engage in localized acts whose ultimate function is to make the system run more smoothly (acts like providing space for the multitude of new subjectivities, and so on). The threat today is not passivity but pseudo-activity, the urge to "be active," to "participate," to mask the Nothingness of what goes on. People intervene all the time, "do something"; academics participate in meaningless "debates," and so forth, and the truly difficult thing is to step back, to withdraw from all this. Those in power often prefer even a "critical" participa-

tion, a dialogue, to silence—just to engage us in a "dialogue," to make sure our ominous passivity is broken.[18]

The clashing of the powerful can-do-ness of capitalism and the feeble can-do-ness of the American Pentecostal reminds me of a joke among immigrant African Pentecostals in New York. A Nigerian pastor was preaching about witches in Africa, how they control or manipulate the lives and behaviors of their neighbors or enemies. He explained that a witch can stop a husband and wife from having children, prevent the man in the city from sending a monthly feeding allowance to his parents in the village, and compel the Christian to skip church on Sunday. He went on and on, emphasizing the magical powers of witches and wizards to manipulate others. After he had finished, a woman stood up and said, "Pastor, in America we do not have that kind of witches. The ones we have here are neither men nor women. They are called *Bills*. Because of piling bills, a Christian will not pay his tithes or send money home. When he is sleeping with his wife and he wants to ejaculate, he remembers the financial cost of raising children in New York City and he does an onanism. He does not come to church on Sundays because he needs to work on weekends to earn more money to cover his shortfall between income and expenses. The fear of bills is the beginning of economic wisdom in New York, and for many residents of the city it surpasses the fear of God. Bills are the witches we face here in New York City. They come into your house and sit on your tables, countertops, and everywhere in broad daylight. They do not need to visit your homes in the night or appear invisible. The mailman or the email system brings the American witches to your home."

She continues, "If the power of a witch lies in the ability to manipulate another person's behavior, then nothing surpasses the American witch. American witches are more powerful than the African ones. In the winter, if you do not offer them part of your paycheck, they can cause you to freeze to death in your own home. Bills can force a loving mother to leave her underage children alone at home and go in search of money. In fact, they can make you do whatever they want and they can do whatever they want with you. Pastor please pray for me. I want deliverance from the American witch!"

This is the power, the can-do-ness of the new economy as seen through the eyes of African immigrants in New York City. Any half-serious critical investigation of the economic conditions in Western democratic societies will reveal that a majority of their citizens and residents are in the strong arms of bills (also known as debt). The people are free, but the corporations who hold their debts manipulate their behaviors and actions. As Lazzarato puts it,

> You are free insofar as you assume the way of life (consumption, work . . .) compatible with reimbursement. The techniques used to condition individuals to live with debt begin very early on, even before entry on the job market. The creditor's power over the debtor very much resembles Foucault's last definition of power: an action carried out on another action, an action that keeps the person over which power is exercised "free." The power of debt leaves you free, and it encourages you and pushes you to act in such a way that you are able to honor your debts [even if, like the proud macho man, you can freely shout in the street "I can do it"].[19]

The "I can do it" that easily rolls off the tongues of citizens of the United States is really not boldness or freedom. This bravado conceals their unbridled obedience to the capitalist system. It covers their acceptance of the parallelogram of market forces as superior power over them that do not require moral legitimization. This obedience often manifests itself as Christo-marketistic religion among certain segments of Christianity, as the abandonment of any concern with social justice. It also shows itself as the Christo-nationalistic religion of neoconservatives who place their country at the center of divine revelation. This form of obedience reveals itself yet in another way: as the liberal religion among the so-called progressives who want to maximize their enjoyment without any cost or sacrifice. Finally, this kind of obedience displays itself as a consumerist religion of the mall, which could not care less about the world situation. In all these cases, obedience is the main, central, dominant virtue demanded by the modern/postmodern authoritarian religions of fundamentalist Christianity, aggressive nationalism, cost-free political liberalism, and sedative, rapacious consumption.

Everybody is claiming "I-can-do-it" amid a thralldom of obedience to some authority, binding power, ideology, pleasure, or private goal. Obedience is ultimately a command that maintains the established order of the economy, sapping the initiative to resist finance capital or late capitalism. The "I can do it" of the modern democratic citizen is always a form of obedience that aligns with the system and does not try to transform it. The "I" in the "I can do it" is not an "I" without the guarantees, support, backing, and approval of the restrictive regnant nomos of its society. The freedom of the "I" in the "I can do it" is a freedom that is demanded by the capitalo-parliamentary institutions, and it is not an expression of the potentiality to-do that is in harmony with the potentiality to not-do.

Capitalism does not quarrel with the "I can" of the individual. The ideology of capitalism is never about drawing a tight circle around the individual about what is included and prohibited. Its focus is on negotiating the exchange between the included and excluded, the nonclosure of the circle of regulations. Capitalist ideology counteracts its order by making space for inevitable transgression of the order. This is how the order and its hold on the individual are strengthened. The point is to manage the inherent transgressions, admitting its failure of closure while using transgressions to strengthen itself.[20] This reminds me of the proverbial mother's instruction to her daughter. The daughter informed the mother that she suspected that her husband was not virile enough to sire and because of this she wanted to divorce him. The mother said to her, "You can discreetly sleep with a virile man of your choice and get pregnant and then ask God for forgiveness, as long as you do not divorce to bring disgrace to our family name."

So the ideology of capitalism does not say to the citizen, "You can not!" In fact, it enjoins transgression to smoothen its functioning. The permission to do, to enjoy your "I can do it" easily (imperceptibly, eventually) shifts to an obligation to do, to strive to meet the impossible demands of the system. This permission or injunction is coming from an insatiable agency in whose reckoning the person can never do enough and is therefore guilty of betraying her desire, which in the first place is the constellation of ideals, expectation, and the "desire of the other" that she has internalized in the course of *disciplining*.

Let us try one more time to dig deeper into the nature of the American Pentecostal's "I can do it." This "I can do it" functions as an abstract universal notion and the individual citizen is an embodiment of it. Under the hammer of late capitalism, fierce competition for jobs, and incessant efforts to possess economic security, the boastful "I can do it" is an affirmation of the individual as an abstract universal capacity to do (work and think). This individual or capacity is violently torn out of a particular lifeworld and social roots and thus the actualization or experience of the capacity to-do is dependent on contingent social circumstances and free choice. But this is only half the story. In order to complete the story, we need to ask under what historical circumstances does the abstract (commodified) "I can do it" become the obvious wise response to this massive economic predicament? In what economic constellations do the sheer impotence and unbearable frustration of a great many individuals in society become masked as the free-choice engendered "I can do it"? According to Žižek,

> This is the point of Marx's analysis of commodity fetishism: in a society in which commodity exchange predominates, individuals themselves, in their daily lives, relate to themselves, as well as to the objects they encounter, as to contingent embodiments of abstract-universal notions. What I am, my concrete social or cultural background [or economics surroundings], is experienced as contingent, since what ultimately defines me is the abstract universal capacity to think and/or to work. Any object that can satisfy my desire is experienced as contingent, since my desire is conceived as an abstract formal capacity, indifferent towards the multitude of particular objects that might—but never fully do—satisfy it. . . . The crucial point here is, again, that in certain specific social conditions of commodity exchange and global market economy, "abstraction" becomes a direct feature of actual social life. It impacts on the way concrete individuals behave and relate to their fate and to their social surroundings.[21]

It is germane to add that it is not that the democratic American Pentecostal citizen is simply more pragmatic and our critique of her boast is merely pedantic. Rather, it is that the tension between the universal frame of commodity exchange (the abstract universal notion) and the impotence of the particular is inscribed into the very nature of the capitalist social formation. This split is even inscribed into the worker or citizen. Her identity is split between its particular and universal aspects. The gap between the particular (her identity, personality, sense of self) and the universal that perturbs it is within her. Indeed, the universal is exploding from within the particular—almost turning the individual into a *universal singularity*, a subject able to participate in the universal without the mediation of the particular. Put differently, the universality of "I can do it" (the interpellation of universal capital) is presented in Western societies—with its usual accent on individualism and free choice—as a particular position.²²

The programmed response to the "hey you" of universal capital or the commands of the "American witch" is the "I can do it." This "I can do it," which is actually an inverted instruction, translates into doing more and more battle against the uncertainty and fragility of lives and social bonds in Western democracies—without sparing a thought on how to transform capitalism. It is easier to fancy how to push the self to work harder, pray a little harder, or more comforting to fancy what more actions he can take in protest within the meaningful framework of democracy than to imagine the end of capitalism. People are running faster and faster only to end up in the same place or even backwards. They are working harder and harder to please universal capital or praying harder and harder to shoo away the American witch—all to no avail.

Working harder and harder appears not to be a "practical" solution or advice. The power of bills or capitalism to condition how persons act in real life needs a moment of critical thinking if the citizens are to extricate themselves from its vicious grip. Both the native-born American Pentecostal and the African-migrant Pentecostal need moments to recognize why the American witch is much more powerful than witches elsewhere. On this point we need to raise the importance of one of Žižek's insights: "There are situations when the only truly 'practical' thing to do is to . . . 'wait and see' by means of patient, critical analysis."²³ We need critical analysis to show us what is happening to our freedom, the exercise of which is not delivering us from acute fragilities of social existence and predicaments of our personal lives.

The distorted freedom that the Westerner celebrates has put human freedom on the path to fast losing its *impotentiality*. Generally, things move from potentiality to actuality, but potentiality does not exist only in act. When potentiality passes into actuality, does it exhaust itself? Giorgio Agamben, following Aristotle, says "no."²⁴ Potentiality does not exhaust itself in actualization. A part of it will always remain, that is, the impotentiality (to "be able not to-do," potentiality to not-be, potentiality that "conserves itself and saves itself in actuality").

There are two types of potentiality: generic and existing. Generic potentiality is the capacity to do something and when a person exercises this potentiality she is altered. A child learns and in the process of realizing her potential she is changed. On the other hand, a scribe has an existing potentiality to write, but also the choice of whether to bring this potentiality into actuality or not. This is the potentiality to not-do or not-be. The scribe is able not to exercise his own potentiality. Agamben sheds light on this form of potentiality, or as earlier indicated, impotentiality.

> This is not to say that human beings are the living beings that, existing in the mode of potentiality, are capable just as much of one thing as its opposite, to do just as to not do. This exposes them, more than any other living being, to the risk of error; but, at the same time, it permits human beings to accumulate and freely master their own capacities, to transform them into "faculties." It is not the measure of what someone can do, but also and primarily the capacity of maintaining oneself in relation to one's own possibility to not do, that defines the status of one's action. While fire can only burn, and other living beings are only capable of their own specific potentialities—they are capable of only this or that behavior inscribed into their biological vocation—human beings are the animals capable of their impotentiality.[25]

Freedom is defined by the ambivalence in human beings' potentiality, by their existing potentiality; they always have the power to-do and to not-do, they are capable of their own impotentiality.[26] Human freedom is not merely the capacity to actualize, to-be or to-do, but also the potential to not-be or to not-do. Freedom, as Agamben sees it, is primarily in the domain of impotentiality, not in actualization. He maintains that it is possible to see how the root of freedom is in the abyss of potentiality. "To be free is not simply to have the power to do this or that thing, nor is it simply to have the power to refuse to do this or that thing. To be free is, in the sense we have seen, *to be capable to one's own impotentiality*, to be in relation to one's privation."[27]

What is happening in the so-called new economy or late capitalism is that the impotentiality that human beings have is being treated as already lost. This is not a mere reframing of freedom or action but the destruction of frame of freedom, the disappearance of the potentiality to not-do or not-be as the support of every potentiality to-do. In terms of political praxis of resistance, the lost represents the vanishing "distance toward the direct hegemonic interpellation—'involve yourself in the market competition, be active and productive!' "[28]

The reason why many people do not recognize that the freedom of choice they exercise, which limits them to an existing frame of possibilities, is destructive of impotentiality is because the new economy or capitalism acts as a "good" master. A good master does not give you prohibitions or infringe on your freedom; rather, he permits you to be yourself, tells you "you can," you can do the impossible. He wants you to experience yourself as free. But actually this freedom is only a step to playing on the desires of the citizens as consumers. The customer has the free choice and permissiveness to consume all he or she wants. Besides, the master's injunction to do is a particular way of exercising freedom that subverts the whole understanding of freedom. The freedom to only do, to only act, is the opposite itself of authentic (full ply of) freedom, because through the severance of impotentiality from potentiality citizens lose their freedom. The effective content of this free and boastful act of "I can do it" is subjugation to capital or market. The *utopia* of the active Western citizen-consumer is precisely the belief in the possibility of complete permissiveness and free choice, a society in which all citizens are completely flexible to the demands of the market and acting like capitalists in the management of their lives, which is now considered as pools of assets. They forget that potentiality and impotentiality are coupled in every action. It is a dream of *"universality without its symptom, without the paradoxical exception that serves the role of its internal negation."*[29]

In summary, the problem of the modern citizen (American Pentecostal) in the new economy is that she can no longer say no to the demands of the market. She is ever so flexible to meet its demands. She is focused on doing, on commission, and not on inaction, omission, the potentiality to not-do. At this point it might serve us well to recast some of our arguments in the theological language of German feminist theologian Dorothee Sölle. What Agamben calls the "irresponsible 'I can do it'" of democratic citizens,[30] their blindness to their incapacities, will be considered in light of Sölle's theological thinking as a result of their being collectively obedient for too long.[31] Following her thought we attribute the estrangement from impotentiality to training in obedience, which is responsible for the good conscience of democratic citizens in their willingness to have only one-armed freedom, the potentiality to-do. This freedom is a consequence of creating societies imbued with religions, creeds, or ethos that accent obedience as the primary virtue of human coexistence rather than Spirit-led/filled creative spontaneity, leavening disobedience, or deliberate potentiality to not-do.

The boastful "I can do it" of the Pentecostal who prides herself as living in a free country like the United States "is in fact a surrender of the sense of possibilities, of that phantasy which bursts all boundaries. As a person limits herself to that which she finds, which she preserves and sets in order, her spontaneity atrophies."[32] According to Sölle, there is something beyond this mere, easygoing obedience and it is resistance, the exercise of spirited, responsible freedom that imaginatively and effectively opposes obedience. I call this freedom the potentiality to not-do, or emancipatory spirituality.

Let me now gather up what we have learned so far. The obvious response to the fragilities inflicted on Pentecostals and all citizens alike by late capitalism or the new economy is the response of the irresponsible "I can do it." The approach here is to throw oneself into late capitalism. The response is like the movement (venture, an inner drive) of the estranged toward union. The end result is something I will call *pentecocapitalism*, the alliance between late capitalism and Pentecostalism that creates a Pentecostal-capitalist resonance machine, to adapt the words of William Connolly who charted the path of the evangelical-capitalist resonance machine.[33]

Pentecocapitalism and God's Subjects

Pentecocapitalism conditions the pentecostal subjectivity by tapping into two deep nerves within popular culture. Pentecostal preachers are able to depict a believer as a person of *consumption*, a follower of Christ sanctioned by God to richly enjoy all things (1 Tim. 6:17), and as a person of *wonder*, in, with, and through whom God's Spirit permeates everyday life. These two dimensions of the believer are tightly woven. Wonders facilitate access to exotic and out-of-reach goods for consumption. Signs and wonders are items of consumption; they are eventually incorporated into the being (existence) of the person through sensory and nonsensory organs. But too much enjoyment of the good and gifts God richly provides to a person can cause constipation in the flow of anointing, inhibit the believer from being an access to and conduit of wonders. A pentecostal preacher once admonished his congregation with these words: "For the fact that God richly gave us all things to enjoy does not mean we should have sex with our spouses every day. That is to be enjoyed sparingly if you want to grow in the Lord, increase your anointing." This admonition bears hints of ethics of Pentecocapitalism that resonate with that of capitalism.

Pentecocapitalism has an ethic of production, the production of the anointing or spirituality that gives access to signs and wonders. Pentecostals employ the technique of the self on the self, the technology of the self to discipline their bodies to become God's subjects, vessels of anointing. There is an appreciable level of *internal disciplining* peculiar (attributable) to pentecostal spirituality. This disciplining is anchored to and feeds on the belief in "calling" or access to the supernatural. The belief is that all believers can wrestle possibility out of impossibility in the sacred or are at least endowed and empowered (Spirit-baptized) to form a new self to transform his or her personal life and do good works on earth. This internal disciplining may remind some of us of Max Weber's discussion of the Protestant ethic and the spirit of capitalism. Weber taught us that workers in nineteenth-century capitalism gave their bodies and souls to the social apparatus that hails them from outside. They responded to the interpellation of capitalism (as per Louis Althusser's "Hey, you") by successfully internalizing and incorporating this hailing from outside. The powers of the system worked on them in the most intimate fashion—from within. According to Rey Chow, "What I consider most decisive about [Weber's] theory is the effective structural collaboration he pinpoints between the power of subjective belief (in salvation) as found in modern, secularized society and the capitalist economism's ways of hailing, disciplining, and rewarding identities constituted by certain forms of labor."[34] What is the equivalent of work ethic in pentecostal spirituality? In the words of Chow, "What is the phenomenon symptomatic of a ferocious and well-rewarded productionism in contemporary" pentecostal spirituality?[35] It is the phenomenon of the massive, proliferating, energetic spiritual (ecclesiastical) entrepreneurship: fast paced growth of church infrastructure (ownership), increasing church attendance, efficient and efficacious ~~tax, tithe~~ profit farming, production of signs and wonders, and the utilitarian razzmatazz (spectacular exhibition) of anointing—all of which have avoided societal transformation like the plague. In order to be, to establish oneself, to be the "authentic" pentecostal self with the valorized anointing, this saved entrepreneur must both be seen to *own* his profitable anointing and exhibit (sell, franchise, project, globalize) it repeatedly. To put it in different terms, the phenomenon is the feverish, simultaneous pursuit of salvation as an *object* and of prosperity as an *abject*.[36] The capitalist-spiritual entrepreneurs are haunted and trapped within the given of *abject* salvation—of calling as abjection.[37]

Colin Campbell in his 1987 book, *The Romantic Ethic and the Spirit of Modern Consumerism*, has offered a supplement to Weber's thesis. Since an economy consists of production and consumption, he argues that some other ethic supplied the impulse that led to increasing consumption that absorbed the ever-growing capitalist production. (Productive capitalism needs a consumptive market to buy all the stuff it is producing.) He traced the impulse to the "Romantic ethic" that stimulates new desires and shapes attitudes toward consumerism. The generation of insatiable wanting (not wants) is based on the emotional experience of imagination—dreams of finer lifestyles and enjoyment of novel goods. This form of imagination he names "imaginative hedonism." And in naming and calling attention to it he shows how the pursuit of wealth alongside the pursuit of pleasure created the modern capitalist society.[38]

Pentecostalism is stimulating new desires and wants, shaping forms of consumerism as it creates or awakens inner longings and impulses that (can) feed productive systems when or where ascetic ethics of the production ethic is (necessarily) not enough. A question suggests itself at this juncture: What economic secrets do the combination of *pneumatological imagination* (à la Amos Yong) and *imaginative hedonism* hold for an active and creative (or dysfunctional and lethargic) capitalist system?

We have talked about production and consumption and now we need to move on to the third dimension of the Pentecostal ethic. Every economy is a set of productive (and capital formation), consumptive, and distributive (income transfers) activities. But what do we say about distribution? Economists tell us that no capitalist system operates without some mechanism for income transfers from income-surplus sectors (areas or persons) to deficit ones. The ethic of transfer of value or social engagement is very functional in pentecostal churches. It is true that there are some pentecostal churches that are involved in social justice projects, but it is truer to say that income inequalities between many pentecostal preachers (chief executive officers of their churches) and their church members are characteristic of the gap between the worker and the CEO in the corporate world or the huge income inequalities of the early twenty-first-century American society.

Concluding Thoughts

Global capitalism has no doubt shaped the character of Pentecostalism, its ecclesial practices, and its adherents' subjectivity. Amid all this there is a tilt toward worship as pure means (WPM) or to recover the same as a lost object they never really possessed. In its current form, WPM directs desires away from the instrumental logic of late capitalism and it may well be a call for an exodus from the imperial virtues shaping the global Pentecostal movement. Alas, as we already stated earlier, capitalism itself is a vast apparatus for the production of pure means. So WPM may after all not represent a desertion or exodus from the capitalist logic.

Despite what we might think of the influence of late capitalism on WPM, philosophically the connection must be grounded. WPM captures something of the (fantasmatic) secret ambition of Pentecostals. One becomes a full Pentecostal not only by sharing the movement's *ethical substance* and being invested in the exchange logic between believers and God, but also by identifying with this secret ambition. It is *pure* worship, to desire and attain the virtue of worship as pure means. Worship gives Pentecostalism its unprecedented vitality and WPM haunts every giving, performance, or production of ordinary worship. WPM requires the repeated failures or aborted efforts of ordinary worship to actualize itself fragmentarily. There is a necessity of succession, repetitions, and failures in the relationship between the two forms of worship: Pentecostals have to first choose (or make the "wrong" choice of) ordinary, instrumental, worship before they can reach worship as pure means, the true speculative meaning of worship, or realize the secret ambition. Direct access to WPM is not possible.[39]

Worship as pure means is an object that Pentecostals long to have and mourn in the precise sense of loss of an object that they never possessed. The secret or the secret ambition erects itself in the very gesture of a withdrawal or loss.[40] This is one thing, one orientation, or a call at the heart of pentecostal sensibility that resists the capitalist logic, albeit it is very fragile and has little chance of success. Even if we are tempted to put a fine point on it we can only, with faltering lips, say it is a kind of weak force, a powerless power. Paradoxically, it is strong enough to (occasionally) escape global capital's power of mediation, to assert its identity and not to allow imperial capital to "sublate" it. WPM flashes forth amid the foaming ferment of the heady brew of Pentecostalism and capitalism. The next chapter presents how we might rightly understand or philosophically ground worship as pure means.

6

Worship as Pure Means

Introduction

"The World"

I saw Eternity the other night,
Like a great ring of pure and endless light,
   All calm, as it was bright;
And round beneath it, Time in hours, days, years,
   Driv'n by the spheres
Like a vast shadow mov'd; in which the world
   And all her train were hurl'd.

—Henry Vaughan (1621–1695)

The opening lines of this poem gave me the imagination and words to capture something about the enigmatic worship as pure means that I want to convey in this chapter. The poem in its entirety advocates for a life devoted to God, to worship of God as the best and worthiest of human existence.[1] Henry Vaughan envisages a pure life—life stripped down to what he regards as its primary telos: worship of God. This is to him the greatest, most fundamental religious and moral truth most of the world has not recognized or taken seriously. Let me now capture in prose what I also saw the other night.

I saw worship the other night, like a great light of pure and endless waves; all ecstatic as it was glorious; all round beneath it, people, in their sexes, classes, races, driven by the spirits, like a vast body moved, on which the world and all her means and ends were hurled and torn. Great worship often follows the patterns of ordinary worship, yet the purposelessness of great worship suddenly transmutes those patterns into something that snatches up and delays the eternal in its desperate fleetingness, to an immaterial, "virtual" medium that has "an absoluteness, a purity, a beauty, which would not be possible in" an ordinary praise and worship.[2] This is the great magic trick of pentecostal worship.

A worship service may be unstructured, disorganized, full of emotion, yet it has a kind of calmness that allows profound transfiguration and produces the form of divine-human relation in which abstraction of far-reaching importance is possible—provided that a particular condition is met. There is the abstraction of the changeable nature of worship during the collective exchange and mingling of emotions, and the abstraction of a concrete, individual, specific pattern of worship. In a worship service, the concrete, particular form of the individual worshiper is undifferentiated in the collective bowl of worship as incense, the lifting up of hands and prayers as effervescent sacrifice despite its specific qualities. Once its incense quality has been abstracted, then one individual's worship has the "same value" as another person's. For Pentecostals, the worship is what makes it possible to "measure" or "evaluate" the worth or social effectivity of all other interactions with God, all other forms of everyday divine-human (group-institutional) interactions, whatever their specific qualitative, tangible determinations might be. In the innermost core of the worship service is to be found the "transcendental" matrix (texture) that constitutes the a priori framework of a concrete, particular objective approach, medium to (relationship with) God. Worship constitutes the foundation for all objective-universal spiritual evaluation. This twofold abstraction requires another abstraction, the impossible possibility of purity, becoming worship as pure means. Worship-maximizing Pentecostals argue for "pure worship," that is, worship as a means not subordinated to an end, not geared to specially calculated utilitarian interest. But this "hope" is only approachable, in my opinion, when worship is also not an end in itself, but a pure mediality without end. It is for this reason that in this chapter I philosophize pure worship as a sphere of pure means and gesturality, means without end, believers *being-in-a-medium* of divine-human relation, allowing worship to be shown as such and not constrained by a predetermined end. Put differently, worship as pure means makes means, the means of divine-human relation, visible as themselves in which the instrumentality of contemporary worship or Christian practices is suspended through the conception of religion as play. The notion of religion as play finds its apogee in worship as pure means. In its nature of purposelessness, play transcends the instrumental demands and constraints of the present given world in the direction of possibilities and not-yet-defined potentialities.[3] Of course, the logic of play is the logic of grace.

As we have shown from the beginning of this book, there is always a twist, a convertible character to pentecostal philosophy. Here we attempt to grasp a dimension of convertibility by asking: Where cometh this uncanniest of all hope—the expectation of pure worship? Is this not a poignant expression of "will to power," the "I can do it" of pentecostal subjectivity? Nietzsche's madman and overman declared God's death and deliberately willed the will to power. The pentecostal holy man and big man split God and wills to be the master, the lord of the earth. Perhaps, it is not from the benevolence of the worship leader, the pastor, or the bishop that we expect our pure worship, but of their own, not God's interest. This story and analysis must wait for a later occasion; for now, we will confine ourselves to understanding worship as pure means. In exploring the uncertain territory of worship as pure means opened by Pentecostals, I do not promise to write a straightforward philosophy or history of pentecostal worship, nor do I elaborate on the genealogy of Pentecostals' thoughts (practices) on worship. This is only an exercise, a *theorein*, a way of viewing the pentecostal practice of worship.

A Theory of Pentecostal Worship

The concept of worship was often located in either of two spaces: the production of substantial good or the utilitarianism of contingent empirical interests. There is an alternative to these two forms of thought. I propose that we consider worship as no longer (not always) passing through the production of substantial good (such as forming a particular people) or the settlement of contingent individual interests, but as going straight through to the evocation of a world from the circulation of emotional and spiritual energies, extracting value from the pure circulation of emotional energy. The performance of worship takes the form of parthenogenesis: meaning and value produce more meaning and value without any longer passing through the "substantialist" production or utilitarian settlement. This view of worship as producing meaning and value is only a starting point and it should be understood as such, a view we will refine as we go along because the process is only a pure mediality, not a pipeline that takes means and produces the *end* of meaning and value. Worship is not identified with meaning. Meaning is a possibility inherent in spirit, a possibility in terms of an interest. As per the third view we are advocating here, we go into worship without putting an "interest" in it and take nothing out of it. Worship wants nothing but to be worship. What worship aims for is that there is nothing to be aimed at. It is aiming that makes no aim to appear other than aiming itself.

Worship is a pure means. A means is pure precisely because its *in-order-to* has not yet been decided. A decided means is no longer a pure means. For instance, worship as a pure means is a courageous openness whose *validity* defies all purposive articulation but represents the commitment of the participants whose self-realization lies in self-transcendence. When worship tries to be useful, placed in the service of utilitarian purpose or particular ambition, it falls to the level of profitability or ritual action, abandoning its openness to surprises. *Pure means is not the opposite of means or ends, but a condition of their possibility.* It is pure mediality.

Pure means does not speak or gesture to a result that we can point to before engaging in a process, motion, or quest. It is the motive process. The concept of worship as pure means gestures to the idea that the motive process of life in the Spirit, the born-again existence, the divine-human relation that unfolds amid gathered believers praising God, is not wholly determined, is not locked into an invariant network of causes and effects. To have an end-means relation presupposes a preexisting totality of possibilities out of which a possibility becomes actualized as an end at the instigation of means. But if one has a worldview in which the new, the *event*, cannot be accounted for by the known chain of causes, preexisting conditions, then the new can emerge, which retroactively creates its own possibility.[4]

Pure means is without goal and without goalessness. It is a world somewhere between end and means. Worship as pure means gestures to the idea that God is not conditioned by means programmed to reach him. Worship as pure means also points to this idea: God is not an end among ends, something we strive to grasp for the time being or for keeps. Somewhere between (beyond) the worlds of means and ends is God, the Unconditioned, and the spirit and truth of pentecostal worship lies in lurching into the liminal, marginal, and "mystical" wonderland between means and end. Worship as pure means is what we may call *being-in-worship*, and it simply means being in one's spirit and being in intimate contact with the Holy Spirit. In its charismatic intensity, pentecostal worship is a pure intermediary between habituated bodies and possibilities of divine phenomena.

Worship as pure means is posited through the activities of the believers as its presupposition. Worship achieves its actuality in the subjective presupposition of the gathered believers, acting as if they are in worship, and it is a site of the Holy Spirit. They recognize themselves in it (worship) as worshipers, their point of reference. This worship is a means, a pure one insofar as the believers believe in it as a site of the Holy Spirit and act accordingly. The mistake will be to view it as a means to an end and not a pure mediality. The means is the media of the means. The means realizes itself as its purport, to use a Hegelian expression. It is in the finite process of the means of worship that the process of participating in worship takes place, and that the beautiful or sublime consciousness or feeling thus arises. Worship grounds itself in the very "foaming ferment" of the subjects acting as if they are worshiping. The foaming ferment is shot through with the facticity of the past (experience of past possibilities is reactivated, the fact of previous encounters with the divine is relived), the present bodily *jouissance* of God, and the coming future. In this ecstatic ferment there are no simple demarcations of time into past, present, and future. Time is an ecstatic temporality! It is in this character of worship as a *virtual* entity (or nonentity) that it represents itself as pure means par excellence.[5]

Under these circumstances and dynamics, the believer thus becomes the subject of worship—which means both that she becomes worshipful and that she enters into worship; she enacts worship and she becomes worshiper. "Both as an internal(ized) capacity and as an external(ized) identity; [worship then becomes the means by which she connects to God by uttering 'I worship You Lord' (or any other song)], as if in an infinite echo, in order to be reborn and replete with God's grace, in an interminable (that is to say, *quintessentially* repetitious) dance of gestures that ensures God's interminably (repeatedly) reauthorized power."[6] Worshiper and worship, grace upon grace, "are thus interlocked in a repetitive ritual display ad absurdum."[7]

The idea of pure means indicates that the means *is* the end, displaced end. The connection is organic and permanent. It is becoming—one of means and end. The means is completely identified with the end. If you have seen the means you have seen the end, and yet there is a no difference. As pure means, the means does not purport to be an end itself, nor is it simply a means to something else or the end. Since it includes within itself both the exalted end (participating in the power of the end, referent) and the means, which conveys the senses, practices, and orientations in their journey to the exalted end, it is at once means and end. The object (worship) provides direct medium to Jesus Christ and participates in the power of God. The means is a *symbol* and hence pure means.

Another way of viewing worship is to consider it in terms of the relationship with the Holy Spirit. Pentecostal worship is about creating the context for the presence of the Holy Spirit, for the Spirit of Christ to move and work among his people. Worship is context, a milieu of the Holy Spirit. In this sense and to this extent, the Holy Spirit is really the pure means in the believer's relationship to and with Jesus Christ. Being-in-Christ presupposes a being-in-the-Spirit. The being-in-the-Spirit is not an end itself; it is not just a *sign* of Christ but also a symbol of Christ (fellowship) with Christ. Being-in-Spirit is not a means to an end either. The Holy Spirit is not only a medium of fellowship with Christ, but an integral person of the Godhead; the Spirit is medium to the Spirit (Godhead). This means she is a means to means. The Spirit is pure means.

The emergence of worship as pure means in pentecostal circles involves or marks a slight adjustment to the interaction of the sacred and the secular. If originally, historically (that is, pre-Pentecostalism) worship was aimed at the sacred, as a means or conduit to the "transcendence," then when it becomes a pure means it also becomes profanatory, to use Giorgio Agamben's word. Worship instead of remaining as something separated unto reaching the divine, as a veritable means to the sacred, is taken back from its confinement as a means to an end, as a heteronomous site of holiness that exceeds the collectivity (the people) and put (restored) into playful use that neither honors nor abolishes its "sacredness." In this way, worship as pure means "deactivates the apparatuses of power and returns to common use the spaces power had seized."[8]

The Pentecostal movement in this act of profanation also exhibits secularization tendencies. The act of transforming worship into pure means not only makes it profanatory, but also makes it contemporary with the current times (*secularum*, of this age). Herein, we see the huge desire of contemporary pentecostal worship music and habits to invert notions of "sacred taste," inherited rhythms, to knowingly transgress the line separating the sacred and the secular. It is neither religious nor secular—a quintessential figure of the profane.

One characteristic of pure means or profanation is that it frees objects and behaviors from generic inscription within given their spheres, and this is what capitalism and its ally, secularization, do well, especially when seen from the standpoint of the sacred sphere. "The activity that results from this thus becomes a pure means, that is, a praxis that, while firmly maintaining its nature as a means, is emancipated from its relationship to an end; it has joyously forgotten its goal and can now show itself as such, as a means without an end."[9]

If academic theologians conceive worship as a creative process that constitutes free persons to become the body of Christ in its practices, then everyday Pentecostal believers may have joyfully forgotten this goal in the *immediacy* of their jouissance or enjoyment of God. Worship is not for the production of communion with Christ. This is left for the habits, virtues, and vigor of the Christian life. Worship is not geared to express the mystery of Christ or the real nature of the true church. This is the prerogative of the Holy Spirit who knits the community of Christ. The worship is not designed to bring about anything but create the context (that has no predetermined end) for the Holy Spirit to work and to move. Worship is context; precisely, worship itself is the context.[10] It is a mediating presence. It is a multisensory *skin* of transimmanent divine-human play, the erotic veil of sublime intimacy teased by the wind.

Worship is pure means because it is not about transforming believers into something, not about becoming a people. They believe they are already the children of God, a born-again people. Worship is about a community that is continually doing something, "perfecting" the kinetic existence and experience of being and doing in the Spirit of Christ. The epistemological problem in pentecostal worship lies not in creating or identifying a community but in believing and seeing that this gathered, already identified community is in spirit and truth. Jesus says *those* who worship God must worship him in *spirit* and *truth*. The matter with Pentecostals is not with the "those" but one of "spirit and truth." In their worldview, spirit and truth is about access and context.

Thus, to repeat, worship is about a community that is continually doing something, "perfecting" the kinetic existence and experience of being and doing in the Spirit of Christ. In the being and doing that is worship in spirit, the barrier between the indicative and imperative, of means and ends, is breached and transformed into the fluidity of simple *means*. Worship is indicative and imperative. It indicates the kinetic reality of God's divine presence breaking forth into the alternative community and making possible the imperative of a being-in-communion, which is the working of *community, potentiality*, and *participation*.[11]

In the next section, we shall endeavor to highlight certain features of the pentecostal worship service that I have noticed as a participant-observer that drove me to conclude that pentecostal worship is a pure means. I want to consider six features of everyday worship and reflect on them to craft *a* pentecostal philosophy of worship. I want to show, as I see in a mirror dimly, what worship as pure means looks like. Hopefully, one day when you the reader come face-to-face with pentecostal worship as pure means you shall know fully even as you are completely grasped by it.

Worship as Matterization of Grace

Watching Pentecostals in intense, fluid praise and worship has often filled me with the idea that worship itself is a "sacrament" of grace; sacramental not as in imparting grace but as grace phenomenalized, materialized, as a visible reality, grace as corporeal, or grace as *real presence*. Let me unpack this by elucidating it in four ways. First, worship is the mirror-play of grace. Grace is purposeless. It is not coded to well-defined goals. The whole idea of worship as pure means is about seeing grace from the human side. God *graces* human beings and they in turn *grace* God. It is like God seeing us and God is *being seen* by us, as Nicholas of Cusa formulated the vision of God. When properly understood, worship is the self-coincidence of grace in itself. In worship the *active* shedding of grace on humanity is identified with the *passive* reception as grace comes together, condensing into itself. Indeed, worship is the *coincidentia* of giving and receiving, outflow and inflow of grace. The logic of worship is the logic of grace.

Second, worship as pure means is a pure gift. The Spirit's presence (and gifts) and human presence (and capacities) are pooled together and distributed between the two parties. The worship is arising only from a principle that is interior to the Spirit-believer relation. The worship is a complete gift and there is no need for reciprocal counter-gift. It is not possible to accumulate worship to be later used or enjoyed by one of the parties. The two parties generate it and both participate in it at the same time. If anything is to be stockpiled, it is not the worship itself, but the memory of it, and that is not what we are talking about here.

Third, worship is an institution. It is the institutional embodiment of responses to grace that are enacted or performed by individuals in their relationships with God. Individuals respond to God in various ways; they cooperate with one another to voluntarily express, celebrate, affirm their relationships with God. The network of responses that emerges out of this affirmative, cooperative process, the institutional framework, is called worship. This framework is not a *means* to accomplish any goal. It is rather a site of cooperative actions, which remains perpetually as a cooperative arrangement not restricted to determined goals. Worship is always a collective, collaborative, composite endeavor, and isolated performance is not part of the framework, as worship requires the gathering of two or three persons. In its composite, aggregative nature, it is a pure means like the "market." This does not mean that the individuals whose collaboration creates worship have no motivation.[12] The accent is on the collaborative.

In this collaborative ambience it appears that each person is sharing his or her energy collaboratively and that collaboration itself is "sharing" him or her. Worship appears to play itself, becoming a result of itself. When a man plays the piano so often and gets very good at it, at some point or moments of play he does not feel that he is playing it, but rather the piano is playing him. The player has passed on some aspect of his spirit to the piano, or as the Japanese (as per the philosophy of "Renri") will say, the tool has acquired the identity of its owner, has harmonized with the owner, or has appropriated the spirit of the owner. When this happens the piano is also "giving" back something of itself to the owner. This is the becoming spiritual of the play. The play is a network partner with the player and the piano and it exists and functions as long as the other partners are together at their ownmost and utmost best and in the harmonious identification with one another. The play is the spirit/soul of the encounter. This spirit is only born, only lives, dies, and resurrects in the encounter. In a moment of intense encounter, the spirit can "possess" the player as if it is a separate power all of its own. With this spirit the play is graceful, a transformation of difficulty into appearance of effortlessness, nonchalance. When worship begins to play the worshipers—as it often does in pentecostal worship services—it becomes *being-with*.

Fourth, worship is the intensification, the ecstasy of the state (dynamics) of *being-with*. It is the stretching out and the opening of space *between* (which is beyond connection and disconnection) worshipers (one with other) and God.[13] Worship is not an immanence in which the one is collapsed into the other or a milieu (or essence) in which a set of persons are immersed. It is a being-with that does not collapse and erase the "between" through which syncopated energies are generated and pass through the persons who are always one with the other, *being singular-plural*.

This *between-ness*, singular-plurality bridges the duality of subject and object, human beings and God, and between human beings themselves.

Worship is both the subject and/or the object of divine-human relationship in an assembly. As a subject, it shows what the Spirit (or human beings) desires and what the relationship desires. As an object, it shows relationship at work.[14] As such it bridges the subject-object divide. It is always a relation. Worship as pure means is an expression of Romans 8:26: the Spirit of the triune God who helps us pray is the same one who receives our prayers. Jesus Christ said, "whenever two or three are gathered in my name I am there in your midst [as the Holy Spirit]" (Matt. 18:20 NIV), and worship gestures to and marks the presence of the Holy Spirit in the community of believers.

Worship, however, is not the model of the divine-human relationship, but of the intensity of denuding it of end and calculation. What worship as a pure means models or presents is not the relationship but rather the stripping bare of the tension within it. In worship the relationship seeks and loses all aim, grasps itself. Worship is exactly this exit from instrumental use of relationship that embodies the divine-human relation. Worship embodies the relation in its infinite coming from *this is* to *that is*, and into presence in which time seems to have completely collapsed. Time appears to have become a mode of eternity, the place or point when it seems the temporal chain of reasons or the invariant network of causes and effects is momentarily broken up or suspended. It is not only time that seems to collapse, as if it is nothing for those in the ecstasy of worship, but the divine-human relation "collapses" into a skeletal airiness, into its pure form.

Worship as Pure Signifier

The emphasis of worship as pure means or pure mediality foregrounds the divine-human relation not as a signifier of anything other than itself or also posits it as not signified by anything in its livingness. At best, it is an empty signifier; it is nothing except a pure mediality, the *thereness* of a relation, a pure presence, and therefore it can stand for everything. This is very much related to the unstructured nature, skeletal airiness of pentecostal worship itself, or rather spirituality.

The ritualized, structured worship is chock full of semiotic meanings and signification, which limit its capacity to be made into popular use as it anchors and defines the divine-human relation. Worship as pure means concretizes the divine-human relation as a means without defining, limiting, its purpose and meaning. Worship transgresses the separation between means and ends, even as it refuses to be anchored by either of them. "There is something playful, irresponsible, carnivalesque about [pentecostal worship] that refuses rationality and the discipline of the everyday: it is there to escape, to vacate; it is liberatingly empty."[15]

It is, indeed, a pure signifier. Worship, not the sharing of the Word or deliverance, is the unary point that "quilts" the whole pentecostal service, the multitude of individuals. But this worship is empty, representing the gulf between the human beings who must worship according to their capacities and abilities and the Divine who is the pure point of grace. This gulf or scission is precisely the passage of the divine, the way of grace coming from "heaven" and journeying back from earth to "heaven." The gulf is the field of mediation between human capacities and free grace, their point of unity. Human capacity to worship and coursing grace occur, entangle in the scission and not in the Divine. Worship is most empty or the gulf biggest when it is at its best. At this point it is purposeless.

When worship is the crown of a pentecostal gathering, people do not stoop to the level of making it instrumental or purposeful. On the contrary, the orientation is to maintain to the greatest extent the distance between purpose and purposelessness, relegating the position of worship to a point rejected from the whole commodity exchange logic, where it matters little if it makes no rational (means-end-circuit) sense. There is now something beyond its presentation in reality, something beyond its descriptive properties. There is now an "unnamable thing" in worship that is more than the worship. Without purpose and with only an unfathomable trait in its core, worship becomes self-referential; it is its own sign. Worship as a pure means is the pure signifier, the master-signifier with no signified.[16] Thus, it is empty.

Now someone may intervene by arguing that by defining worship as a pure means I have drained it of all effective contents, all "pathological" objects or particularity. Not exactly, there is still something that is "less than nothing" in pentecostal worship. The very point where the worship is purified of all instrumentality or particular purpose, its empty form appears as *objet petit a* (Lacan), the object cause of desire. Pentecostals act pentecostally when the content of worship becomes the form of worship itself; that is, when worship becomes empty. This is an emptiness that separates the "true believers" from the false brethren, an emptiness that drives the desire for God. The empty form of worship becomes a source of jouissance. The worship (the singing, the moans, the clapping, the dancing, the jerking, and the "slaying") is best enjoyed when it is in its neutral, empty form. This is the imperative to "enjoy!" hidden in the pentecostal worship in its supposedly best form. The Pentecostal is a Christian who, when she is among others of her kind, requires a free worship (allusion to Kant here). You know you are freely worshiping the Lord when you raise yourself to reject all "pathological" purposes of the "worships" out there in the name of Spirit-filled worship. It is precisely when Pentecostals distance themselves from others and pathological particularity of worship that they fall under the sway of the inflexible imperative to enjoy.[17] Let us continue with our philosophizing of pentecostal worship by further examining its "emptiness" and the object cause of desire that seems to emerge from it when it is nothing, a mere void.

Worship as Heidegger's Greek Jug

The more I think of worship as pure means and the void at its center, the more my mind is drawn to Martin Heidegger's analysis of the Greek jug (vase). Worship as pure means is like an empty shell made of music and spiritual gifts and wrapped up in emotions and intersubjective focus. If you are able to unwrap it and crack the shell, you will only find a material void, site of purposelessness, pure means staging a play between form and emptiness. Praise and worship as means—with its panoply of exultations, thanksgivings, music, song, dance, tongues-speaking, prophecies, silence, and slaying in the spirit—can hold the communion aspect of religious life. But the holding that constitutes the means "is not so much the function of the means as the void the [panoply] surrounds."[18] It is as if worship as pure means always retraces "the outline of Heidegger's thing," which is actually no thing.[19] As Heidegger describes the jug:

> The emptiness, the void, is what does the vessel's holding. The empty space, this nothing of the jug, is what the jug is as the holding vessel. . . . Sides and bottom, of which the jug consists and by which it stands, are not really what does the holding. But if the holding is done by the jug's void, then the potter, who forms the sides and bottom on his wheel, does not, strictly speaking, make the jug. He only shapes the clay. No—he shapes the void. For it, in it, and out of it, he forms the clay into the form. From start to finish, the potter takes hold of the impalpable void and brings it forth as the container in the shape of the containing vessel. The jug's void determines

all the handling in the process of making the vessel. The vessel's thingness does not lie at all in the material of which it consists, but in the void that holds."[20]

When pentecostal worship is viewed through Heidegger's account of the thing, the worshipers are the potters; they shape the void. And to quote Mark C. Taylor, "Whether form brings forth void or void brings forth form remains obscure. What does seem clear is that the thingness [pure mediality, materiality] of every [worship as pure means] is the no thing of the void."[21]

There is no surefire way for worshipers-potters or worship leaders to immediately grasp the importance of form or void in a praise and worship service in order to transform it into a pure means. They can start with panoply (the usual materials) and the void forms around the space in between the materials. Or they can start with the void (instrumentality, calculations, purpose drained off from the outset, total openness to the Holy Spirit) and then form the materials from the emptiness—this is an impossible possibility. If void produces worship as pure means as much as the panoply produces worship as pure means, then worship is in an important sense *about* nothing, to paraphrase Taylor. "Nothing, it seems, is the generative void or creative emptiness in and through which things [worship in spirit and truth] arise and pass away."[22] May we say that just as the Greek potter in the strict sense does not make the jug, as Heidegger argues, the worshiper-potter does not ultimately create this nothing?

Before we proceed to discuss the object cause of desire as promised, let us examine one of the ways the void of pure means appears in worship; that is, how ends fall off from means in worship to generate worship as pure means. Here I want to draw from the thought of F. W. J. Schelling as it relates to the state of no conation. In his third draft of *The Ages of the World*, Schelling makes the point that a person can arrive at this state of no willing through two routes.[23] On one hand a person can withdraw from all desires in the worship service and thus strive toward no particular purpose. On the other, another person who abandons himself to all desires, obsessions, and cravings can unwittingly reach the state of no conation. Schelling explains that this occurs, "Since this person too only desires the state in which they have nothing more to will."[24] But this state of no conation flees from both types of people, "and the more zealously they follow it, the farther it distances itself from them."[25] This is why the second option of starting with a void and working toward worship as pure means is an impossible possibility. It presupposes "the will that wills nothing, that desires no object, for which all things are equal and is therefore moved by none of them."[26] This is not attainable by human beings.

From Means to Means: The Pursuit of the Real of Worship

The route to worship as pure means, pure void, or desubstantialized self-relating negativity is the search for the unfathomable object cause of desire, precisely *objet petit a*, to use Lacanian terminology. Pentecostal worshipers are often looking for that mysterious X that accounts for the *most-anointed, out-of-this world* worship. So they go on stripping down the worship of positive symbolic features, yet that exhilarating worship cannot be pinned down to a specific feature. Nonetheless, two worship services, which are alike in all positive features, can exhibit palpable differences in the experience of anointing. The unfathomable X is what accounts for the unmistakable difference, the gap between the two worship services. Whether the gap exists or not does not matter; either way it must be presupposed or fantasmatically constructed if the believers are to make sense of the structural (emotional, connectivity) gap between the services. The object that makes all the difference when there is no perceivable or conceivable positive difference is the *objet petit a*. To get this nonexistent difference that exercises great powers of effectivity worship is desubstantialized. Is this not exactly the process of the emergence of the Cartesian subject? The subject arises from the desubstantialization of the human being (through the process of universal doubt and momentary passage through radical madness) to the point where what is left is a self-relating negativity of a pure *cogito*.

Here it appears that worship and subjectivity in their kernels are characterized, as it were, by a Schellingian violent gesture. The disappearance of "pathological" content in worship as pure means, far from signaling the end of worship, does something else. It gestures to the emergence of subjectivity, a new pentecostal subjectivity, the "barred" subject. WPM in itself suggests that for those engaged in it there is already a split in them: between the human person (with wealth of substantial content) and subject qua the void. It appears WPM is the musical (praise-and-worship) counterpart of the believer's self-emptying for Jesus Christ. The two forms of subjectivity are connected by (impossible) pure desire, not a desire for something, by direct desire for the void of worship by a subject of God. All this is to say that there is an intersection between subjectivity and worship and the intersection takes the shape of "pure desire," that is, "a desire which is not a desire for something, a definite object, but a direct desire for the lack itself. (Say, when I truly desire another person, I desire the very void at the centre of his subjectivity, so that I am not ready to accept any positive service in return.)"[27]

The pentecostal believer who approaches the void of WPM by stripping off all specific positive symbolic features from the worship also strips bare herself. In fact, the desubstantialization of worship is also the desubstantialization of the believer. It is the believer's desubstantialization (the removal of all personal and social features from the self that may hinder the move toward WPM) that "transubstantiates" an ordinary worship into WPM. Or at least the desubstantialized subject (worshiper) is the libidinal foundation of WPM or the minimum idealization needed to support WPM.

In a self-reflective way, this foundation is "always already mirrored back" into the worship itself.[28] This can be witnessed in the songs and abject positioning of the body or bodily remainder (after desubstantialization, self-emptying has done its work) in the worship service. The Holy Spirit is asked to melt and mold the self in total submission to this transimmanent power. When the Spirit is felt to be doing this work you might hear "Yes!," "Once More!," or "More!" This verbalization stands for the ever increasing desubstantialization of the believer. "It indexes the attitude of actively endorsing the passive confrontation with the *objet petit a*."[29] This is where the song about "melt me, mold me" continues. It says "fill me," meaning "let me have that unfathomable X that makes the difference where there is no difference." But the subject cannot be filled with *objet petit a*. The *objet petit a* cannot fulfill desire. Desire is not caused by *objet petit a*, it only sets desire in motion and cannot bring it to its full satisfaction. The best that can happen is ecstatic rupture (with shaking bodies, closed eyes, moaning and shouts, speaking in tongues, tears falling from the cheeks to the garments and to the ground, and so on), whereby the subject identifies with the object cause of desire.[30]

There are other reactions in moments of intense worship. While one face is displaying ecstatic rupture, the other may seem to be provocatively staring at the invisible Holy Spirit as if to say, "Give me more before I will ever be moved or hit the floor." There is another with an instrumental attitude, working too hard, highly concentrated, engaged in a hard task as if such techniques will lead to the expected breakthrough to ecstasy. And yet there is still another person who looks at all that is happening with indifference. The hands are clapping, the lips are moving with the rhythms of the songs, but there is a bored stare.[31]

Worship as Kantian Duty

We have emphasized WPM as desubstantialization of ordinary worship, the removal of "pathological" content from ordinary service. We have talked about worship as pure means, reminding the readers of the act of doing something for its own sake, but then our notion points beyond the notion of end in itself. Let us examine three types of means-end relationships. First, when something is a means to another thing, means and end are externally related. The means is present for the sake of the end. Second, instead of an action being means to something else, it is an end in itself. So we are told human beings must be treated as ends in themselves. In this second case it cannot always be argued that cause and effect are internally related. More importantly, means and ends are not reciprocally interchangeable. The third type of means-end relationship brings us to a case where means and ends are reciprocally related. There is an inner teleology that binds them together in an autopoietic being, emergent self-organizing system. This being, system, or organism is self-creative. In this kind of system "every part is reciprocally both end and means." For "the parts of the thing combine of themselves into the unity of a whole by being reciprocally cause and effect."[32]

The notion of WPM goes beyond these three types of mean-end relationships. In this last case, end is separated, split, severed from means, and ends and means become an apparatus of pure means, creating and capturing means without end. In the worship, drive, goal is separated from aim (the path toward the goal). Or rather, the goal becomes the experience of the path, the aim itself. Here there is a permanent failure to achieve the "finite" goal as the aim itself becomes somewhat "infinite." As Žižek puts it, "In the very failure to achieve our intended goal, the true aim is always achieved."[33] It seems WPM has become a partial object, means severed from the body (symbolic order) of ends, and an "organ without body" emerges.

By detaching ends from means, life-in-the-Spirit can be detached from the various instrumental ends, "pathological contents," and move toward non-capitalist, non-prosperity-gospel profanation, engaging in the very difficult task (the impossible possibility) of resisting late capitalism's gigantic apparatus of pure means, which separates everything from itself and is exhibited in its separation from itself as a spectacle. Thus WPM as a pure means opens up pentecostal worship with its profound connection to instrumental logic, relieving of its connection to ends of prosperity gospel, logic of exchange and commodification, reciprocity, and ideals of late capitalism. This is how Giorgio Agamben describes the activity that results from freeing an object or behavior from its genetic inscription within a given sphere: "The activity that results from this thus becomes a pure means, that is, a praxis that, while firmly maintaining its nature as a means, is emancipated from its relationship to an end; it has joyously forgotten its goal and can now show itself as such, as a means without an end."[34]

The movement from three types of means-end relationships, I thought, would take this whole analysis of WPM beyond the force field of Kantian philosophy. Moving beyond Kant actually brought us back to him in a way that illuminates a crucial aspect of pentecostal spirituality. Paradoxically, WPM ends up looking like a Kantian duty. When worship is stripped of any "pathological" interest, goods, or motivations, it is transformed into a Kantian ethical act. Worship now overlaps with "doing one's duty." The pentecostal commitment, unconditional commitment to pure worship, turns into the "law of worship," which stands beyond the pleasure principle. This "transubstantiation" of worship into duty does not mean that Pentecostals are caught in a pseudo-concrete act of purity. It is simply that the very "transubstantiation" bears witness to the freedom that ultimately defines life-in-the-Spirit. Is not a Kantian ethical act the ultimate exercise of freedom? Freedom is an act grounded only in/by itself. It is the predicate of a subject who is not bound by the chain of "pathological" interests/urges or who breaks up the network of causes and effects.

Limit and Excess of Worship as Pure Means

In order to end this section of the chapter characterizing WPM, let us examine its limit and excess. The limit of worship as pure means is worship itself, that is, the pentecostal mode of worship. We can read this statement in two ways: there are instrumental and playful relations of worship. First, WPM will be done in, or can never really take off, in Pentecostalism because of the regnant nature of the prosperity gospel and other calculative interests that are fostered by or inhabit the movement. This is to say the generative forces, the factors that propel worship in the first place for many Pentecostals will not take a back seat to a serious commitment to worship as play. From this perspective worship as its own limit means that the most formidable obstacle to the further development in any group's or individual's spirituality is ordinary worship. This reasoning assumes an evolutionary schema; ordinarily, people grow from ordinary worship to WPM. At some point in their spiritual growth and development they realize that the generative forces of worship have grown too big, leaving the playful relations of worship (the divine-human relations) etiolated. So some dialectics of forces and relations move in a way to elevate relations above forces, but then they maintain that the frame of relations never really catches up in the consumerist-desires-all-things pentecostal world in late capitalism.

This is indeed a simplistic way of examining the dialectics of generative forces of worship and the playful relations of worship. The relationship between these two forces is not evolutionary. The playful relation of worship can formally subsume the instrumental, generative forces of worship as it meets (founds) them in the nave of the church or the common space of the storefront church, and then change the generative forces here a little, there a little, in such a way as to gradually bring both in line. In doing this, WPM does not need to drive ordinary worship as if they are both bound by some teleological divine mandate.

No one can exactly say for any one group or person when the internal contradictions of ordinary worship have become an insurmountable obstacle to WPM or predict periods or a specific time when relations and forces will come in accordance. Ordinary worship is capable of transforming itself through its very inadequacy and impotence, so to speak. At any moment the excessive failures of instrumental worship may well lead to WPM because ordinary worship is constitutive of WPM. This is what I meant by WPM meeting ordinary worship in the nave or common space. WPM emerges only from the surplus failures of instrumental worship. If we subtract the excessive failures or aim to directly choose purity (the Kantian duty of worship), we lose WPM. This is the coincidence of failure and success, limit and excess, sinner and saint that disruptive grace enacts as the impossible possibility of worship as pure means.

Let me expatiate on what I mean when I say any direct choice of WPM will constitute a fundamental blockage to attaining it. While it is true that worships that are not pure means are failures, it is truer to say that failure is the only path to the truth of worship as pure means. We must repeatedly fail in reaching toward the goal of WPM and sometimes experience worship as a nightmare. The path opens up from here only if we recognize our failure as the form of success. If we remain *faithful* to the goal of WPM, after the failure we can discern a way forward. In the failure we can discern the perspective for overcoming it. In trying to actualize WPM it often first changes into its opposite and it is by passing through the failure itself that the ideals of WPM become actuality. There is no direct path to WPM. In the worship service the believers are not directly confronted with a choice between bad worship and WPM. The only choice is between no worship and bad worship, and what tips the balance in favor of WPM is the realization that non-WPM is human instrumentality, purposes, and hubris in the guise of true surrender to the Holy Spirit. The so-called bad worship is the solid material base that allows fleeting WPM to shine through.

"Bad worship" is like what Hegel says about the phallus: it is both an instrument of urination and insemination, a conjunction of the high and low, when he is illustrating the two readings of "Spirit is a bone."[35] If we see only failure in the failures, then we are like those in Hegel's reasoning who can only discern the phallus as the organ of urination. But to see a possible path to success from the failures is to be like those who can also discern the phallus as an organ of insemination, the higher functions of generation. Hegel's point is that we do not directly go for the best option or proper result with our first choice, but only through repeated failures. The choice of "insemination" comes only through repeatedly choosing "urination"; we arrive at the true choice via the wrong choice. If we tried to directly choose worship as pure means, we would infallibly miss it. WPM emerges through repeated ordinary worships, instrumental worships, or purposeful worships as their aftereffect.[36] But is there a fundamental obstacle to WPM that failures and preliminary "wrong choices" cannot fix?

Concluding Thoughts

What really separates Pentecostals from worship as pure means today? Is it just about an inadequate number of failures of ordinary worship? Of course, it is the instrumental logic, the symbolic economy of exchange in today's pentecostal worship and lifestyle, you declare. But I say unto you, the gap that separates Pentecostals from WPM is inherent in worship. Worship is itself split between purpose and purposelessness. As Giorgio Agamben taught us in *The Kingdom and the Glory*, worship (glorification) is always needed as a support of power, as a cover for the crack between being and praxis in the conception of God, which the concept of *oikonomia* introduced into the Christian understanding of God. For Agamben glorification is the "glorious nutrient of power."[37] Doxological acclamation (the praise that human beings give to God, glorification) is, Agamben argues, "perhaps, in some way a necessary part of the life of the divinity."[38] What Agamben is saying, precisely, is that glory is the substance of God's power and God depends on glorification. "Perhaps glorification is not only that which best fits the glory of God but is itself, as an effective rite, what produced glory; and if glory is the very substance of God and the true sense of his economy, then it depends upon glorification in an essential manner."[39]

If glorification plays such an important function, as Agamben demonstrates in his book, then worship, which produces glory by glorifying, cannot be totally rendered as purposeless. Worship definitely serves a purpose in the divine-human economy. Yet, we should be careful to note immediately that the process of glorification reveals the theodoxological inoperativity of the power machine. Inoperativity, as we saw in chapter 1, is at the heart of and an internal motor of glorification.[40] The tension in worship, its split character, seems to be well captured by the following statement by Agamben, from his comment on the empty throne of power (referring to Ezekiel's vision of God's *kabhod* and the Western democratic system):[41]

> *The empty throne is not, therefore, a symbol of regality but of glory.* . . . The throne is empty not only because glory, though coinciding with the divine essence is not identified with it, but also because it is in its innermost self-inoperativity and sabbatism. The void is the sovereign figure of glory. The apparatus of glory finds its perfect cipher in the majesty of the empty throne. Its purpose is to capture within the governmental machine that unthinkable inoperativity—making it its internal motor—that constitutes the ultimate mystery of divinity.[42]

Note well that the purpose, the instrumental value, of glorification is to produce inoperativity, which is precisely to end the instrumental functions of glorification; that is, to have a utilitarian glorification "whose functions are not executed but rather displayed."[43] With this apparent coincidence of purpose and purposelessness it is obvious that the gap that separates Pentecostals from worship as pure means is inherent in worship itself. When we think worship has been delivered of all "contents" and is now nothing we then discover that there is something that is less than nothing in it.

We have come a long way from the introduction where I made a case for the notion of split God in Pentecostalism and proceeded to deepen our knowledge of this notion as it operates across and between various spheres of social practice. The discourse has portrayed the notion of a split God as an *apparatus*.⁴⁴ Agamben defines apparatus as "anything that has in some way the capacity to capture, orient, determine, intercept, model, control, or secure the gestures, behaviors, opinions, or discourses of living beings."⁴⁵ In what remains of the chapters of case studies, I will examine the interactions between the pentecostal apparatus and West African believers. I have chosen West Africa as a site for the last case study because I have some deep knowledge of the regnant form of Pentecostalism in the region. Besides, I have already published a scholarly work on Pentecostalism in one of its major countries.⁴⁶

I would like to quickly add that to consider West Africa, or any other place for that matter, as a site for the pentecostal apparatus is to assume that it is a place where the apparatus achieves actuality. But this assumption should not be construed to mean that the investigator can simply match features of the apparatus to extant practices and then declare how the apparatus imposes itself on believers. The apparatus does not have an independent existence apart from the practicing Pentecostals; it is not a mega-entity, a transcendent substantial reality, aware of itself and controlling them as puppets. What we expect to see in chapter 7 is the dialectics of the interaction between the apparatus of split God and Pentecostals. What this means is that while the apparatus has the power to ground pentecostal activities, it is a virtual/ideal entity (nonentity) that can only exist as the subjective "presupposition" of engaged or pentecostally subjectivized West Africans. Borrowing from the words of Slavoj Žižek from a different context, let me end by stating that the apparatus

> exists only insofar as subjects act as if it exists. Its status is similar to that of an ideological cause like Communism or the Nation: it is the substance of the individuals who recognize themselves in it, the ground of their entire existence, the point of reference which provides the ultimate horizon of meaning to their lives, something for which these individuals are ready to give their lives, yet the only thing that really exists are these individuals and their activity, so this substance is actual only insofar as individuals believe in it and act accordingly.⁴⁷

7

Everyday Form of Theology

Between Pentecostal Apparatus and Prosaic Existence

Introduction

Our investigation of the interaction between the apparatus of the split God and West African Pentecostals will focus on an everyday form of theology in the region. This requires that we find a veritable lens that can help us peer deeply into the discourses, practices, and aesthetics of West African Pentecostalism. Such a lens should also enable us to continue to demonstrate how Pentecostalism contests, befuddles, and transforms the categories and boundaries of orthodoxy. As we stated in the introduction to this book, piety and danger are extimate in pentecostal everyday theology. The pentecostal worldview is essentially split from within. There is a part that is faithful to the received tradition of Christian faith or conservative biblical orientation, and there is always another path that threatens to exceed the bounds of the faith, to make common cause with liberal, secular forms of explanation or understanding. These two are at the heart of the pentecostal worldview and coconstitute a tension that is always at the brink of breaking loose but not quite there yet.

We also noted in the same place that in Pentecostalism piety and danger make common cause with paleonomy. Pentecostals' everyday theology is a *paleonomic* gesture in the sense that it simultaneously erases and preserves the Christian tradition. Paleonomy, according to Jacques Derrida, is the "maintenance of an *old name* in order to launch a new concept."[1] It is the strategy of a person who wants to conquer from within a system.

"A paleonomic gesture requires us to stand inside and outside a tradition at the same time, perpetuating the tradition while breaking with it, and breaking with the tradition while perpetuating it."[2]

Given all this, how best do we proceed with the task of this chapter?[3] I will use a novel approach, which I call *microtheology*. Microtheology seeks to create a space within theology and to dispel its boundaries by identifying the subtle ways, the motility of small acts, disparities, and the small errors that give birth to the practices and reflection we call the everyday form of theology. It opposes itself to the search for definite contours that mark shifting or final boundaries of theological discourse. So instead of constructing a system or framework to trace the limits of a theological framework, or engaging in archaeological operations to discover layers or fragments of meanings that accent the contingency of theology, microtheology originates in the present and speaks into the present.

Microtheology's focus on the small, beautiful, and ugly mundane actions enables the scholar to observe how life interpreted at the deepest level percolates up as subtle acts of everyday existence. Microtheology reveals how humans' concern with the ultimate works its ways into concrete acts. The tiny, minute acts become a window into an embodied interpretation of ultimate concern, existential questions, or theological apparatuses.

Pentecostalism is ever making minute shifts in orthodoxy. Nowhere is this more evident than in West Africa where Pentecostalism is always trying to effect a tiny displacement of the rigid lines between tradition and novelty, mainline and margin. The central locus of divine-human encounter in the worship service and the primary theological activity of West African Pentecostals is not the Eucharist or preaching but prayer. More precisely, prayers as hedged, sustained, and driven by praise and worship anchor both beliefs and practices and characterize the Christian life. Prayers are objective, relational, and dispositional. The prayer-spirituality has as its objective the attainment of human flourishing as empowered by the Holy Ghost, building and sustaining of better relationships with God and with human beings (relational), and living a life of Christlike holiness (dispositional). This chapter presents the theology of West African Pentecostalism through the lens of worship-fed prayers. The theology is discerned from the everyday beliefs, practices, and affections, and from all that is ordinary and prosaic in the existence of West African Pentecostals.

I will use the metaphors of self-presentation and self-interpretation as a framework to analyze this prayer-infused worship. Each person in everyday social interaction produces for himself meanings; he guides and controls his identities and generates pleasures for himself within the interplay of meanings and identities. Thus this chapter focuses on the ordinary believer's creative and interpretative capacities to rework materials from the clergy before they are consumed in the face of recalcitrant reality. Everyday theology is a second-order product of the correlation method. The method of correlation that Paul Tillich made famous charges theology to be relevant to the immediate context of its recipients by responding to the questions asked or obstacles confronting the people in a given social situation.[4] But this theology produced by the church, preacher, or theologian has to be reworked in daily social circumstances. Correlated theology undergoes another round of correlation in the hands of the people, at the popular cultural level in the West African pentecostal community. The people make their own theology out of the resources and insights provided by the pulpit (armchair) system.

This does not mean that resources and insights for what can be called the popular-correlation method are only provided by the pulpit-correlation method. Believers do not passively consume the "products" of the pulpit. Their very consumption makes them into producers. The pulpit products produce a people who creatively produce their own *wearable* theology to further fit their "bodies," their lifestyles in the here and now, or to circulate meanings and pleasures. The original sermon, preaching, or correlated theology is "a discursive structure of potential meanings and pleasures that constitutes a major resource of popular [correlation theology]."[5] This resource and others are employed by believers to produce meanings and pleasures and to resist or evade the containment or disciplinary efforts of the pulpit or social system. Their point is not to overturn or raid the existing social system or religious epistemic system but to nudge it to yield spaces for survival, the preservation of some sense of identity, and production of meaning and pleasure. Indeed, everyday theology is constructed and sustained by the interface of everyday life, the messages and teachings of the *pulpit industry* (church), and the social situation of the people as it currently bears on the pursuit of human flourishing.

We will limit our study of everyday theology to three areas pertaining to human flourishing: meaning, identities, and pleasure. John Fiske makes the triplex of meaning, pleasure, and identity and the relationship between them an important lens for the study of popular culture. He says, "Culture is the constant process of producing meanings of and from our social experience, and such meanings necessarily produce a social identity for the people involved . . . Within the production and circulation of these meanings lies pleasure."[6] Our task of constructing the theology of West African Pentecostals is to show how people live their spirituality to make meanings, construct identities, and find pleasures. The generation and regeneration of meanings, identities, and pleasures are not without constraints. They are always produced within the circumscriptions of the social system that envelopes the believers and the boundaries patrolled by the clergy or the hierarchical authorities of the church. Contrary to the celebrated semiotic democracy and brotherhood of believers in pentecostal churches, there is some panoptic power over the people. The disciplinary energy of the clergy is always quick to deploy its moral, aesthetic, suasive, and legal powers to control the meanings, pleasures, and social identities of the people.

Pleasures in Worship

In the study of everyday theology it is vital to understand how the people use the products and services of the churches "to their own interest and find pleasures in using them to make their own meanings of their social identities and social relations."[7] Scholarly works on bodies of Pentecostals, however, have exclusively focused on the disciplining of the body, exerting of control over the body to support their spiritual quest or sustenance of salvation and holiness. Pleasures of the body or participation in pentecostal worship as motivated by pleasure, pleasure that centers on spiritual power to create new meanings in believers' lives, and the pleasure of evading the traps of Satan have not received adequate scholarly attention. There are also pleasures that certain believers derive from disciplining their bodies or internalizing the disciplinary regimes in themselves. The body and its pleasures are important in understanding the human nature and material form of the pentecostal worship service.

Birgit Meyer has shown that pentecostal worship is a fabric of material and sensory experiences, an aesthetics of persuasion. "One of the most salient features of Pentecostal/charismatic churches is their sensational appeal; they often operate via music and powerful oratory, through which born-again Christians are enabled to sense the presence of the Holy Spirit *with* and *in* their bodies."[8] Annalisa Butticci says that the Prayer City of the Mountain of Fire and Miracles Ministries in Nigeria "was purposely created to accommodate massive crowds of prayer warriors and to shape the emotional, sensory, physical and collective experience of prayer."[9] She describes a typical public collective prayer session with these words:

Thousands of men and women fight their battle against demonic spirits and manifest miraculous touch of the Holy Spirit by throwing their bodies to the ground . . . shaking, trembling, rolling, and screaming at the top of their voices. The smell, sound, touch, and sight of so many people furiously praying is overpowering. . . . The massive movement and sound of the crowd and the multi-sensory experience of this spiritual and social catharsis are all overwhelming.[10]

A pentecostal worship service is a means of release as much as re-creation, devotion as much as display, piety as much as play. Praise and worship is often an intense, pleasurable social experience in West African churches. Together worship and worshipers' bodies become a site for the production of ecstasy, jouissance, and bliss. For some believers the pleasures come from the excitement of the body and its senses; for others they are from pure contemplation of the divine or a possible encounter with the Holy Spirit. The former pleasure, though it is given space in the worship, is also surveilled so that it does not exceed its limits. Pastors and their assistants are always equipped with clothes to cover exposed upper female thighs or quickly carry out women who appear to threaten the purity of the gathering when they are "slain" in the spirit. Rules and unruliness are always watched so that the pleasures and excesses of the body (especially the female body) do not undo social control or pollute the anointing deemed to be circulating in the assembly.

During my visits to pentecostal churches in West Africa, I have observed the power and supposed dangers of pleasures of worship services. The human body—in the intense moment of worship, especially in deliverance services—breaks down into its animal nature and, existing in that state of fracture, falls to the ground and displays serpentine movements. The believer's body eventually convulses in muscular spasms before collapsing into stillness, which signifies the end of the state of the fracture. The whole episode symbolizes orgasmic pleasure just as any demonic possession can offer. Is this a manifestation of possession by demons or an extreme case of jouissance (erotic bliss) when the body breaks free of social control or the norms it had incarnated? The correct answer does not really matter. Whichever is the case, the members of the deliverance team will quickly move to cut off such a pleasure that threatens social control and corporate anointing. The human body in its animal realism, writhing on the ground with hands pressed to the sides, represents not only loss of behavioral control, but also a disruption of semiotic, social categories. More importantly, the *spectacle* of the transformed, liminal, or grotesque body is a reminder of the fragility of the categorical boundaries of formal or official theology.

Use of Language: Creating New Meaning and Identity

It is not only the spectacles of bodies writhing on the ground that challenge categorical boundaries of formal theology. Common expressions of daily conversations convey theological interpretations that not only indict nonpentecostal practices, but also celebrate pentecostal sensibility. Take, for instance, the common expression used in Ghana to describe a well-received worship service: "The anointing was great." This phrase asserts both divine visitation and emotional energies given and received during the service. And this is only one dimension of the meaning. As Kwabena Asamoah-Gyadu argues, the expression is also a subtle "critique of the staid and over-formalized liturgical forms of worship found in historic mission denominations."[11] In West African Pentecostalism, language in the form of common expressions is often used to create new meanings, formulate dynamics of identity, stage a battleground between forms of aesthetics, and to differentiate between inferior and superior or past and future.

The biblical language as a system is tactically appropriated and expressed as a "display" in the public to affirm community membership and identity. The quaint terminology of the old King James Bible, for instance, constitutes a cultural capital, which can be spent to acquire respectability in everyday life or deployed to extend the power of Spirit-filled words over personal and social existential spaces. The use of the language in this way serves to affirm or resist commonly accepted meanings in ways that acknowledge the transitory nature of most daily interpersonal encounters. Biblical language "is not [always] used to convey social, common meanings inherent in it as a system, but the unique transitory meanings of its speakers."[12]

There is more to language use in everyday West African pentecostal theology. The everyday use of theological or religious language is often based on associative relation rather than logical connection, involving a great deal of parallel processing. A West African Pentecostal in prayer says, "Holy Ghost sword, shear, shear, shear; I cut the bars of iron asunder." *Holy Ghost sword* simultaneously means he has taken up the sword of the

Holy Ghost in his hand or there is now an imaginary sword in his hand that is empowered by Jesus, and he is announcing that Jehovah Nissi is now fighting for him. Holy Ghost is not just the name of the Third Person of the Trinity; it is a cliché that articulates the dominant worldview and ideology of West African Pentecostalism. The name metaphorizes the power, invisibility, and adoration motifs of Pentecostals. The invisible Holy Spirit represents and performs the supernatural power of God as he is evoked by a spiritual warrior's adoration.

Shear, shear, shear is the whistling sound of the sword's blade as it slices through the defenses of the prayer warrior's enemies. The man's voice that makes the whistling sound is accompanied by his right hand furiously cutting the air like a blade. The punning meaning that arises as his hand becomes a physical sword as well as a spiritual sword of God—and his voice duplicating the killer-sound of the sword-hand—brings together many images, sounds, and words in an associative freedom that is both liberating and threatening in its embodiedness.

I cut the bars of iron asunder is what the whole prayer exercise accomplishes as the pentecostal warrior frees himself from the spiritual cages or imagines himself being re-created as a new, triumphal person. In this particular prayer session and its use of language, three disparate but simultaneous bodies—the man, the Holy Ghost, and that of the implied new man—are in play and giving resources to each other. Understanding this prayer is not about *deciphering* the logic of the sentence or structure of theological discourse. Comprehension requires *reading*—the ability to bring "oral, vernacular culture to bear" upon the sentence, requiring "the parallel (not sequential) processing of words and image, of puns within words, of puns between words and image."[13] This ability to assess vernacular culture of the spiritual warrior opens up the deep structure of his prayer. At once he is calling on supreme power and exuding power, imaginatively re-creating himself through performative speech to give his life a new meaning, and thus forging a new social identity. Pleasure is attached to this social identity because it is rooted in his new born-again identity and the joy of belonging to a vivifying body of Christ. The pleasures produced from this kind of spiritual exercise are of practical use, functional and relevant in the day-to-day negotiation of social experience on the micropolitical level.

Everyday theology brings to received (pulpit, official, scriptural) theology everyday oral culture that underlies, precedes, exceeds, subverts, contests, and affirms it. Everyday theology is full of contradictions: it contains the meanings of pulpit theology and those that insist that the people's theology is theirs to use and that they do not require pastoral or academic theologians' approval. Resistance and affirmation are always present in it and this ambiguity marks its creativity. Only those who bring an inappropriate set of criteria to judge it think this ambiguity or complexity undermines its creativity and aesthetic appeal. To avoid this, we at least need to pay attention to how pleasures are produced at the intersection of meanings and identities, and how pleasures help to generate the people's theology.

Sweetness of Jesus's Blood: Meanings in Pleasures

The clock strikes 4:00 a.m. on Saturday morning in Brooklyn, New York. The Nigerian Pentecostal church has just concluded its night vigil that began at 10:00 p.m. the previous day. Leftover wafers and small cups of juice rest on the Holy Communion table at the right corner of the sanctuary, in front of the altar space. An eleven-year-old boy named Emmanuel walks over to the pastor, who is clearing the table, and asks to drink from one of the cups. He has asked during past communion services, which happens only on the first Friday night of the month, but the pastor has never obliged him. This time the pastor agrees. Emmanuel drinks the red juice and exclaims, "Jesus, your blood is sweet!" He then licks his lips, rolling his tongue over them to suck in the remnants of the liquid. This is his first time of drinking the communion wine, because in this particular church children under the age of thirteen and not yet baptized by immersion are not permitted to partake in the Holy Communion.

Why did this child literally characterize the juice as the sweet blood of Jesus? He clearly knew that the juice was not the blood of Jesus; he had seen the pastor pour the red juice from the Kedem grape juice bottle during preparations for the service. He was also not schooled in the niceties of the theology of transubstantiation. Adults spoke about the juice as the blood of Jesus but simultaneously regarded it as the juice from the Kedem bottle. The adults might have thought that pastor's utterances in consecrating the cups of juice endued them with spiritual powers, but they did not believe they were actually drinking the physical blood of Jesus. The child was different. His acceptance of the liturgical truth places him outside the meanings and power of the dominant adult belief system.

Is there really a contradiction between the child's belief on the actual (transformed) nature of the juice and that of the adults? Not really. First, following Jacques Rancière I will argue that the boy and the adults are caught up together in a particular distribution of the sensible, in one way of framing a sensory space and determining how the transcendental presents itself to sense experience.[14] In their shared sensorium, the thing-in-itself and its representation/symbol, the invisible and visible, can exchange their properties. This relation is both asserted and denied in everyday theology. Second, let us not forget that Emmanuel knew that the "blood" he drank after the service came from the Kedem juice bottle. Before he drank, the adults had partaken of the consecrated juice, felt its materiality of life and supervening spiritual power coursing through their bodies, and believed the contact to heal them physically or spiritually. The adults and Emmanuel were not concerned with blood, not blood from wine or juice, but with the "blood principle," the materiality of sensuous encounter, bodily engagement that underlies and precedes pentecostal spirituality and the vitality of life/existence. In West African Pentecostalism, religion is tasted, touched, smelled, seen, heard, and danced. In the committed engagement with the Spirit the body becomes a *religious machine*. The pentecostal body is an apparatus for seeing, hearing, tasting, dancing, incorporating, and feeling the numinous. I use the term *religious machine* not to say that pentecostal religious experience is mechanistic, rule-governed, calculable, or linear. The term is used to gesture to the virtuosity of the pentecostal body in divine-human interactions to both produce and consume religious goods (for example, semiotic commodities and emotional energies).

Let us press further our description of material and embodied sacraments with the example of anointing oil. Olive oil is used for cooking and when it is consecrated it becomes anointing oil for rubbing on the body or head. As anointing oil it is sacramental and used for religious purposes only. But in everyday pentecostal practice in West Africa, anointing oil can also be poured into a boiling pot of food in a use that is neither religious nor sacrilegious. The believer in the kitchen frees the anointing oil from the binary opposition to use it to generate new meanings and pleasures for her. This behavior is a key part of everyday theology and social practices. Religious objects, ideas, or practices are often pried apart from their original uses and contexts and are combined in a new social and signifying context that reworks their original meaning or symbolic value. The assortment of anointing oil and food, derived from a transimmanent bricolage, could be termed *cooked sacrament*, a semiotic-numinous delicacy with a culinary edge.

Shopping as Spiritual Guerrilla Warfare

Just as religious objects can be pried apart from their original uses, Pentecostals "profane" the sacred aura and meaning that attend to window shopping in the "cathedrals of consumption," opening it up into new possible uses and meanings without demonizing it. There is a new kind of shopping that has emerged in West Africa as poor Pentecostals encounter the lure and forces of modern goods that late capitalism offers. I call this buying practice *born-again shopping*. This is a term that describes Pentecostals who visit marketplaces and malls, engage in window shopping, sensuously consume wares, and occasionally touch them or pray at or over them without spending money.[15]

The approach is a guerrilla tactic that invades the physical and "psychic" spaces of the goods in the market in the hopes that God will eventually provide the money to buy them or cause them to come to the person as a gift. In born-again shopping, the commodity is constructed as the object of the pentecostal voyeuristic look, which places the believer in a position of special power over it and gives him possession of the commodity, or at least of its image. The pleasure of doing this translates the promises of wealth-and-health gospel, which is rooted in cargo-cult mentality, into everyday relevance in the period between their pronouncement and fulfillment. Born-again shopping is not only about pleasure; it is also a tactic of the poor and weak to establish themselves in a controlling position over the market-commodity system that assiduously renders them powerless and dependent. It is important to understand that the shape of everyday theology is socially determined by the weight of the world, excessive suffering, the gravity of social existence; the abrasive forces of information and meanings from the dominant, oppressive social system that assault them, which have to be reworked for personal and socially pertinent meanings; and the fluidity of daily existence, their intransigent social experiences.

Prayer as the Locus Classicus of Everyday Theology

The everyday theology that we have set forth is best exemplified by the deep structure of prayer. The everyday practices of believers live under the sign of *meaning structure of prayer*. Prayer gives rise to or anticipates thought that guides everyday practice. It anticipates thought because practices that give form to meaning are already an interpretation. Prayers in turn live under the logic and teleoaffectivity of everyday practices. We might say that everyday theology, for West African Pentecostals, is a sort of unity-of-prayer-and-practice. This is to say that prayers craft everyday theology and the prayers are also forms of practice.

Together everyday practices and prayer—constituent parts of everyday life—function under the *sign* of power, the projection of traditional and modern, spiritual and nonspiritual, forms of power into the daily, microsociological experiences of Pentecostals. The centrality of prayer and its imbrication in everyday practices derive from the sociohistorical significance of power in West Africa. As Matthews Ojo writes:

> I am convinced that nothing occupies the attention of Africans as much as power, particularly its manifestation, whether in the form of material wealth, political and social statuses, traditional privileges like chieftaincy titles, colonial heritage, etc. . . . Power is focal to social relations for most [Africans], amid a social milieu where "power" whether in terms of ethnic linkages, financial resources, filial relations, and business connections have been able to achieve. Crucial to the life and activities of Charismatic movements is the articulation and appropriation of new forms of power in very pragmatic terms to mediate and address [their] contemporary felt needs.[16]

In West African pentecostal communities, power is primarily accessible through intimate relationship with the Holy Spirit and prayer. Prayer is the concrete analysis of a given social situation, scripture, and theology in order to change social circumstances and their interpretation. Prayer analyzes the specific crisis of inherited theology, its particular cultural situation, and its present predicament. Prayer does the same for personal or social predicaments. The pentecostal prayer retrieves from practical existence the forms theology must take if it is to effectively translate Christianity into the African culture. The attentive eye that the prayer warrior brings to examining how various forms of theology touch the ground in real life enables her to discern the theological ideas that constitute meaning for her. In this way prayer enables theology to both respond to the questions in a culture's creative self-interpretation and to challenge them.

Prayer does all these within the available modes of exchange in West Africa. Pentecostal prayer in West Africa pivots around four principles or modes of exchange, enabling it to socially determine the diverse orientations of everyday theology or practices. These modes of exchange also reflect communal norms about power or the intercourse between powers of being. An analysis of oral prayers and published prayers reveals that the intercourse between humans and the Holy Spirit is structured around the four pragmatic notions of pure gift, reciprocity (gift and counter-gift), plunder and redistribution, and instrumental faith.[17] In the mode of pure gift, God's response to human needs is taken to be a gratuitous act of benevolence. When God gives in this mode, the gift is complete and there is no need for a reciprocal gift. God is expected to show God's superiority and believers accept his gifts without making return gifts, positioning themselves as children, clients, and servants of an omnipotent chief. An example of such a divine gift is the pure pleasure that bodies experience during worship services. In the mode of reciprocity, there is gift and counter-gift. Pentecostals believe that offering, fasting, and other disciplinary efforts can be directly exchanged for divine blessings and approval. The prayer language of the man who used his hand as a sword that we described earlier embeds this logic. He hopes to exchange time and energy expended in prayers for personal transformation.

Under the mode of plunder and distribution, the divine-human intercourse is solicited and sustained in order for the Pentecostal believer to acquire the necessary power to plunder the resources of enemies or nonbelievers and redistribute them for personal gains and the work of God's kingdom. Born-again shopping is an example of this principle of intercourse.

Finally, we have instrumental faith. Most West African Pentecostals perceive faith as the power of universal exchangeability in transactions of the spiritual realm or intercourse with the Holy Spirit. Faith is accumulated in order to acquire goods or translate "spiritual blessings that are hanging in the air" into physical goods and accomplishments. Here spiritual intercourse has taken the form of commodity exchange, and faith-as-money is the intermediary. It appears that with faith (as indexed by the name-it-

and-claim-it gospel) believers can bypass the usual groveling and pleadings before a deity and move on to an exchange transaction that is presumably grounded on mutual consent between deity and human beings. At any rate, the consent of God might not even be solicited at all times, because, as the faith-drenched Pentecostals claim, "you shall decree a thing and it shall be established unto you" (Job 22:28 NIV). They believe that faith can produce wealth at will and this partly explains the rise of born-again shopping. The prayer warrior swinging his hand as an imaginary sword and shouting "shear, shear, shear" is also drawing on instrumental faith to create the new man.

In any given prayer session or round of daily experience, these principles or modes of exchange operate simultaneously and in mutual interrelationship. So when I highlight one mode as characteristic of a prayer form or daily transaction, it is only to indicate that this form is dominant, while the others are subordinated to it. In the long-going rapid-fire prayers or everyday practices of West African Pentecostals the different modes of exchange turn over quickly.

It is germane to mention that the practices that constitute an everyday form of theology do not represent a domain of practices separate from these four principles or modes of exchange. Daily practices of Pentecostals are deeply connected to the modes of exchanges or a complex combination of them such that the principles can be used to shed light on them. But this should not be construed to mean that the organizing principles of daily practices derive from them. The principles of divine-human intercourse may have originated from human-to-human exchanges or from everyday theology of African traditional religions, which subsequently transferred to a new register. Whatever their source, they are today under the power, logic, and allure of the notion of the split God.

Senses and Sensation: Aesthetics of Practice

In chapter 3, we discussed Annalisa Butticci's work on *real presence* among West African Pentecostal immigrants in Italy.[18] Let us recapitulate. The immigrants, acting against the background of the notion of a split God, long for and construct or constitute real presences by throwing their bodies and their objects into a clearing or gap in order to sustain, expand, and exploit it. Let me unpack what *gap* or *clearing* means in this context as it is connected with the *Lacanian* Real. Butticci's skills in excavating the depths of pentecostal aesthetics of worship helped me to identify the underlying structural principle of sensuality of the human-divine encounter. I identified this principle using Jacques Lacan's triad of the Imaginary-Symbolic-Real. There is an idealized self-image of what African Pentecostals want to be (*imaginary*). There is God (the *Big Other*) whom they want to impress through impassioned prayers, dance, and gifts and who implores them to give the best of themselves to God and to the world (*symbolic*). They have a symbolic identification with God. The Real is the same God for whom they try the "impossible possibility," demanding of themselves a crucifixion of the flesh in order to experience the jouissance of heaven on earth, to enjoy the expanded possibilities of life in Italy. This Real that is God resists the Pentecostals' grasping or full understanding no matter how close they approach him. They approach him with the full complement of the body and its senses, but they can never "represent" him. The Real transpires or shines through their reality, forever slipping through their fingers, as Slavoj Žižek would put it. What we can discern as the Real in the divine-human encounter are "traces" left behind on the body surfaces or in the psyche. Such traces include the fragile moments of smiles, laughter, radiant faces, sweaty bodies, pleasures, feelings of elevation and empowerment, emotions, sense of new possibilities, and so on. These traces at best remind us of the leftover glory of Jehovah that shone on Moses's face after he saw but just the backside of God. Despite their strong belief in the transimmanence of the divine, the Spirit of God cannot be fully mediated, represented, or captured. The Spirit remains enigmatic and untouchable. The Real in our Lacanian-Pentecostal triad can be likened to the unstable temporal presence, the imperceptible, ungraspable gap between the past and the future. And the real presences that Butticci analyzes in this book are constructed or constituted by human beings throwing their bodies and their objects into this clearing or gap in order to sustain, expand, and exploit it.

The role of bodies and senses—the aesthetics/*aisthesis* of religion—are crucial in the study of Pentecostalism. Any teasing out of the everyday form of theology can ill afford to ignore how believers employ their bodies and senses to enable religious experiences. The study of everyday theology cannot afford to ignore how believers establish portable links with the power of the Holy Spirit, and how they receive and sustain anointing on immigration documents. Scholars will reap huge dividends when they pay attention to how the body serves as a weapon (through its capacity to touch and sanctify objects, to vocalize spiritual commands and prayers, to feel the presence of God in job interview rooms, etc.) in the struggle for survival.

Birgit Meyer argues aesthetics—sense and sensational forms—is central not only to understanding how Pentecostals and charismatic Christians sense the presence of the Holy Spirit, but also to their politics. "Understanding religion as offering a particular aesthetics, which forms religious subjects by tuning their senses and enabling modes of embodying the divine through sensational forms, bring together sensation and power. Aesthetics is not outside power structures but enmeshed with them."[19]

To ignore aesthetics in any analysis of the everyday form of theology is to ignore the role of bodies (its discipline and technology of the self) as the weapons of the weak, the body as site for the manifestation of the divine, and how a pentecostal aesthetics of persuasion is mobilized through the staging of miracles and healing on the body. We have argued in the introduction and chapter 3 of this book that the pentecostal belief in the miraculous and real presence is a pointer to the split God. Part of that argument goes like this: the starting point for grasping the Pentecostal view of God as split is to focus on their inclination toward the "non-All," non-whole, of reality. Because Pentecostals believe that there are cracks in reality, tears in the phenomenal curtain over the noumenal that allows "miracles" to eventuate or spirit-filled believers to access things-in-themselves, their actions cannot reflect a harmoniously ordered God.

The Miraculous in a World of the Split God and Split Reality

Scholarly works on African Pentecostals have invested a lot of energies and publications on grand macro narratives and events, painting the big sociological picture. It is time to develop microsociological analyses, showing how African Pentecostals flow from situation to situation as they draw from their religious and cultural capitals. These will provide insights to inform models of the everyday form of theology or the study of its organization. It is also time to understand what animates African Pentecostals' view of how reality is ordered and how their reality responds to various forms of spiritual energies from situation to situation.

The study of the organization of everyday forms of theology of West African Pentecostals must pay adequate attention to the relentless construction, deconstruction, and reconstruction of their understanding or practical notions of destiny and miracle. Underlying African Pentecostals' interpretations of their world and ensuing day-to-day theologies of hope and survival are a joint, rejiggered conceptualization of *destiny* and *miracle*, the ordering and responding complexity of God. The spiritual energies relating to these two notions or dynamics constantly invite and capture African Pentecostals' loyalties. They believe that these enable them to move not only beyond their inherited boundaries and capabilities, but also beyond the obstacles to human flourishing they encounter in their lifeworlds. Responses to greetings or questions that take the form of "God dey!," "To God be the glory," "It is God," or "Na God" are affirmations of the joint operations of the miraculous and destiny in believers' existence. These utterings are shortened discourses of a certain social-political imaginary, the naming of certain revolutionary futures worked by God-talk, supernatural allegiance, agents' decisions, and social practices.

Let us first examine the issue of destiny.[20] Afe Adogame, in his study of African Pentecostal immigrants in Europe, points us to the thinking that there is no accident in their world, everything happens according to God's plan.

> In fact, the stories of illegal immigration and unapproved residence permits are sometimes legitimized as sacred narratives. Pastors encourage members (undocumented immigrants) not to "look at their past histories or present predicaments, but look forward to God's future plan for and with them," "*I do not care* how you came to this country. It was not by any mistake, but by God's perfect design. God brought you to this country for a purpose."[21]

In this kind of world where all things are in God's firm control, the responses to greetings are constant reminders of this key belief. Now a typical philosophical theologian might think that, in such a world tightly controlled by God, the expectation for the new and surprises will be minimal. But this is not the case. I-don't-care theology is not vested in the niceties of systematic or tightly argued constructive theology. The concern is with what people do and experience—their daily functionings. Religion or communion with God is a capability that is valued for its own sake as well as for the functionings it enables. Miracles, surprises, irruptions of events, which boost functionings, are always welcome. This is the God-drenched world of the *expected unexpected*. God controls a world that is very unruly, punishing, and frustrating, and God's reign is indexed by the appearance of the unexpected at any time to alleviate human sufferings, to cover shortfalls in functionings. The sudden irruption of the unexpected is the outworking of individual destiny or purpose that God has put in place. Destiny (order) works through freedom of irruptions, by disrupting the order of things/beings. In fact, the unexpected, the power of the unexpected, or contingency is almost equated with God or God's action.

Existence and Social Analysis: The Grounding of an Everyday Form of Theology

The beauty of Adogame's book lies in the fact that it potentially offers raw materials for crafting the everyday form of theology of West African migrants in Europe. The subliminal aspect of the book is that there are positions inherent in Adogame's thought, but that he himself did not comprehend their implications deeply enough. The book focuses on theologies that are acted out. The transnational dimensions of immigrants' lives are important and the author does nice work of situating them in concrete demographic, political, economic, social, and legal settings in both host and home communities. Adogame rightly notes how "[t]he lived experiences of African Christian immigrants shape their spiritual/religious lives, just as theologies are constructed from these experiences and the reservoir of indigenous religious worldviews retained by them in their 'new homes.'"[22]

Despite this insight the author often hesitates to follow his own leads and insights, fails to deepen the reader's sociological understanding of how "non-theologians" forge liberatory theology and religious sensibilities in the concrete crucibles of everyday life. One has to be extremely patient and skillful to read the inner grooves of the lines of his text in order to decipher that he is always making an attempt to construct what we have called the everyday form of theology that never comes through. The author is unconsciously always piecing together a theology from below, a theology of the street that responds to existential needs of people in the here and now, a theology of resistance and liberation by ordinary folks.[23]

African Christian Diaspora presents, in unsteady steps, a sociology that might undergird an everyday form of theology and everyday forms of resistance. It attempts to present the story of a marginalized people resisting domination, alienation, degradation of their humanity, and marshaling theologies to make sense of their conditions and their praxes. The acts of African immigrants in host societies show that they have not consented to dominance and they have not given up on theological reflection. Their theorization of their daily experiences posits a God whose ordering and responding complexity counters that of the governing structures of their host nations.

An everyday form of theology is emerging from African Christian immigrants who are mindful of their embeddedness in structures of domination, discrimination, and oppressions as these are generated by the dynamics of race, class, gender, documentation, nationality, language/accent, and empire. This theology is a work and way of being that seeks to liberate migrants from all that thwarts flourishing life. Drawing from daily experiences, scripture, and pretheoretical doctrinaire theology, African immigrants develop a set of theoretical constructs to frame their experiences, to organize and guide their work and way of being.

Adogame is a sociologist who has done an admirable job of providing the ethnographic data and sociological insights for philosophers or theologians to construct how to extract the key forms and contents of everyday theology and to ground the theoretical-theological constructs of ordinary Pentecostals in the very existential conditions that gave rise to them in the first place. There are two issues in the preceding statement: methodology of extracting an everyday form of theology (microtheology) and the philosophical grounding of theoretical constructs of ordinary folks (some philosophy of existence).

The foregoing discussions in this chapter suggest that "academic theology" will not be a good partner in the first task. Academic theology, which usually functions under the sign of *logos*, is not a good tool for those interested in the kind of everyday form of theology we have put forward in this chapter.[24] The theology I have extracted is from the practices of participants' lives under the sign of *meaning*. This is a meaning that gives rise to or anticipates thought. It anticipates thought because the practices that give form to the meaning are already an interpretation. Using the techniques of microtheology, I brought them (*logos* and meaning) together under the symbol of *existence*, the temporospatial continuum where logos and meaning both stand in and stand out. Existence transcends religion.

By this approach, I have interpreted Pentecostalism as a dimension of the adherents' existence, and not only as an external reality that demands integrative thinking or a window into reality that makes events and happenings intelligible. In general, this is what an everyday form of theology under the symbol of existence demands. We must understand meaning in order to live in the aura of the logos, but we must function in the aura of logos in order to understand or articulate meaning. The ensuing outcome of this approach situates everyday theology of West African Pentecostalism not only in existence; it is also an interpretation of existence.

Existence is about how to produce, reproduce, sustain, and cause to flourish human lives in social communities and with and through nature that encompasses and exceeds human beings. This is a universal principle of ethics (life) that always demands concrete fulfillment and is instantiated (phenomenalized) in cultures, modes of life, and ways of being. Since we are concerned with an everyday form of theology, how did we articulate it in a work like this in the light of material existence? To this end, we need to ask: What is the content of such a theology? What does it recognize as the agonistic striving of its subjects/adherents/addressees? What does it posit as their hope? The content of this theology is the improvement of material life, by agonistically striving against or negating obstacles to the realization of this content and harboring hope for the realization of what is lacking in the actualization of the content.

The driving interest of West African pentecostal theology is not so much a negative critique of social existence, but rather about what conditions are necessary for an affirmation of social existence that could at the same time be critical of the obstacles to improvement in material life. It is a theory (method and content) about the conditions of possibility of living well that presupposes spending eternal life with Jesus Christ.

The addressees of this theology are essentially and primarily people who live in misery and under the social weight of oppression, state neglect, and necrophiliac capitalism, whose immediate interest in social emancipation finds expression in economic terms. These are people who are continually expecting the *messianic arrow of time* (in the form of the new, happiness, prosperity, and redemption) to cut across, to leap into, to erupt, and to disrupt their historic arrow of time, which is an eternal recycling of the same surplus suffering.

And to continue with Walter Benjamin's metaphor, each moment of fasting, prayer, praise and worship, and scripture reading is seen as the small door through which the messianic arrow might enter, when the discontinuous time erupts into the repetitive continuous history of "suffering and smiling." Theology and those subject to theology are working to find and stand in that messianic gap (or flashes of it) that erupts in the repetitive history of the same in order to push back the flow of excess suffering from the past and anticipated download of additional suffering from the future. The quotidian struggle of the subjects is to transform the weighty historic time into the light messianic time, or to put it differently, to hold down messianic time and transform it into historic time. This is their existential struggle. This is the reality (human victims' material needs) that is before theology, the prior assumption of theology and religious practice, but it is in turn constituted by theology as a discourse by a community of victims.[25]

Earlier I stated that there are two issues in the preceding statement: methodology of extracting an everyday form of theology and the philosophical grounding of theoretical constructs of ordinary folks. Earlier I stated that the task of extracting the key forms and contents of everyday theology and grounding the theoretical-theological constructs of ordinary Pentecostals involved two things: philosophy of existence and microtheology. We have dealt with the first of the two but the second two remain, which will now bring these reflections and the whole chapter to a (provisional) conclusion.

Concluding Thoughts: Microtheology of Everyday Life

The preceding analyses derive from my microtheological approach to the interactions between the pentecostal apparatus and believers in West Africa. This is not the method of "academic theology," with preference on knowledges stored in books. In a certain sense, academic theology is an interpretation and reinterpretation of texts of theologians, philosophers, and others. It is an exercise in textual reading, textual criticism, and the mining of meanings from texts. The texts are usually academic essays and books, and not the tactics of everyday life, popular uses of theological language, or habits and thoughts of ordinary folks. Everyday theology, as we have shown, can be an excellent source of theology for academic theologians or it can stand all by itself. My move here to accent everyday acts as sources of theology is not an attempt to reveal the subtle, subterranean movements of the divine life in quotidian human existence. It also does not express a desire to work out any notion of religious a priori in human life or social existence. For me, everyday theology is where we can take a bird's-eye view of the kind of spirituality that is under the sway of a split God, or at least is where we show the way Pentecostals materialize their jouissance in a set of practices that are ultimately informed by the notion of a split God. It is also where we can discern the stirrings of West African Pentecostalism's yes and no to the totality of Christianity's interpretation of life or existence. Everyday theology is also the principal source for microtheology, a minimally explored dimension of pentecostal scholarship. Microtheology investigates what people actually do in social situations with their faith, identifies what kind of interactions actually happen that are evidently marked and colored by beliefs, and ferrets out the theological meanings of such interactions.

Pentecostal theology has made admirable strides in many areas, but it is still focused on global-level, large-scale constructive projects or macro configuration of thoughts. The key thinkers of the Pentecostal movement are only grappling with the grand theories of spirituality, doctrines, kingdom of God, pentecostal distinctive of baptism in the Holy Spirit, pneumatology, interreligious dialogue, Pentecostal principle, and the formulation of global theology, to name just a few. These efforts give short shrift to the local, face-to-face, ephemeral patterns of everyday life, small aspects of encounters, and the flux and variation of the social life of Pentecostals. Apart from a few exceptions, the major thinkers have so far ignored interactional situations and interaction rituals of the social world of Pentecostals. This need not be so. Theologians need innovative ideas, tools, and frameworks to theorize and theologize about the everyday life of ordinary Pentecostals. The tools of their regular constructive/systematic theologies are too cumbersome, blunt, and ill-suited for this new task. They need to turn to what I have named earlier as *microtheology*, which is more suited for the task. Microtheology will complement and expand traditional macrotheological approaches to pentecostal spirituality.

Microtheology is an interpretative analysis of everyday embodied theological interactions and agency at the individual, face-to-face level. The study is one of everyday social interactions of individuals or small groups that demonstrate the linkages between spirituality (practices and affections) and embodied theological ideas (beliefs). Theologies, beliefs, and doctrines play an important role in structuring the daily, microsociological experiences of Pentecostals, and theologians need to understand these influences. Social interactions are like sociological transformers, taking the powerful current of theology "from above and distributing it in voltages" that the micro-moments can take, mixing it with some emotional energies as resources, and turning it into spirituality.[26] To put it differently, spirituality (practice) takes the strain of theology from above, breaking it down, mixing it with some emotions as motivations, and turning it into an everyday form of theologies (beliefs) as outcomes. Real, useable theologies issue from the hard-bitten consumers of theologies generated within the customary or hierarchical orders.

I need to quickly state that the approach to theology I am trying to develop in this chapter is not limited to studying how theology from above is transformed when it touches the ground. It also seeks to understand the role of microaggressions and microaffirmations—in this case microtheological aggressions and microtheological affirmations—that Pentecostals display in everyday life as they interact with people who are higher, at the same level, or lower in power. In what ways do Pentecostals engage in theological microaggressions against non-Pentecostals in interactional situations? What about the use of microaffirmations in interactional situations and for fostering moral solidarity and trust? What roles do microaggressions and microaffirmations play in social dominance or in the acceptance or rejection of status among Pentecostals in everyday life? Besides, microtheology offers historical analyses of shifts in rituals of everyday life, microstructural shifts in standards of interactions, and boundary-marking rituals and anti-rituals.

To do all this well we need expertise in *thick* cultural analysis and competence in micro-empirical observation of social interactions. I will illustrate this set of skills by analyzing the hand movements of the African Christian on hearing bad news. This view describes spirituality as seen from below, from the angle of the behaviors, gestures, conversations, and situations in which theology is actually acted out. I observed pentecostal women in Kalabari (Nigeria) make circular motions with their clenched right hands over their heads and then snap their fingers to intimate the rejection of bad news. When a woman hears bad, frightening news she makes the cyclical motion with her hand while saying *E Tamuno oke* ("my God form a hedge of protection around me"). The making of the cyclical motion with a clenched hand signifies ritual cleansing of the self. The hand is clenched to symbolize an egg that is often used in traditional rituals of purification. In the setting of African traditional religions (ATR), a priest performing the ritual of cleansing takes an egg in his palm, makes a circular motion over the body of the client from head to toe, and then throws the egg hard on the earth to break it into pieces. By this he signifies that the pollutions, curses, and evil intrusions in/over the person have been collectively transferred to the egg, neutralized, and dispersed to the four winds. The client is thus decontaminated, hence, free from danger. The pentecostal woman who does the circling motion with her right hand is representing this ritual in a shorthand way. But when she adds *E Tamuno oke*, she is transferring the ritual from the registers of ATR into those of Christianity.

The woman's micro-act speaks volumes about her embodied theologies and cultural milieu. She might not go to ATR priests for consultation and she might even excoriate them as "demonic," but her bodily motion draws from two forms of *regimes of discourse*. Her microtheology works on a diagonal trajectory between the ideas of ATR and Christianity. While the woman does not have the theological sophistication and language to craft a global theology, her diagonal trajectory daily opens a new alternative, an everyday form of theology that creates a third regime of discourse. She is able to navigate her situations in new ways by connecting the two religious discourses and claims and by creating a new commonality among them. Herein lies the originality of theology at the micro, everyday level. At this ground level, theology is always conjoined with practice; rejiggered doctrine is wedded with spirituality.

Theology moves about as actions, microaggressions, enculturated bodily expressions, or underlying patterns of behavior. In this kinetic rendezvous with existence, theology does not symbolize belief as in clarification of doctrines, nor does it prescribe what behavior ought to be as in dogmatic ethics; it is behavior. Everyday behavior not only rescripts theology; it also represents the agonistic but correlational relations that Pentecostals have with it. The everyday form of theology is a dynamic theory of human flourishing that is routinely enacted by individuals in their daily encounters and situations. It is a reflection that is born in and borne by their praxis. Pentecostal theologians need to begin to focus on this kind of spirituality from below, theology as actually acted out.

Another example that illustrates expertise in thick cultural analysis and competence in micro-empirical observation come from Afe Adogame's 2013 book, *The African Christian Diaspora*. He gives some weight to the everyday situational dynamics in his analysis of transnational Pentecostalism, paying attention to immediate social experiences of African migrants in their interactions with fellow Pentecostals. Adogame in this book exhibits the theoretical impulses of Erving Goffman without being conscious of them. His attention to details in micro-situations is revealed in this passage:

> In actual fact, theologies are acted out from simple exchanges of pleasantries "How are you?" and the response it evokes among

Ghanaians, such as "By God's grace"; or Nigerian replying: "We thank God," "God dey!," "E go better!," "We go survive!," "To God be the Glory!"; or further as some Kenyan-led churches are accustomed to responding: "I am blessed and mightily favoured." Such wide-ranging responses elicit narratives woven around day-to-day life experiences. . . . It is indeed a matter of conjecture how and in what ways such theologies of "everyday life" partly verbalized by African Christians can enrich "classroom" theologies common among many Western Christians.[27]

Goffman's analysis of daily rituals in everyday life provides us with a powerful tool to elaborate on what Adogame calls "theologies of everyday life." Goffman is noted for analyzing the role of everyday expressions (such as "How are you?," "Good night," "Hello," and "Goodbye") in social structures and showing that they are not meaningless. They mark and enact social relationships, beliefs, and symbolic acts in the structures of social existence. The greetings, as Adogame has recorded, indicate how Christians regard their relationships and daily life. They are considered as practices and processes acted out in the sacred presence of God. These greetings and their responses are not just meaningless expressions or acts, but are important rituals. They are rites of those who believe they live their daily lives in the presence of God and are subjects of God's grace. The responses not only show respect for God, but they also constitute the person-to-person encounters as sacred. In the lifeworld of Nigerian or Ghanaian *born-agains*, reality is divided between the profane and sacred realms, which are viably permeated and integrated by the unseen world. Certain everyday rituals, like responses to greetings and blessings of food before eating, confer sacredness on what is profane. In particular, responses to greetings stand not only as palpable means of this conferment, but also as a marker of religious identity, a presentation of self in everyday public life.

There is a fine-grained liberatory aspect to these verbal rituals. If we think of social life as taking place in an ecology of struggles between God and Satan (which includes oppressive powers of society) over the life of believers,[28] then in order to maximize one's chances of survival and success, it is usually necessary to explicitly define one's allegiance or hope in the struggle.[29] "E go better!," "We go survive!," "To God be the Glory!," and their equivalents are used to define, invoke, or sustain the sacred canopy over the ecology of a person's everyday life. And they are also used to mark (nudge or hail) daily transitions to microvictories.

These responses enact daily resistance to destructive powers of evil, of the devil that ever threatens life. They are regarded as daily "prophetic utterances" to ward off the "satanic or demonic arrows" that fly in the daytime. Thus, the verbal rituals are at least doing three things: marking transitions, accentuating relationship with the divine, and enacting resistance to potential attacks on flourishing life.

Adogame, a sociologist, made his fine-tuned observations because he was interested in capturing something of the "theologies of everyday life" of the Pentecostals he was studying.[30] Adogame's commitment to the microsituational is founded on his belief that "religion is usually not thought out in the agora of theology, but lived out in the marketplace of Africa. Their theology is not in books but in their heads, thoughts, utterance and day-to-day actions and life modes. In the diaspora, there is a certain resilience of the action-orientedness of African Christianities."[31]

Adogame's analysis points to the vast potentials of the sociological and theological constructs that undergird the everyday life of migrants. In order for pentecostal theologians to properly understand, interpret, and advance "theologies of everyday life" as set forth by sociologists and anthropologists such as Adogame, they need to crosswire James Scott's notion of subalterns' resistance to authority and domination and Goffman's interaction ritual analysis. Scott enjoins us to investigate the *public and hidden transcripts* of oppressed people in their interactions with power. Goffman shows us how incidents, interactions, the chain of encounters over time, and situation as an emergent property shape individuals.[32] An everyday form of theology is a dynamic reflection on encounters and situations by individuals, a reflection that is not separate from their praxis. Pentecostal believers reflect on the common realities of everyday life theologically in ways that recognize the interplay of structures (of society and situations) and their own agency. The scholarly community needs the kind of microsociological analyses that Goffman is famous for in order to enable theoretically oriented theologians to engage with this emerging theology.

Some readers may be thinking at this point that microtheology's focus on individual (micro) actions constitutes a path onto solipsistic theology. Microtheology as an everyday *form* of theology is not solipsistic. It aims to capture in its *form* of theology the actions that express the *import* of theology. Actions or acts (which by definition are social) are the concrete materials, the *contents* through which the import (the meaning-making interpretation of life, the meaning-giving depth or end of religion) is experienced. Microtheology is the concrete analysis of theology in order to change it. It analyzes the specific crisis of inherited theology, its particular cultural situation, and its present predicament.

Microtheology reveals both the beautiful and ugly parts of theology. Systematized, immanently consistent, theology crafted in the dusk of the day is an erudite "high" that presents the beautiful and comforting parts of a religion minus the ugly and disturbing counterparts. By concealing the unbecoming parts, systematized theology panders to civilization's longing for order, control, protection, and boundary. Microtheology retrieves from practical existence the forms theology must take if it is to effectively translate its religion into the culture. The attentive eye that microtheology brings to examining how theology touches the ground in real life enables the theologian to discern the theological ideas that constitute meaning for a set of believers. In this way microtheology enables theology to both respond to the questions in a culture's creative self-interpretation and to challenge it. As it does all these it is evaluating and reanimating itself in order to remain as a font of meaning-giving ideas. Thus, microtheology performs an important service for theology. Without microtheology pentecostal theological ideas might soon turn into ghosts, living on and having a life of their own when the human bodies and social flesh that originally carried them have long decayed. The cultivated, refined, and erudite theology must feed from the trough of the practical and worldly wisdom and adaptations of microtheology to fend off all spectrality.

In sum, to understand the spirit of a period of theology the "texts" we must read are not the works of intellectual sublimity of systematic theologians or even the more practical pastors, but the imaginative and evocative uses to which they are put. This is not a rejection of intellectualism, but to note that the relevant text for an interpreter of the theological spirit of any period of Pentecostalism is *textflesh* (as against textbooks). Textbooks are narrow compared to textflesh, which is a rhizomatic site of textbooks, reworked texts, embodied actions, and meanings. The "theological spirit" of an age emerges only after immanently consistent theology has been put to use (evaded), inserted into the fluid dynamics of daily existence. This reworking of theology between the hammer and anvil of existential microtheology is either affirmative or powerfully resistant and contradictory to received theological wisdoms and meaning.

Conclusion

Ethical Implications of a Split God

In these final pages, I would like to engage very briefly with the "theological" excess, the religious "too muchness" that informs the everyday lives of Pentecostals as a result of the notion of a split God. I want to bring to our attention an excess, a surplus charge that flows into daily social life from the split God.[1] These concluding pages will present four instances of the excess that comes from within the life of the pentecostal subject and the surplus charge that comes from the outside, from the wider social and cultural contexts. In more precise terms, this unconcluding postscript will offer a short meditation on the theological excess, the particular significance of the notion of a split God and show how it defines Pentecostal ethics in wider, existential terms. What makes this meditation interesting is that it works to show how cultural or political pluralism emerges out of the core of the notion of a split God. The paradox is that it is really this notion of a split God that the cultured despisers of religion regard as marking Pentecostalism as exclusivist and fundamentalist that is most deeply invested in pluralism and nudges its adherents toward a radical love of others in the midst of life.

The four examples illustrate or exemplify what it means to be in the midst of everyday social life with this notion: to interact with a religious Other, to be subjected to the possibilities and impossibilities of daily existence, the multifarious ways in which the pentecostal subject is summoned to respond to the inoperativity, the lack of "essence" of the human animal. The force of the notion of a split God drives the interaction with the religious Other not only because it permeates the very fabric of everyday life, but it also shapes the *ethical substance* of pentecostal communities. The notion of a split God gestures to a theology of radical alterity, whether or not Pentecostals are fully conscious of it. There is always, as we have demonstrated throughout this book, the gap, the incursion, the Other, or some kind of obstacle embedded or introjected in the life of the subject, being, or order of being. What are the existential valences, the theological aspects of this gesture in everyday life?

The Pentecostals' inclination toward the split image of God, ontologically incomplete reality, and split self shows that alterity is immanent to the construction of pentecostal identity. Despite all the efforts to "domesticate" God, there is still an uncanny strangeness to him. God eludes their grasp; the imperative of "Speak-up" glossolalia means they are not fully determined by their context; the dwelling of the Holy Spirit in them means that every Pentecostal is in herself dislocated, and the much-sought-after anointing or Spirit baptism cannot be fully captured, represented, or symbolized. The split image suggests that the Godhead is not only "structured precisely around an openness" to alterity; uncanniness, uncanny strangeness, is also internal to the believer's consciousness of him.[2] What is familiar is ultimately grounded on strangeness: God moves in mysterious ways, the unfinishedness of reality means that it is also a stranger to itself, and the believer is indeed a stranger to herself. There is no easy way to interpret these various forms of strangeness and thus there is a deadlock, which the proliferation of interpretations struggles to cover up.

All the preceding illustrations are important in understanding some of the cultural conflicts between Pentecostals and other (religious and nonreligious) groups. They are crucial to answering the question: Who is my neighbor? Pentecostals often attribute intergroup conflicts to *external differences* between them and others. There may be some truth in this, but it is also possible that such conflicts might well indicate the uncanniness internal to Pentecostals' construction of identity. More precisely, as psychoanalytic philosopher Eric Santner's thought suggests, the differences between Pentecostalism and its Other may signify "the possibility of shared opening to the agitation and turbulence *immanent* to any construction of identity, the *Unheimlichkeit* or uncanniness internal to any space and every space we call home."[3]

The point is that the enigma of the Other that Pentecostals think is an obstacle to integration with the Other is also an enigma within/of Pentecostalism.[4] What eludes the Pentecostals' grasp about the Other eludes not only their own grasp about themselves, but also the Other's grasp about itself. This is the point Santner is making, and Slavoj Žižek also makes this point about any effort one culture makes to understand another culture.

> The limit that prevents our full access to the Other is *ontological*, not merely epistemological. . . . this means that the Other (say, another culture I am trying to understand) is already "in itself" not fully determined by its context but "open," "floating." . . . We effectively "understand" a foreign culture when we are able to identify with its point of failure: when we are able to discern not its hidden positive meaning, but rather its blind spot, the deadlock the proliferation of meanings endeavors to cover up.[5]

Thus the way to understand another culture, according to Žižek, is through its enigma, what about itself that eludes its grasp.

> In other words, when we endeavor to understand the Other (another culture), we should not focus on its specificity (on the peculiarity of "their customs," etc.); we should rather endeavor to encircle that which eludes their grasp, the point at which the Other is in itself dislocated, not bound by its "specific context." . . . I understand the Other when I become aware of how the very problem that was bothering me (the nature of the Other's secret) is already bothering the Other itself. The dimension of the Universal emerges when the two lacks—mine and that of the Other—overlap.[6]

There is a dimension of the force of the notion of a split God that permeates practices of everyday life that could possibly complement the kind of intercultural understanding both Santner and Žižek are advocating here. There is an internal alienness within Pentecostalism as there is alterity, uncanniness, strangeness in the Other, and all sides are trying to grasp it even as it keeps slipping through their fingers. There is, therefore, a possible point of contact to develop mutual understanding. Pentecostals in the singularity of their own out-of-jointness occasioned by the split God can open up to the internal alienness of the Other.[7] This can enable them to shift their antagonistic relationship with the Other from the register of external *differences* between cultures to shared opening to internal alienness. From Santner's point of view, this kind of shift in logic marks the point at which they truly enter the *midst of life*; that is, when they "truly inhabit the proximity to [their neighbor], assume responsibility for the claims his or her singular and uncanny presence makes on [them] not only in extreme circumstances but *every day*."⁸ There is a cultural pluralism implied in the split-God notion from Santner's perspective.

Let us now turn to the second example. This study has shown that Pentecostalism demystifies the sacred. And this is discernible in the way it locates God both within and outside the sacred. Pentecostals place God in (*en*) it and nominate the same as its anchor and guarantee. The sacred is conceived as an opening to a "beyond" (which is not necessarily always transcendent), a space that creates, harbors, or provokes new possibilities. We noted in chapter 4 that Pentecostalism's two-pronged position on the sacred (godly and special mundane events or "potentiality" and "virtuality") is always mediated by the playful character of the pentecostal spirit. Pentecostalism "profanes" the sacred without abolishing the sphere of the sacred. It *deactivates* the aura that attends to the rites and stories (myths) of the sacred sphere. Yet it is this profanation and belief in God who is beyond the sacred as its anchor that, at the same time, places Pentecostals not only in the midst of the sacred, but also in the *midst of life*. How can a people who are so invested in the beyond, the noumenal, be so embedded in the everyday, phenomenal life? In the past when much of pentecostal everyday life was driven by eschatological hope, apparently, this paradox was not well noticed.

I will turn to Franz Rosenzweig's theology, under the pressure of Santner's interpretation, to explain this paradox.⁹ The key here is Rosenzweig's theory of the state and of revelation. His interpretations of the state and divine revelation show that the state as a mode of temporalization and revelation is an intervention into "sovereign temporalization." Revelation opens the eyes of believers to see in and beyond the state's ceaseless effort to control life, found and augment its institutions that "overcome" the damages caused by the inevitable passage of time. In the words of Santner, the divine revelation that Rosenzweig is theorizing "is nothing but our opening to this 'beyond' that our life in the midst of institutions never ceases to produce. *Rosenzweig's paradox*, if I might call it that, is that our opening to this 'beyond' is the very thing that places us in the midst of life."¹⁰

The major move I make to transform Rosenzweig's conceptualization of the connection between state and revelation into a pentecostal framework is to transpose the state into the sacred, that is, to *re-cognize* Rosenzweig's theory of the state as a viable theory of the sacred. Once this recognition is made and accepted then the rest of the transformation of frames works itself out, so to speak. Let me begin by restating

Rosenzweig's theory of the state and point out its uncanny resemblance to the theory of the sacred. He posits sovereignty or state as a "solution" to the problem of the passage of time. For God's people eternity has already come in the midst of time, but the state repeatedly "strives to give nations eternity within the confines of time."[11] As he puts it,

> The world's people as such are without orbits; their life cascades downhill in a broad stream. If the state is to provide them with eternity, this stream must be halted and damned up to form a lake. The state must seek to turn into an orbit that pure sequence of time to which the people as such are committed. It must transform the constant alternation of their life into preservation and renewal and thus introduce an orbit capable, in itself, of being eternal.[12]

This view of the state as a mode of temporalization is remarkably close to a theoretical perspective on the sacred. In chapter 4, we saw that what is sacred in any society is believed to always have a purchase on eternity; that is, it is believed to transcend the passage of time. The sacred always claims for itself the capacity to transcend the ravages and passage of time. Following sociologist Richard Fenn and philosopher Quentin Meillassoux, we argued that the conception of the sacred in most societies has been "reduced" to the effective practices and procedures directed by a society to enable the cosmos and nomos to maintain themselves against the threat of chaos by strengthening and renewing the ethos. One of the primary roles of religious imagination and the habits of other organs overseeing the forbidden aspirations of people is to explain, control, and predict the pattern of appropriate responses to the passages, damages, and surprises of time. The sacred (in such societies) is how a society oversees life with regard to continuity between the past and the present and the future. The key goal of the practices and procedures of the sacred-as-religion or sacred-as-state is to control the passage of time over life and society's institutions by subordinating the "virtualizing power of time" to a superior power or set of powers. The aim of the controlling intent is to ensure that novelties, radical (or unauthorized) ruptures, do not emerge to defeat all continuity between the past and the present and the future.

Just as Rosenzweig critiques this view of the state/sovereignty/sacred as unstable and one that hinders the emergence of new possibilities, Pentecostals, as we have demonstrated in chapter 4, also have an alternative to this view to the sacred.¹³ For them the sacred is the site of possible and impossible possibilities, surprises, novelties, and contingencies. The state in its mode of temporalization, of attempting to stem the passage of time, Rosenzweig argues, "introduces standstills, stations, epochs into the ceaseless sweep of this life."¹⁴ What revelation does, according to Rosenzweig, is to give believers the resources to intervene in this state's capture of life and time, to destabilize this hegemonic power of the state (sacred) that claims the power or foundation to authorize or legitimate the new. Revelation (which is for him also love's "divine" imperative) opens the eyes of the believers to "what remains/insists in and beyond the drama of authorization/legitimation."¹⁵

There is always an opening in the core of the temporal machine of the state, in the hegemonic control of the possibilities by the sacred; that is, there is always a remainder or surplus in any system, "totality," order of being, socio-symbolic network, that exceeds control. This locus of excess, the opening, allows for new possibilities to emerge. This is "a site where the possibility of unplugging from the dominance of the sovereign [sacred] can open. Indeed, that opening *is* what Rosenzweig understands by revelation."¹⁶

Ultimately, for Rosenzweig it is our capacity to look "beyond" the state's capture of life that puts us in the *midst of life*. The Pentecostals' orientation to look beyond the regnant understanding of the sacred, to profane the sacred, is the very attitude that places them not only in the *midst of life*, but also in the sacred, a space that creates possibilities for new or excluded possibilities. Reading Santner compels me to expand the pentecostal conception of sacred to include not only the inner logic of Rosenzweig's understanding of revelation, but the out-of-jointness that our analysis of the split God suggests is at the core of pentecostal identity and that of its Other. The sacred thus includes

> the space of human possibilities organized around the claims made upon me by the Other insofar as he or she is singularly out-of-joint with respect to the social intelligibility produced by [the symbolic order]. The Other who invades my life with his or her passionate claims on my attention, desire, and care is, in other words, an Other filled with too much pressure, a surplus of excitations that have, to some extent, always already been organized as impossible.¹⁷

Once again under the pressure of Santner's and Rosenzweig's thoughts we have identified one more hint about how the notion of a split God could possibly influence everyday ethical life or enable Pentecostals to enter into *the midst of life*, to inhabit the proximity of their neighbor or the Other.

Our third example concerns worship as pure means (WPM). We argued in chapters 1 and 6 that WPM is a "work" of inoperativity and that this inoperativity is at the heart of being and praxis of God. WPM as pure mediality (re-)presents worship as exposition of human beings as *argōs*-being. Is it not conceivable that the Pentecostals' orientation to (drive to, obsession with) WPM is an unrecognized way they are grappling with the purposelessness that is at the core of human beings, the surplus of being, or the real within the human being, even as they are grabbed or claimed by the instrumental logic or mesmerizing story of global capitalism? Before we proceed any further let me explain what I mean by *argōs*-being because it holds a key to comprehending the argument I will be making here. Aristotle wonders if nature left man without a function, work (*ergon*) that is proper to human beings or if they are essentially workless (*inoperoso*), functionless (*argōs*).

> For just as the goodness and performance of a flute player, a sculptor, or any kind of expert, and generally of anyone who fulfills some function or performs some action, are thought to reside in his proper function [*ergon*], so the goodness and performance of man would seem to reside in whatever is his proper function. Is it then possible that while a carpenter and a shoemaker have their own proper function and spheres of action, man as man has none, but left by nature a good-for-nothing without a function [*argōs*]?[18]

Aristotle quickly retreated from this thought and supplied the answer: "Activity of the soul [is] in accordance with virtue." This is the essence of human beings, at least and insofar as she is in the *polis* and it is the end she pursues. Today, we are no longer quick to identify what is the proper timeless function of human beings. And we even regard community as *inoperative* as it is only the experience of *compearance* (as Jean-Luc Nancy has taught us). Community or the notion of the community, according to him, is not based on some essence, idea, or project. As he argues in his *The Inoperative Community*, the community is not about communion, an essence, but about being-together, being *ex-posed* to one another.[19] So, and rightly, Giorgio Agamben argues that human action cannot be regarded as a means that makes sense only with respect to an end.[20] Thus, it is not totally out of place for Pentecostals to understand worship not with regard to a particular end, but as a sphere that corresponds to the *argōs*-standing of human beings.

This has implications for how we think about ethics in everyday life. To flesh this out, we need to connect with Rosenzweig's concept of the *metaethical self*. The self is different from personality, which is an assemblage of common human predicates; it is the generic dimension of a human being. The individual can be subsumed under the concept of the universal, which Rosenzweig represents with the equation $B=A$, the taking up of the distinctive (B, *das Besondere*) into the general (A, *das Allgemeine*).[21] "Personality is always defined as an individual in its relation to other individuals and to a Universal. There are no derivative predications about self, only the one, original $B=B$.[22] The self is the something singular, particular, irreplaceable, not generic, and nonsubstitutable about a human. This pure gap in any series of human identifications or classification is what Santner calls the self or metaethical self.

> The self, that is, signifies *the part that is not part* (of a whole), a nonrelational excess that is out of joint with respect to the generality of any classification or identification. . . . [It] is not some other, more substantial self behind the personality, not, that is, some sort of true self that, say, assumes a distance to the social roles of personality; it is, rather, a *gap* in the series of identifications that constitute it.[23]

Like worship as pure means, that is, worship at the zero-point of "pathological content," the metaethical self is also empty of predicative determinations. Again, like WPM, the metaethical self is emptied of teleology; it resists entrance into any teleological subsumption.[24]

> One day the self assaults man like an armed man and takes possession of all the wealth in his property. . . . Until that day, man is a piece of the world even before his own consciousness. . . . The self breaks in and at one blow robs him of all the goods and chattel which he presumed to possess. He

becomes quite poor, has only himself, knows only himself, is known to no one, for no one exists but he. The self is solitary man in the hardest sense of the word: the personality is "the political animal."[25]

This solitary self resists being made part of any larger or higher purpose by the symbolic order. The metaethical self cherishes purposeless activity. "The self is, in a fundamental sense, *good for nothing*, a rupture in the very logic of teleological evaluation."[26] To put it in the words of Žižek from another context, the self, the *defiant character* of a person (*B=B*) that Rosenzweig theorizes represents "that which, in me, resists the blissful submergence in the Good is . . . not my inert biological nature but the very kernel of my *spiritual* selfhood, the awareness that, beyond all particular physical and psychical features, I am 'me,' a unique *person*, an absolutely singular point of spiritual self-reference."[27] This does not mean that the self does not or cannot appreciate teleology. The point being made is that the metaethical self resists teleological integration into structured wholes, which is always executed on the basis of the predicates that inform or undergird personality. The self, or this character of human beings, the capability of purposelessness (inoperativity) is what in Rosenzweig's view truly distinguishes humans from all other creatures.

The thought and language of Rosenzweig and Santner can help us to clarify the ethical dimension of worship as pure means in the light of the uncanny strangeness that inhabits any identity or human being—the enigma. This is the metaethical self, the tautological kernel of *B=B*. This suggests that any deliberate endeavor to communicate, to inhabit the proximity to the Other, must involve a willingness to approach the neighbor, the Other, in the precise sense of what Freud calls the *Thing* (*Ding*). There is an unfathomable X (abyss) to the Other, "the neighbor-Thing," a radical otherness, an impenetrable core, mysterious and elusive. The Other (the real of the Other, its uncanny strangeness) cannot be integrated into the pentecostal universe or symbolic order. What is important to realize is that in the encounter with the Other Pentecostals must reject

> the ethical domestication of the neighbor—for example, what Emmanuel Levinas did with his notion of the neighbor as the abyssal point from which the call of the ethical responsibility emanates. What Levinas obfuscates is the monstrosity of the

neighbor, monstrosity on account of which Lacan applies to the neighbor the term Thing (*das ding*), used by Freud to designate the ultimate object of our desires in its unbearable intensity and impenetrability. One should hear in this term all the connotations of horror fiction: the neighbor is the (Evil) Thing which potentially lurks beneath every homely human face.[28]

Let me find other language to restate this ethical demand. To this end, let us turn to Jesus Christ's supplementation of the commandment on adultery in the Hebrew Bible and to Richard Wagner's alternative supplementation of the same commandment in order to set the background for my own supplementation of another commandment. Jesus said in Matthew 5:27 (NIV):

> You have heard that it was said, "You shall not commit adultery." But I tell you that anyone who looks at a woman lustfully has already committed adultery with her in his heart.

Wagner says:

> The commandment saith: Thou shalt not commit adultery! But I say unto you: Ye shall not marry without love. A marriage without love is broken as soon as entered into, and who so hath wooed without love, already hath broken the wedding. If ye follow my commandment, how can you ever break it, since it bids you to do what your heart and soul desire?—But where ye marry without love, ye bind yourselves at variance with God's love, and in your wedding ye sin against God; and this sin avengeth itself by your striving next against the law of man, in that ye break the marriage-vow.[29]

About loving the Other, Jesus says in Matthew 5:43–45 (NIV):

> You have heard that it was said, "Love your neighbor and hate your enemy." But I tell you, love your enemies and pray for those who persecute you, that you may be children of your Father in heaven. He causes his sun to rise on the evil and the good, and sends rain on the righteous and the unrighteous.

And I humbly supplement it in this way:

> The commandment says: "Love your neighbor! But I say unto you: You shall not love your neighbor without loving the uncanny strangeness, the impenetrable, mysterious core in him or her. If you love your neighbor without loving his or her unfathomable monstrosity, you are already guilty of hatred and you are angry with him or her and you shall be in danger of judgment.

At the heart of the three ethical implications of the notion of the split God that we have managed to uncover under the pressure of Rosenzweig's philosophy and theology is the metaethical self in the *midst of life* (living with the neighbor). This metaethical self appears to materialize one split among a series of splits in the components that constitute the divine-human relation. First, the metaethical self indicates that the human being is dislocated in herself; there is a crack in her that lies between her personality and her metaethical self, the split in any series of human predicates that ground personality, the gap between $B=A$ and $B=B$. One of the key insights of Rosenzweig's *The Star of Redemption* is that the life of the Jew is penetrated by radical alterity, out-of-jointness, and is characterized by internal alienness. The Torah demands, according to Rosenzweig, that Jews be open to other human beings and be always conscious of the implication of differences, the uncanny strangeness of the Other in the *midst of life*. This is the responsibility that comes with the enigma/singularity of election. The life of the Jewish nationality is not fully captured by the generic predicates of other historical peoples, but by a gap or excess in the series of predicates that normally distinguish historical peoples. In fact, the Jewish collective self (or metahistorical destiny) appears to be like the metaethical selfhood, $B=B$.[30] The final form of split that I want to point out is the one Rosenzweig identifies in God. His interpretation of the Shekhina presents God as split.

> The Shekhina, God's descent upon man and his sojourn among men, is pictured [thought of] as a dichotomy [separation, cut] taking place in God himself. God himself separates himself from himself, he gives himself away to his people, he shares in their sufferings, sets forth with in agony of exile, joins their wanderings.[31]

Given all this, is it not conceivable that behind the notion of a split God or the inflection of thought that led to it are the ideas of the pentecostal variant of metaethical selfhood, historical destiny (which is not a displacement or replacement of the metahistorical destiny of the Jews), and belief that God is still willing and does suffer with human beings? In Pentecostalism the Holy Spirit may be functioning in some respect as, or has somewhat subsumed, the idealization or conceptualization of the Shekhina. As Jürgen Moltmann puts it, "The idea of the Shekinah points towards the *kenosis of the Spirit*, God renounces his impassibility and becomes able to suffer because he is willing to love."[32]

There are readers who will not accept the pentecostal notion of a split God and its link to God's renunciation of his impassibility and to Pentecostals' thirst for the (near) palpable God's presence (real presence, some Shekhina presence) because for these readers it would be tantamount to accepting as "true" many other things they despise about Pentecostalism. What can I say? In the words of the priest at the end of a long conversation with Josef K. in Franz Kafka's *The Trial*, let me say to them, "It is not necessary to accept everything as true, one must only accept it [notion of a split God] as necessary."[33]

At last, we have come to our fourth and final illustrative example. I demonstrated in chapter 1 how tongues-speech not only ends up in symbolic castration (the entrance of the speaker into the symbolic network of society, which displaces, constrains, tames, or neutralizes the impossible-Real in/that is glossolalia), but also demands the tearing down of historical-cultural predicates in relating to God. The former I called interpreted glossolalia and the latter form I called noninterpreted glossolalia (the empty "Speak up"). Here we want to only focus on the symbolic castration as a form of *seduction*, as an incorporation into the symbolic network that creates internal ethical conflicts or internal alienness in the pentecostal subject. In another version of Laplanche and Santner's conception of *seduction*, I want to suggest that the incorporation of glossolalia into the domain of language normativity, into socio-symbolic affirmation, is a form of *seduction*.[34]

The translation or incorporation is immediately a sort of summoning forth (*ex-citation*) from the past and *throwness* into the world (1 John 2:16) and overproximity to desire of the divine Other.[35] When glossolalia is translated and you say the Spirit tells you this, what does the Spirit want? God has spoken once; twice the faithful, disciplined believer must hear. The congregation or the person needs to respond to the *ex-citation*, "calling out" of the interpreted language, an enigma of the divine Other's desire. So the person who feels concerned sets out to translate this enigmatic desire or message. This round of translation, which arrives at some sort of determinate demands, often allows for meaningful negotiation with the enigmatic message. The negotiation puts the person both inside and outside the symbolic network.

The point I want to make is that the distinction between glossolalia (hot from the mouth of the speaker) and interpreted glossolalia is not simply horizontal, a difference between inscription/subjection into the symbolic network or not. There is also a "vertical" distinction between the two ways the same believer can be interpellated. On one level of the divine desire, the individual recognizes herself as a part within God's totality in the name of which she has been called forth. While on the level of the symbolic network, she is encouraged to "contract" from the interpellation of God's totality, to have affective attachment to the symbolic network as a kind of obscene supplement to the divine interpellation.[36] The "call" of the "Big Other" of society that gave "voice" or intelligibility to the glossolalia sets up a struggle between the $B=A$ (God's totality) and $B=B$, which resists the impact of the divine voice.[37]

All this suggests that the incorporation of glossolalia into the sociosymbolic relations may also encourage transgressive enjoyment of what that wider world has to offer, or, at least, a "transgressive enjoyment structured in fantasy."[38] The incorporation may, on a general note, be a (secret) symbolic "getting off" point on the enigmatic traumatic demands of a Spirit-filled life. We might say, then, "getting into" a Spirit-filled life includes a dimension of "getting off," a (promise of) normative reentrance to society. This is the tension or split in everyday life: subjection and *seduction*.[39] Every Pentecostal is in herself dislocated. Alterity or uncanny strangeness, as we noted earlier, is immanent to the construction of pentecostal identity. There is always a surplus charge that comes from within the life of the pentecostal subject and from his or her wider social and cultural contexts. This is the theological excess, religious too-muchness that informs everyday life of Pentecostals as a result of the notion of a split God. This excess may be a source of the microtheological aggressions and microtheological affirmations Pentecostals display in everyday life as they interact with others in wider contexts. Microtheological analysis can, as we saw in chapter 7, help not only to investigate how to deflect microaggressions, but also help us to decipher how to use microaffirmations in interactional situations to foster moral solidarity and trust.

Notes

Preface

1. This way of phrasing my thought was inspired by Katerina Kolozova, *Toward a Radical Metaphysics of Socialism: Marx and Laruelle* (Brooklyn: Punctum Books, 2015), 13.

2. Daniel Olukoya, *Prayer Passport to Crush Oppression* (Lagos: Mountain of Fire and Miracles Ministries Press, 2006).

3. Slavoj Žižek, *Organs without Bodies: On Deleuze and Consequences* (New York: Routledge, 2004), 172.

4. About subjectivity, Hegel states in *Jenaer Realphilosophie* (1805–1806): "The human being is this night, this empty nothing, that contains everything in its simplicity—an unending wealth of many representations, images, of which none belongs to him—or which are not present. This night, the interior of nature, that exists here—pure self—in phantasmagorical representations, is night all around it, in which here shoots a bloody head—there another white ghastly apparition, suddenly here before it, and just so disappears. One catches sight of this night when one looks human beings in the eye—into a night that becomes awful." Donald Phillip Verene, *Hegel's Recollection: A Study of Images in the Phenomenology of Spirit* (Albany: State University of New York Press, 1985), 7–8. On the power of understanding, he writes: "That an accident as such, detached from what circumscribes it, what is bound and is actual only in its context with others, should attain an existence of its own and a separate freedom—this is the tremendous power of the negative." G. W. F. Hegel, *Phenomenology of Spirit*, trans. A. V. Miller (Oxford: Oxford University Press, 1977), 19.

5. Jean-Luc Nancy, *Being Singular Plural*, trans. Robert D. Richardson and Anne E. O'Byrne (Stanford: Stanford University Press, 2000), 37.

6. The split God is a product of Pentecostal *productive imagination*, as Kant is wont to put it. The scriptural or orthodox idea of God is their basic, universal category of understanding; everyday practices constitute the particular data of experience or sensation, and imagination operating at the border of these two schematizes them. Here imagination, under the pressure of sensations and

sensual desires, reorganizes or refigures an already synthetic knowledge of God and the outcome is a split God, arbitrary figures of productive imagination. God is at once more than and one with Power-God, Hand-God, or Glory-God. In the imagination of Pentecostals, God appears to have been transformed from a centralized communion of three hypostases to a decentralized network of partial organs defined, differentiated, and distributed by deeds. With desire rather than repressive hermeneutic or orthodoxy driving the figuration of the divine, God becomes deed or autonomous images of deeds. God is what God does for me (us). God is defined through his deeds as perceived in the concrete lives of individuals or, in different terms, deed precedes essence. Essence has collapsed into deeds; the signified has collapsed into the signifiers. Deeds are by nature split. A deed is self-divided between the action and its trace, the agent and her act, the action and its limit, antecedent productive will and its exterior form, representation, realization, or the deed and its arbitrary count-as-one. Indeed, the Pentecostal notion of a split God does not oppose the orthodox notion of God; it only exposes a caesura or "night of the world" in it when it collides (colludes) with lived experiences of a certain class of believers.

7. In one sense this statement could be interpreted as the worship of "gods" in God, or the loss of God in God's ownmost-gods. Is this very peculiar to Pentecostalism? Jean-Luc Nancy once wrote: "Judaism is an atheism with God. Protestantism, on the other hand, is a theism without God. Catholicism is the worship of all gods in God, or the loss of God in all gods. Islam is the pure proclamation of God to the point where it becomes an empty clamor. Buddhism is the worship of God in all gods or the loss of all gods in God." See Jean-Luc Nancy, *The Inoperative Community*, trans. Peter Connor, Lisa Garbus, Michael Holland, and Simona Sawhney, foreword Christopher Fynsk (Minneapolis: University of Minnesota Press, 1991), 128.

8. G. K. Chesterton, *Orthodoxy* (San Francisco: Ignatius Press, 1995), 145.

9. This paragraph is inspired by Slavoj Žižek, *The Indivisible Remainder: On Schelling and Related Matters* (London: Verso, 2007), 57–59, and F. W. J. Schelling, *Philosophical Investigations into the Essence of Human Freedom*, trans. Jeff Love and Johannes Schmidt (Albany: State University of New York Press, 2006). Schelling writes:

> The principle raised up from the ground of nature whereby man is separated from God is the selfhood in him which, however, through its unity with the ideal principle, becomes *spirit*. Selfhood *as* such is spirit; or man is spirit as a selfish [*selbstisch*], particular being (separated from God)—precisely this connection constitutes personality. Since selfhood is spirit, however, it is at that same time raised from the creaturely into what is above the creaturely; it is will that

beholds itself in complete freedom, being no longer an instrument of the productive [*schaffenden*] universal will in nature, but rather above and outside of all nature. Spirit is above the light as in nature it raises itself above the unity of the light and the dark principle. Since it is spirit, selfhood is therefore free from both principles. (33)

10. On this point see Nimi Wariboko, *Nigerian Pentecostalism* (Rochester: University of Rochester Press, 2014).

11. Slavoj Žižek, "The Abyss of Freedom," in F. W. J. Schelling, *Abyss of Freedom/Ages of the World* (Second Draft, 1813), trans. Judith Norman (Ann Arbor: University of Michigan Press, 1997), 58.

12. Birgit Meyer, "Aesthetics of Persuasion: Global Christianity and Pentecostalism's Sensational Forms," *South Atlantic Quarterly* 109, no. 4 (2010): 741-63.

13. The analysis in this paragraph was inspired by Žižek, "Abyss of Freedom," 62.

14. See Schelling, *Philosophical Investigations*, and Schelling, *Abyss of Freedom/Ages of the World*.

15. Slavoj Žižek, *The Puppet and the Dwarf: The Perverse Core of Christianity* (Cambridge: MIT Press, 2003), 87.

16. Is the split God not an unexpected or (il)logical fallout of a *strong-force* God, marked by the logic or metaphysics of omnipotence and divine interventionism, to use the language of John Caputo? Since God is the strongest force of all and every aspect/dimension of God's self is absolutely the same, then fractals of the Godself can be variously deployed in an extravagant display of divine omnipotence without the loss of Godliness or Godhood. While this view of the split God locates it within *strong theology* with its fantasy of divine power, we should add that the Pentecostal notion of split also gestures to a certain hermeneutic of the desire for God that refuses to contain or close off the *name* of God as a totalized entity, but strives to affirm the name as an *event*. In this latter sense, the notion of split God is the (ambiguous) symbol or poetics of Pentecostals' passion for power and natality. John Caputo, *The Weakness of God: A Theology of Event* (Bloomington: Indiana University Press, 2006).

17. Slavoj Žižek, *The Sublime Object of Ideology* (London: Verso, 2008), 241-44.

18. The adjective *ordinary* is used here to designate everyday form of practice, lived pentecostal practice, rather than academic theology. What matters here is not superiority/exceptionality versus low class or humbug, but the praxis/theory distinction. Though I bring critical theory as a frame of reference to interpret an everyday form of theology from lived pentecostal practices, this should not be construed to mean ordinary Pentecostals will stop being "ordinary" when they start to think philosophically. The distinction between academic Pentecostals

and ordinary Pentecostals is based on a praxis/theory distinction that serves to underwrite my appropriation of critical theory, which easily lends itself to deep appreciation of the truths of pentecostal praxis.

19. Wariboko, *Nigerian Pentecostalism*.

20. Ebenezer Obadare, "The Spirit of Yoruba Liberalism," *Marginalia*, February 16, 2017: http://marginalia.lareviewofbooks.org/spirit-yoruba-liberalism/, accessed February 17, 2017.

Introduction

1. Slavoj Žižek, *The Monstrosity of Christ* (Cambridge: MIT Press Verso, 2009), 59.

2. Nimi Wariboko, *Nigerian Pentecostalism* (Rochester: University of Rochester Press, 2014).

3. Slavoj Žižek, *The Puppet and the Dwarf: The Perverse Core of Christianity* (Cambridge: MIT Press, 2003), 125–26.

4. Giorgio Agamben, *Nudities*, trans. David Kishik and Stefan Pedatella (Stanford: Stanford University Press, 2011), 102.

5. Agon Hamza, "A Plea for Žižekian Politics," in *Repeating Žižek*, ed. Agon Hamza (Durham: Duke University Press, 2015), 235.

6. Here I have played around with Alfred Sohn-Rethel's words in his *Intellectual and Manual Labor: A Critique of Epistemology*, trans. Martin Sohn-Rethel (London: Macmillan, 1978), 20.

7. The two quotes are from Slavoj Žižek, *The Parallax View* (Cambridge: MIT Press, 2009), 17.

8. Adrian Johnson, *Žižek's Ontology: A Transcendental Materialist Theory of Subjectivity* (Evanston: Northwestern University Press, 2008), 166.

9. Jean-Luc Nancy, *The Inoperative Community*, trans. Peter Connor, Lisa Garbus, Michael Holland, and Simona Sawhney, foreword Christopher Fynsk (Minneapolis: University of Minnesota Press, 1991), 19.

10. Nancy, *Inoperative Community*, xxxvii.

11. I have adapted Jean-Luc Nancy's words for my purposes here. See Nancy, *Inoperative Community*, 30.

12. I have adapted the words of Slavoj Žižek, *Less Than Nothing: Hegel and the Shadow of Dialectical Materialism* (London: Verso, 2012), 267.

13. The quotes are from Žižek, *Less Than Nothing*, 267.

14. My thinking and some of my words here draw from Žižek, *Less Than Nothing*, 267, 280–81.

15. Slavoj Žižek, *Organs without Bodies: On Deleuze and Consequences* (New York: Routledge, 2012), 12.

16. Adrian Johnson, "'Freedom or System? Yes, Please': How to Read Slavoj Žižek's *Less Than Nothing: Hegel and the Shadow of Dialectical Materialism*," in Hamza, *Repeating Žižek*, 18.

17. Gavin Walker, "Žižek and Marx: Outside in the Critique of Political Economy," in Hamza, *Repeating Žižek*, 197, inspired this train of thought.

18. Adam Kotsko, "The Problem of Christianity and Žižek's 'Middle Period,'" in Hamza, *Repeating Žižek*, 245-48, and Sead Zimeri, "Islam: How Could It Have Emerged after Christianity?," in Hamza, *Repeating Žižek*, 257-58, inspired this thought.

19. Frank Ruda, "How to Repeat Plato: For a Platonism of the Non-All," in Hamza, *Repeating Žižek*, 47.

20. See Johnson, "'Freedom or System?,'" in Hamza, *Repeating Žižek*, 19.

21. Virginia Burrus, "The Heretical Woman as Symbol in Athanasius, Epiphanius and Jerome," *Harvard Theological Review* 84, no. 3 (1991): 232, quoted in Harvey Cox, *Fire from Heaven: The Rise of Pentecostal Spirituality and the Reshaping of Religion in the Twenty-First Century* (Reading: Addison-Wesley, 1995), 328.

22. Jacques Derrida, *Positions*, trans. Alan Bass (Chicago: University of Chicago Press, 1982), 71.

23. Gerhard Richter, *Thought Images: Frankfurt School Writers' Reflections from Damaged Life* (Stanford: Stanford University Press, 2007), 1.

24. Paul Tillich, *The Protestant Era* (Chicago: University of Chicago Press, 1948), 75.

25. Richard McNemar, "The Mole's Little Pathways," in Nathan Hatch, *The Democratization of American Christianity* (New Haven: Yale University Press, 1989), 81.

26. For a discussion of the expressionists and impressionist pictures of Jesus Christ in a different context, see Terry Cross, "Tillich's Picture of Jesus as the Christ: Toward a Theology of the Spirit's Saving Presence," in Nimi Wariboko and Amos Yong, *Paul Tillich and Pentecostal Theology: Spiritual Presence and Spiritual Power* (Bloomington: Indiana University Press, 2015), 71-83.

27. Lee Smolin, *The Trouble with Physics: The Rise of String Theory, the Fall of a Science, and What Comes Next* (Boston: Houghton Mifflin, 2006), 15-16.

28. Žižek, *Less Than Nothing*, 166.

29. Ruth Marshall, *Political Spiritualities: The Pentecostal Revolution in Nigeria* (Chicago: University of Chicago Press, 2009), 213.

30. Nimi Wariboko, *The Pentecostal Principle: Ethical Methodology in New Spirit* (Grand Rapids: Eerdmans, 2012), 151-54.

31. Carl Raschke, "The Monstrosity of Žižek's Christ," *Journal of Cultural and Religious Theory* 11, no. 2 (2011): 11-20, 16.

32. Hatch, *Democratization of American Christianity*, 65.

Chapter 1

1. Mark C. Taylor, *Altarity* (Chicago: University of Chicago Press, 1987), 101, inspired this series of thought.

2. Taylor, *Altarity*, 168.

3. Taylor, *Altarity*, 54–55.

4. Anne Norton, "Pentecost: Democratic Sovereignty in Carl Schmitt," *Constellations* 18, no. 3 (2011): 393–94.

5. Norton, "Pentecost," 397.

6. Martin Heidegger, *Poetry, Language, Thought*, trans. Albert Hofstadter (New York: Harper and Row, 1971), 202, quoted in Taylor, *Altarity*, 43–44.

7. Mark C. Taylor, *About Religion: Economics of Faith in Virtual Culture* (Chicago: University of Chicago Press, 1999), 40–42, inspired this section.

8. Taylor, *About Religion*, 42–43.

9. The traditional pentecostal interpretation is that the languages the disciples spoke in Acts 2 were foreign, strange to them. A disciple spoke a language he or she did not previously know how to speak before the pouring out of the gifts of the Spirit. The belief is that the Spirit supernaturally endowed the disciples with a new capability to speak new languages they had not learned in the past. This perspective implies three things: the disciples did not cognitively understand their own utterances; if they did, then they also had the spiritual capability to understand what was coming out of their animated mouths; and they spoke a kind of unintelligible language, but each member of the audience experienced the miracle of hearing the disciples in his or her native/particular language. There are a few Pentecostals who champion the third option, but a majority of them tend to lean toward the first option given their experiences with glossolalia. With the gift of glossolalia persons speaking in tongues do not often understand what they are saying, except in cases where they also receive the gift of translation or another person is spiritually endowed to understand their utterances and interpret the words pouring out of their mouths. In all options, the starting point for analysis of Pentecostals is that the disciples, at least initially, did not know or understand what they were saying. See Frank D. Macchia, "Glossolalia," in *Encyclopedia of Pentecostal and Charismatic Christianity*, ed. Stanley M. Burgess, 223–35 (New York: Routledge, 2006).

10. Jacques Lacan, *The Ethics of Psychoanalysis 1959–1960*, bk. 7, of *The Seminar of Jacques Lacan*, ed. Jacques-Alain Miller, trans. Dennis Potter (New York: Norton, 1992); see also Slavoj Žižek, *In Defense of Lost Causes* (London: Verso, 2009), 89.

11. Jacques Lacan, *The Four Fundamental Concepts of Psycho-Analysis*, ed. Jacques-Alain Miller, trans. Alan Sheridan (New York: Norton, 1977); see also Clayton Crockett, *Interstices of the Sublime: Theology and Psychoanalytic Theory* (New York: Fordham University Press, 2007).

12. Slavoj Žižek, *The Puppet and the Dwarf: The Perverse Core of Christianity* (Cambridge: MIT Press, 2003), 112.
13. Giorgio Agamben, *The Time That Remains: A Commentary on the Letter to the Romans* (Stanford: Stanford University Press, 2005), 95, 137.
14. Agamben, *Time That Remains*, 23.
15. Agamben, *Time That Remains*, 23.
16. Agamben, *Time That Remains*, 26.
17. Agamben, *Time That Remains*, 124.
18. Slavoj Žižek, *The Indivisible Remainder: On Schelling and Related Matters* (London: Verso, 2007), 169.
19. Robin Horton, *Patterns of Thought in Africa and the West: Essays on Magic, Religion and Science* (Cambridge: Cambridge University Press, 1993), 25.
20. Horton, *Patterns of Thought*, 25–26.
21. F. W. J. Schelling, *Abyss of Freedom/Ages of the World* (Second Draft, 1813), trans. Judith Norman (Ann Arbor: University of Michigan Press, 1997). In this section of the chapter, I am going to combine my reading of the second and third drafts of Schelling's *Ages of the World* and Žižek's interpretation of the second draft to provide a succinct summary of its main ideas as they bear on our purpose here.
22. Andrew Bowie, *Schelling and Modern European Philosophy* (New York: Routledge, 1993), 105, quoted in Žižek, *Indivisible Remainder*, 37.
23. Slavoj Žižek, "Abyss of Freedom," in Schelling, *Abyss of Freedom/Ages of the World*, 17.
24. Žižek, "Abyss of Freedom," 30.
25. Žižek, *Indivisible Remainder*, 71.
26. Schelling, *Abyss of Freedom/Ages of the World*, 181–82.
27. Žižek, *Indivisible Remainder*, 72.
28. F. W. J. Schelling, *Philosophical Investigations into the Essence of Human Freedom*, trans. Jeff Love and Johannes Schmidt (Albany: State University of New York Press, 2006), 31–34; see also 36–37.
29. This is how Žižek explains this Schellingian point: "The Good always involves a harmonious unity of sensual and spiritual—it is a Spirit which penetrates and illuminates nature from within and without forcing itself upon it, renders it ethereal, deprives it of its impenetrable inertia; whereas true 'diabolical' Evil is a pale, bloodless, fanatical spiritualism which despises sensuality and is bent on violently dominating and exploiting it. The diabolical spiritualism, a perversion of the true spirituality, is the obscure Ground which has 'attained itself,' its selfhood—that is to say, has reached the Light and posited itself as such." *Indivisible Remainder*, 69.
30. For Schelling, evil is attributable to the split itself in the Absolute between ground and existence. But the fact that creation exists attests that good (expansion) prevails over evil (contraction). Since God has his power of the center

in himself and his nature is perfect, God always uses his freedom to choose the good. See his *Philosophical Investigations*; also see Žižek, *Indivisible Remainder*, 66–67.

31. Žižek, "Abyss of Freedom," 15.

32. Žižek, "Abyss of Freedom," 15.

33. Immanuel Kant, *Critique of Practical Reason* (New York: Macmillan, 1956), 152–53.

34. Adrian Johnson, *Žižek's Ontology: A Transcendental Materialist Theory of Subjectivity* (Evanston: Northwestern University Press, 2008), 208.

35. Paul Tillich, *Systematic Theology, Volume 1: Reason and Revelation, Being and God* (Chicago: University of Chicago Press, 1951), 16–17, 221–30; Paul Tillich, *Systematic Theology, Volume 3: Life and the Spirit, History and the Kingdom of God* (Chicago: University of Chicago Press, 1965), 283–94.

36. Tillich, *Systematic Theology*, 1:221, 228.

37. Tillich, *Systematic Theology*, 1:16–17, 221–30; *Systematic Theology*, 3:283–94.

38. Crockett, *Interstices of the Sublime*, 92.

39. Giorgio Agamben, *The Kingdom and the Glory: For a Theological Genealogy of Economy and Government*, trans. Lorenzo Chiesa with Matteo Mandarini (Stanford: Stanford University Press, 2011).

40. Agamben, *Kingdom and the Glory*, 207–11, 221, 230.

41. Agamben, *Kingdom and the Glory*, 242–43, 230.

42. Agamben, *Kingdom and the Glory*, 230.

43. Agamben, *Kingdom and the Glory*, 198–202.

44. Agamben, *Kingdom and the Glory*, 208.

45. Moses Maimonides, *Guide to the Perplexed* (Chicago: University of Chicago Press, 2010), bk. 1, chap. 64, 156–57; see also Agamben, *Kingdom and the Glory*, 198–99.

46. Agamben, *Kingdom and the Glory*, 211.

47. For inoperativity that comes at the eschaton, that is, postjudicial inoperativity, see Agamben, *Kingdom and the Glory*, 239–42, 245.

48. Giorgio Agamben, *Nudities*, trans. David Kishik and Stefan Pedatella (Stanford: Stanford University Press, 2011), 98; see also William Robert, "Nude, Glorious, Living," *Political Theology* 14, no. 1 (2013): 123.

49. Agamben, *Nudities*, 111.

50. Robert, "Nude, Glorious, Living," 123.

51. Eric L. Mascall, "Primauté de la louange," in *Dieu vivant* 19 (1951), quoted in Agamben, *Kingdom and the Glory*, 220. I am relying on Agamben's interpretation here.

52. Mascall, "Primauté," 112, quoted in Agamben, *Kingdom and the Glory*, 220.

53. Mascall, "Primauté," 114, quoted in Agamben, *Kingdom and the Glory*, 220.

54. Agamben, *Kingdom and the Glory*, 220–21.
55. Agamben, *Kingdom and the Glory*, 248–49.
56. Agamben, *Kingdom and the Glory*, 248–49.
57. This sentence should not be interpreted as suggesting that there are only two options available theologically, namely, a strict classical theism or a split-God model that contains contradictions. A wide variety of options exists between these two extremes, for example, open theism and even some versions of process theology. Once we take seriously the pentecostal notions of God at the grassroots level, we will discover that these notions are contesting the boundaries of classical theism that official pentecostal theologians or preachers argue embeds the pentecostal doctrine of God. Or at least they will be forced to look for other models of God outside classical theology that best fit what Pentecostals are doing on the ground. Thus, to reiterate, I am not writing as if these are the only available theologies. Rather, I have only analyzed and described everyday pentecostal practices in ways that will show how ordinary Pentecostals (knowingly or unknowingly) do not limit themselves to classical theism and that in some respects their views of God make common cause with open theism and process theology.
58. Slavoj Žižek, *The Sublime Object of Ideology* (London: Verso, 2008), 42–43.

Chapter 2

1. Jean-Pierre Vernant, *Mortals and Immortals: Collected Essays* (Princeton: Princeton University Press, 1991), 141.
2. Nimi Wariboko, *God and Money: A Theology of Money in a Globalizing World* (Lanham: Lexington Books, 2008), 99–105.
3. Robin Horton, *Patterns of Thought in Africa and the West: Essays on Magic, Religion and Science* (Cambridge: Cambridge University Press, 1993).
4. Horton, *Patterns of Thought*, 207–10.
5. Here I am going to adapt Richard Fenn's theory of religion as elucidated in his "Sociology and Religion: Searching for the Sacred," in *The Oxford Handbook of Religion and Science*, ed. Philip Clayton and Zachary Simpson (Oxford: Oxford University Press, 2006), 253–70.
6. Fenn, "Sociology and Religion," 258.
7. Fenn, "Sociology and Religion," 259.
8. G. W. F. Hegel, *Jenenser Philosophie des Geistes* in *Sämtliche Werke*, ed. Johannes Hoffmeister (Leipzig: Felix Meiner, 1931), 20:180–81, quoted in Georges Bataille, *The Bataille Reader*, ed. Fred Botting and Scott Wilson (Oxford: Blackwell, 1997), 279.
9. See Nimi Wariboko, *Ethics and Time: Ethos of Temporal Orientation in Politics and Religion of the Niger Delta* (Lanham: Lexington Books, 2010), 47–48; Nimi Wariboko, *The Depth and Destiny of Work: An African Theological Interpretation* (Trenton: Africa World Press, 2008), 38–39.

10. It is important for me to state at this juncture that my move to link African Pentecostals' view of or approach to discernment by starting from local ATR practices should not be construed to mean that these features are peculiar to ATR or African Pentecostalism rather than as broadly shared features of Pentecostalism in other parts of the world. Second, Pentecostals' appropriation of the ATR is both a continuity of the past and a rupture.

11. See Nimi Wariboko, *Nigerian Pentecostalism* (Rochester: University of Rochester Press, 2014).

12. Kevin Madigan and Jon D. Levenson, *Resurrection: The Power of God for Christians and Jews* (New Haven: Yale University Press, 2008), 22.

13. Nimi Wariboko, *The Pentecostal Principle: Ethical Methodology in New Spirit* (Grand Rapids: Eerdmans, 2012), 19–35.

14. Jean-Luc Nancy and Federico Ferrari, *Being Nude: The Skin of Images*, trans. Anne O'Byrne and Carlie Anglemire (New York: Fordham University Press, 2014), 33.

15. See Giorgio Agamben, *Nudities*, trans. David Kishik and Stefan Pedatella (Stanford: Stanford University Press, 2011), 1–2; Amos Yong, "Spiritual Discernment: A Biblical-Theological Reconsideration," in *The Spirit and Spirituality: Essays in Honor of Russell P. Spittler*, ed. Wonsuk Ma and Robert P. Menzies (London: T. and T. Clark, 2004), 84–101.

16. Here I have adapted Martha Nussbaum's description of the pupils for my purposes. See her *The Fragility of Goodness: Luck and Ethics in Greek Tragedy and Philosophy* (Cambridge: Cambridge University Press, 2007), 412.

17. Agamben, *Nudities*, 57–90.

18. Emmanuel Levinas, *Totality and Infinity*, trans. Alphonso Lingis (Pittsburgh: Duquesne University Press, 1961), 61, 170.

19. Erik Peterson, "Theology of Clothes," in *Selection*, ed. C. Hasting and D. Nichol (London: Sheed and Ward, 1954), 2:56–57, quoted in Agamben, *Nudities*, 64.

20. Agamben, *Nudities*, 102.

Chapter 3

1. Nimi Wariboko, *The Depth and Destiny of Work: An African Theological Interpretation* (Trenton: Africa World, 2008), 4–14, 233–38.

2. I have reworked Albino Barrera's phrasing for my purpose here. See his *God and the Evil of Scarcity: Moral Foundations of Economic Agency* (Notre Dame: University of Notre Dame Press, 2005), 219.

3. Annalisa Butticci, *African Pentecostals in Catholic Europe: The Politics of Presence in the Twenty-First Century* (Cambridge: Harvard University Press, 2016).

4. Mark C. Taylor and Carl Raschke, "About *About Religion*: A Conversation with Mark C. Taylor," accessed June 14, 2015, http://www.jcrt.org/archives/02.2/taylor_raschke.shtml, 3.

5. Slavoj Žižek, *Event: A Philosophical Journey Through a Concept* (London: Penguin Books, 2014), 133–34.
6. Slavoj Žižek, *The Most Sublime Hysteric: Hegel with Lacan*, trans. Thomas Scott-Railton (Malden: Polity Press, 2014), 43.
7. Slavoj Žižek, *Absolute Recoil: Towards a New Foundation of Dialectical Materialism* (London: Verso, 2014), 20.
8. F. W. J. Schelling, *Philosophical Investigations into the Essence of Human Freedom*, trans. Jeff Love and Johannes Schmidt (Albany: State University of New York Press, 2006), 51–52.
9. Hegel's words as quoted in Žižek, *Event*, 128.
10. Žižek, *Absolute Recoil*, 168.
11. G. W. F., Hegel, *Phenomenology of Spirit*, trans. A. V. Miller (Oxford: Oxford University Press, 1977), 89.
12. Adrian Johnson, "'Freedom or System? Yes, Please': How to Read Slavoj Žižek's *Less Than Nothing: Hegel and the Shadow of Dialectical Materialism*," in *Repeating Žižek*, ed. Agon Hamza (Durham: Duke University Press, 2015), 24.
13. Slavoj Žižek, *Less Than Nothing: Hegel and the Shadow of Dialectical Materialism* (London: Verso, 2012), 37.
14. Žižek, *Less Than Nothing*, 144.
15. Ruth Marshall, *Political Spiritualities: The Pentecostal Revolution in Nigeria* (Chicago: University of Chicago Press, 2009), 190–93, 212–14.
16. Afe Adogame, *The African Christian Diaspora: New Currents and Emerging Trends in World Christianity* (London: Bloomsbury Academic, 2013).
17. Adogame, *African Christian Diaspora*, 22.
18. Chinua Achebe, *Things Fall Apart* (New York: Anchor Books, 1994), 22.
19. According to Italian sociologist Annalisa Butticci, "Na God," a common pidgin English expression in West Africa, captures the sense of awe.

> *Na God* is an expression in West African Pidgin English that means "It is God." When people unexpectedly hear good news, experience a miracle, receive a gift, or when something right or remarkable happens, that is when we might hear Nigerians and Ghanaians say "Na God." This expression is much more than a mere exclamation; it is part of a way of experiencing the world, acknowledging the presence of the supernatural powers, and communicating and mediating experiences of daily life. *Na God* is part of the aesthetics with which African Pentecostals reiterate their link with God and with their community.

Annalisa Butticci, introduction to *Na God: Aesthetics of African Charismatic Power*, ed. Annalisa Butticci (Rubano: Grafiche Turato Edizioni, 2013), 6.

Chapter 4

1. Richard Fenn, *Key Thinkers in the Sociology of Religion* (London: Continuum, 2009), 1–4. This rendition of what I think Pentecostals mean by miracle benefited from my understanding of Fenn's concept of the sacred.

2. Richard Fenn, "Sociology and Religion: Searching for the Sacred," in *The Oxford Handbook of Religion and Science*, ed. Philip Clayton and Zachary Simpson (Oxford: Oxford University Press, 2006), 259; italics in the original.

3. Nimi Wariboko, *The Depth and Destiny of Work: An African Theological Interpretation* (Trenton: Africa World Press, 2008), 37–39.

4. *Agu-nsi* is an Igbo word that has been adopted in Kalabari. The Kalabari word for carved or sculptured idol is *ẹkẹkẹ-tamụnọ*, and *ẹkẹkẹ* means stone, piece of stone, or rock.

5. Robin Horton, *Kalabari Sculpture* (Lagos: Department of Antiquities, Federal Republic of Nigeria, 1965), 8–9; see also Robin Horton, "The Kalabari Worldview: An Outline and Interpretation," *Africa* 32, no. 3 (July 1962): 204. Horton relates the story of how a spirit who misbehaved was summoned before an assembly of its worshipers, found guilty, and fined. Robin Horton, "A Hundred Years of Change in Kalabari Religion," in *Black Africa: Its People and Their Cultures Today*, ed. John Middleton (New York: Macmillan, 1971), 194–98.

6. Horton, "Kalabari Worldview," 204. I have heard of at least two cases of gods that have been disrobed of their powers. One is the *Owu Akpana* (shark) cult and the other is *Ogboloma* (called *Kun-ma* in Okrika, also a Niger Delta community) cult.

7. Richard Fenn, *The Return of the Primitive: A New Sociological Theory of Religion* (Aldershot: Ashgate, 2001), 59.

8. Fenn, *Return of the Primitive*, 60.

9. Fenn, *Return of the Primitive*, 60.

10. Portions of this section bear repeating from chapter 2.

11. From hereon I am going to adapt Richard Fenn's theory of religion as elucidated in his "Sociology and Religion," 253–70.

12. Fenn, "Sociology and Religion," 258.

13. Fenn, "Sociology and Religion," 259.

14. Fenn, "Sociology and Religion," 257–58.

15. If a person does not like the course of her life on earth, she goes to a diviner to change her *so* or *fiyeteboye*. The process of changing destiny is called *bibibari* (altering or nullifying the spoken word, recanting). The person visits a diviner to let *Teme-órú* (the supreme goddess) know that the person would like to change how he or she wants to live his or her life course on earth. Once the change of destiny is effected, the new *so* (which becomes a new point of fixity) determines the whole course of the person.

16. Slavoj Žižek, *Event: A Philosophical Journey through a Concept* (London: Penguin Books, 2014), 128.

17. Slavoj Žižek, *The Most Sublime Hysteric: Hegel with Lacan*, trans. Thomas Scott-Railton (Malden: Polity Press, 2014), 157.

18. I have borrowed the term *mindful ignorance* (*docta ignorantia*) from Catherine Keller. See her *Cloud of the Impossible: Negative Theology and Planetary Entanglement* (New York: Columbia University Press, 2014), 165. By the term, Keller, relying on Nicholas Cusa, refers to "not only the maximum mystery but the misty unknowns of all relations." See Catherine Keller, "The Entangled Cosmos: An Experiment in Physical Theopoetics," *Journal of Cosmology* (September 2012): 2.

19. Slavoj Žižek, *The Fragile Absolute: Or, Why Is the Christianity Legacy Worth Fighting For?* (London: Verso, 2008), 89.

20. Jacques Lacan, *The Ego in Freud's Theory and in the Technique of Psychoanalysis 1954–1955*, bk. 2, of *The Seminar of Jacques Lacan*, ed. Jacques-Alain Miller, trans. Sylvana Tomaselli (New York: W. W. Norton, 1991), 229, quoted in Žižek, *Most Sublime Hysteric*, 64.

21. Slavoj Žižek, "Christianity Against the Sacred," in Slavoj Žižek and Boris Gunjević, *God in Pain: Inversions of Apocalypse* (New York: Seven Stories Press, 2012), 58.

22. This sentence was inspired by Slavoj Žižek, *The Parallax View* (Cambridge: MIT Press, 2009), 67.

23. G. W. F. Hegel, *Elements of the Philosophy of Right* (Cambridge: Cambridge University Press, 1991), 204–5, quoted in Žižek, *Parallax View*, 66.

24. Jeffrey Kripal, *Authors of the Impossible: The Paranormal and the Sacred* (Chicago: University of Chicago Press, 2010), 9.

25. Kripal, *Authors of the Impossible*, 9.

26. Mark C. Taylor and Carl Raschke, "About *About Religion*: A Conversation with Mark C. Taylor," accessed June 14, 2015, http://www.jcrt.org/archives/02.2/taylor_raschke.shtml, 2.

27. Taylor and Raschke, "About *About Religion*," 3.

28. Keller, *Cloud of the Impossible*.

29. I need to clarify this interpretation of her thinking. As a follower of Whitehead, she will agree that in abstract form possibilities do function as "external objects," but as real possibilities/potentialities, they carry the relational density of the past.

30. Keller, *Cloud of the Impossible*, 188–92, quote on 188; see also 131–32, 145, 152–53, 164–65.

31. Keller, *Cloud of the Impossible*, 145.

32. Catherine Keller, *Face of the Deep: A Theology of Becoming* (London: Routledge, 2003).

33. Catherine Keller's preferred term is *Resolute*, not the Hegelian Absolute. It is a third place between Absolute and "Dissolute." See her, *On the Mystery: Discerning God in Process* (Minneapolis: Fortress, 2008), 173–76.

34. Keller, *Cloud of the Impossible*, 146. She is citing Charles Hartshorne here.

35. Slavoj Žižek, *In Defense of Lost Causes* (London: Verso, 2009), 140.

36. Slavoj Žižek, *Absolute Recoil: Towards a New Foundation of Dialectical Materialism* (London: Verso, 2014), 33. Žižek adds, "What characterizes a really great thinker is that they misrecognize the basic dimension of their own breakthrough" (34).

37. Keller, *Cloud of the Impossible*, 17.

38. Here I am applying the distinctions of Jacques-Alain Miller, "Le nom-du-père, s'en passer, s'en servir," www.lacan.com, quoted in Žižek, *Defense of Lost Causes*, 327.

39. Žižek, *Defense of Lost Causes*, 327; see also Slavoj Žižek, *Less Than Nothing: Hegel and the Shadow of Dialectical Materialism* (London: Verso, 2012), 496.

40. Keller, *Cloud of the Impossible*, 148–50.

41. Keller, *Cloud of the Impossible*, 157.

42. The latter—no underlying oneness—more precisely represents the overall focus of her theological and philosophical thought over the years. Creativity would not be for her the One.

43. For the meaning of *en*, see Keller, *Cloud of the Impossible*, 177, 191. See also her *Face of the Deep*.

44. In (en)? As we have shown earlier, the realm of the sacred exceeds what is religiously, doctrinally, and institutionally referred to as theistic God.

45. Nimi Wariboko, *The Pentecostal Principle: Ethical Methodology in New Spirit* (Grand Rapids: Eerdmans, 2012), x, 131, 151, 186, 203.

46. See also Žižek, "Christianity Against the Sacred," 50, where he relies on Giorgio Agamben to make the same point, that the profane is inherent to the sacred.

47. Giorgio Agamben, *Profanations*, trans. Jeff Fort (New York: Zone Books, 2007), 75.

48. Quentin Meillassoux, "Potentiality and Virtuality," *Collapse: Philosophic Research and Development* 2 (2007): 71–72.

49. Meillassoux, "Potentiality and Virtuality," 74.

50. Meillassoux, "Potentiality and Virtuality," 72.

51. Meillassoux, "Potentiality and Virtuality," 73n7.

52. Žižek, *Less Than Nothing*, 230.

53. Keller, *Cloud of the Impossible*, 138–42, 150–51. She certainly understands relationalism to be largely—but never entirely—subject to regulation. This is why she argues against intervention *ex nihilo* in her work.

54. For an excellent discussion of real presence, see Annalisa Butticci, *African Pentecostals in Catholic Europe: The Politics of Presence in the Twenty-First Century* (Cambridge: Harvard University Press, 2016).

55. Gilles Deleuze, *The Logic of Sense*, trans. Mark Lester with Charles Stivale (New York: Columbia University Press, 1990).

56. Deleuze, *Logic of Sense*, 7.

57. Butticci, *African Pentecostals*.

58. Žižek, *Less Than Nothing*, 608.

59. In a different interpretation of her work, one could say that she overrides the distinction between the phenomenal and the noumenal through her focus on materiality of human relationality. The inaccessibility of *Ding an sich* is not the apophatic for her, but the depth and margin of entanglement between things may be. But yes, she does not trust anyone's claim to know the thing in itself, to master pure presence epistemically. She only respects conjectures, and vivid, transformative glimpses, breakthroughs and breakouts. But she does not respect epistemic mastery of the mystery.

60. Žižek, *Less Than Nothing*, 609.

61. Alain Badiou, *Theoretical Writings* (London: Continuum, 2004), 43.

62. Alain Badiou, *Being and Event*, trans. Oliver Feltham (London: Continuum, 2005).

63. In the language or manner of Keller's thought, we should suspect any prophet or prophetess who claims to have perceived the "full ply of possibilities" as in all of the Sacred.

64. Fenn, "Sociology and Religion," 259.

65. Meillassoux, "Potentiality and Virtuality," 67.

66. Meillassoux, "Potentiality and Virtuality," 73.

67. Meillassoux, "Potentiality and Virtuality," 69.

68. Meillassoux, "Potentiality and Virtuality," 73n7: "The virtualizing power of time, its insubordination to any superior order, lets itself be known, or is phenomenalized, when there emerges a novelty that defeats all continuity between the past and the present. Every "miracle" thus becomes the manifestation of the inexistence of God, insofar as every radical rupture of the present in relation to the past becomes the manifestation of the absence of any order capable of overseeing the chaotic power of becoming."

69. There is, perhaps, what we may call a *Pentecostal unconscious* that has deep relations to the scared as the full plenum of possibilities along with its chaotic depths. The unconscious itself has been symbolized as an ocean, an oceanic plenum.

Chapter 5

1. Slavoj Žižek, *The Most Sublime Hysteric: Hegel with Lacan*, trans. Thomas Scott-Railton (Malden: Polity Press, 2014), 23.

2. Nimi Wariboko, *Nigerian Pentecostalism* (Rochester: University of Rochester Press, 2014).

3. Žižek, *Most Sublime Hysteric*, 23.

4. For a discussion on Pentecostalism as a religion of play, see Nimi Wariboko, *The Pentecostal Principle: Ethical Methodology in New Spirit* (Grand Rapids: Eerdmans, 2012), 161–95.

5. Slavoj Žižek, *Absolute Recoil: Towards a New Foundation of Dialectical Materialism* (London: Verso, 2014), 372–73.

6. Quoted in Slavoj Žižek, *Less Than Nothing: Hegel and the Shadow of Dialectical Materialism* (London: Verso, 2012), 19.

7. Antifragility goes beyond resilience or robustness. A fragile system breaks under stress, disorders, or volatility. An antifragile system not only withstands shocks, stress, disorder, uncertainty, and volatility; it also benefits from them. Late capitalism, and more precisely finance capital, renders most persons' and institutions' lives fragile to undermine their freedom.

8. William E. Connolly, *The Fragility of Things: Self-Organizing Processes, Neoliberal Fantasies, and Democratic Activism* (Durham: Duke University Press, 2013), 31.

9. Slavoj Žižek, *The Parallax View* (Cambridge: MIT Press, 2009), 61.

10. Potentiality, as Aristotle taught us, consists of the potential to-do and the potential to not-do, which is called *impotentiality*. There is more discussion on forms of potentiality in the pages ahead.

11. Žižek, *Parallax View*, 202.

12. Giorgio Agamben, *Nudities*, trans. David Kishik and Stefan Pedatella (Stanford: Stanford University Press, 2010), 44–45.

13. Žižek, *Parallax View*, 181, 318–20.

14. William E. Connolly, *Capitalism and Christianity: American Style* (Durham: Duke University Press, 2008).

15. Nimi Wariboko, *Economics in Spirit and Truth: A Moral Philosophy of Finance* (New York: Palgrave Macmillan 2014), 19–32.

16. "Here one encounters the Lacanian difference between reality and the Real: 'reality' is the social reality of the actual people involved in interaction and in the productive processes, while the Real is the inexorable 'abstract,' spectral logic of capital that determines what goes on in social reality." Slavoj Žižek, *Violence: Six Sideways Reflections* (New York: Picador, 2008), 13.

17. Maurizio Lazzarato, *The Making of the Indebted Man* (Los Angeles: Semiotext(e), 2012), 8–9.

18. Žižek, *Parallax View*, 334.

19. Lazzarato, *Making of the Indebted Man*, 31.

20. Slavoj Žižek, *In Defense of Lost Causes* (London: Verso, 2009), 29.

21. Žižek, *Violence*, 149–50.

22. Žižek, *Violence*, 142–57, inspired this paragraph. I am indebted to his insights on capitalism.

23. Žižek, *Violence*, 7.

24. Giorgio Agamben, *Potentialities: Collected Essays in Philosophy*, ed. and trans. Daniel Heller-Roazen (Stanford: Stanford University Press, 1999).

25. Agamben, *Nudities*, 44.

26. Agamben, *Nudities*, 43–44; Agamben, *Potentialities*, 182.

27. Agamben, *Potentialities*, 182–83.
28. Žižek, *Parallax View*, 383.
29. Žižek, *Most Sublime Hysteric*, 137.
30. Agamben, *Nudities*, 44–45.
31. Dorothee Sölle, *Beyond Mere Obedience*, trans. Lawrence W. Denef (New York: Pilgrim Press, 1982).
32. Sölle, *Beyond Mere Obedience*, 51.
33. Connolly, *Capitalism and Christianity*.
34. Rey Chow, *The Protestant Ethnic and the Spirit of Capitalism* (New York: Columbia University Press, 2002), viii.
35. Chow, *Protestant Ethnic*, 111.
36. The word is used in the sense made popular by Julia Kristeva. Chow defined it as "the often culturally tabooed condition of an excessive, rejected being that nonetheless remains a challenge to the body that expels it." Chow, *Protestant Ethnic*, 147–48. According to Kristeva, "The jettisoned object, is radically excluded and draws me toward the place where meaning collapses. . . . It is something rejected from which one does not part, from which one does not protect oneself as from an object. Imaginary uncanniness and real threat, it beckons to us and ends up engulfing us. It is thus not lack of cleanliness or health that causes abjection but what disturbs identity, system, order. What does not respect borders, positions, rules. The in-between, the ambiguous, the composite." Julia Kristeva, *Powers of Horror: An Essay on Abjection*, trans. Leon S. Roudiez (New York: Columbia University Press, 1982), 2, 4, quoted in Chow, *Protestant Ethnic*, 148.
37. I have adapted Chow's phraseology to my limited purpose here. See Chow, *Protestant Ethnic*, 152.
38. Colin Campbell, *The Romantic Ethic and the Spirit of Modern Consumerism* (London: Blackwell, 1987).
39. This will be further discussed in the next chapter.
40. This way of putting the matter is informed by Slavoj Žižek, "Christianity Against the Sacred," in Slavoj Žižek and Boris Gunjević, *God in Pain: Inversions of Apocalypse* (New York: Seven Stories Press, 2012), 43–71, quote on 57–58.

Chapter 6

1. Henry Vaughan, "The World," accessed June 24, 2015, http://www.poetryfoundation.org/poem/174701.
2. Tennessee Williams, "The Timeless World of a Play," in *The Rose Tattoo* (New York: New Directions, 1951), 5.
3. Nimi Wariboko, *The Pentecostal Principle: Ethical Methodology in New Spirit* (Grand Rapids: Eerdmans, 2012).

4. Slavoj Žižek, *Less Than Nothing: Hegel and the Shadow of Dialectical Materialism* (London: Verso, 2012), 229–31.

5. I am indebted to Slavoj Žižek, "The Necessity of a Dead Bird: Paul Communism," in *Paul and the Philosophers*, ed. Ward Blanton and Hent De Vries (New York: Fordham University Press, 2013), 180–81.

6. Stathis Gourgouris, "Paul's Greek," in *Paul and the Philosophers*, ed. Ward Blanton and Hent de Vries (New York: Fordham University Press, 2013), 375.

7. Gourgouris, "Paul's Greek," 375.

8. Giorgio Agamben, *Profanations*, trans. Jeff Fort (New York: Zone Books, 2007), 77.

9. Agamben, *Profanations*, 86.

10. It is important at this juncture to clarify what I mean by worship as a pure means. Some might argue that bringing about the space in which something or anything might happen, namely, that the Holy Spirit can work and move, is precisely the goal of pentecostal worship and thus constitutes a very particular means-end relationship. This does not defeat my argument that worship is a pure means; *pure* means by definition a medium/mediality through which things can happen and is not "purity" in an absolute sense. To be in church and enter into a worship that is only the context of the Holy Spirit, a context that is not tied to specific or instrumental ends or economic logic of reciprocity is to reach the point of worship as pure means. Pure means names a medium that is not predetermined for an end, but it does not mean that at the end of their experience participants would say absolutely there is no end at all to their involvement. Indeed, the concept of pure means names or conceptualizes the ultimate goal of pentecostal worship when not adulterated.

This insight about context furnishes us an incompletable passage by which an impossible truth might appear or be conceived. The philosophical concept of worship as pure means (WPM) is not simply meant to capture the idea of a context in which the Holy Spirit freely *compears*, but an ex-position of what is true in the context, and on the basis of this knowledge to conceive what in the worship appears as a withdrawal or subtraction of something, as a pure event. (G. W. F. Hegel, *Hegel's Science of Logic*, trans. A. V Miller [Atlantic Highlands: Humanities Press International, 1989], 588, inspired the construction of the second sentence). What appears as an event is neither a human possession, nor a *project*; what is given is only a formal relation to it. This amounts to the "unworking," the *inoperativity* of end. The context is "neither ground, nor an essence, nor a substance. But it appears, it presents itself, it exposes itself, and thus it exists as communication" (Jean-Luc Nancy, *Inoperative*, 28). Context is worship communicating itself to worshipers, "both immediately—because it communicates *itself*—and in a mediated way—because it communicates" (49). Context "being immediate and mediated, is itself the rendition of the [worship] that it mediates, it is the emergence of its own [mediality]" (49).

11. This paragraph is inspired by Brian Blount, *Then the Whispers Put on Flesh: New Testament Ethics in an African American Context* (Nashville: Abingdon Press, 2001), 72–73. For the conceptualization of participation, potentiality, and participation, see my *The Charismatic City and the Public Resurgence of Religion: A Pentecostal Social Ethics of Cosmopolitan Urban Life* (New York: Palgrave Macmillan, 2014), 104–8, 152.

12. This way of styling my thought owes much to James Buchanan, *What Should Economists Do?* (Indianapolis: Liberty Fund, 1979), 31–32.

13. Jean-Luc Nancy, *Being Singular Plural*, trans. Robert D. Richardson and Anne E. O'Byrne (Stanford: Stanford University Press, 2000), 5–6.

14. Jean-Luc Nancy and Federico Ferrari, *Being Nude: The Skin of Images*, trans. Anne O'Byrne and Carlie Anglemire (New York: Fordham University Press, 2014), 17.

15. John Fiske, *Reading the Popular*, 2nd ed. (London: Routledge, 2011), 170.

16. Slavoj Žižek, *The Most Sublime Hysteric: Hegel with Lacan*, trans. Thomas Scott-Railton (Malden: Polity Press, 2014), 32–33.

17. Žižek, *Most Sublime Hysteric*, 157–62.

18. Mark C. Taylor, *About Religion: Economics of Faith in Virtual Culture* (Chicago: University of Chicago Press, 1999), 205.

19. Taylor, *About Religion*, 205.

20. Martin Heidegger, "The Thing," in *Poetry, Language, Thought*, trans. Albert Hofstadter (New York: Harper and Row, 1971), 168–69.

21. Taylor, *About Religion*, 206; see also Mark C. Taylor, *Altarity* (Chicago: University of Chicago Press, 1987), 83–85.

22. Taylor, *About Religion*, 246.

23. F. W. J. Schelling, *The Ages of the World: Third Draft* (c. 1815), trans. Jason M. Wirth (Albany: State University of New York Press, 2000), 24–25.

24. Schelling, *Ages of the World*, 25.

25. Schelling, *Ages of the World*, 25.

26. Schelling, *Ages of the World*, 24.

27. Slavoj Žižek, *The Plague of Fantasies* (London: Verso, 2008), 250.

28. Žižek, *Plague of Fantasies*, 35.

29. Žižek, *Plague of Fantasies*, 41.

30. It is conceivable that in some rare cases the repeated failures in "securing" *object petit a* might lead to a crisis of faith, a spiritual conversion away from Pentecostalism or what Lacan calls "subjective destitution." This is "an abrupt awareness of the utter meaningless [sic] of our social [religious] links, the dissolution of our attachment to reality [God] itself—all of a sudden, other people are de-realized, reality itself is experienced as a confused whirlpool of shapes and sounds, so that we are no longer able to formulate the desire." Slavoj Žižek, "Only a Suffering God Can Save Us," in Slavoj Žižek and Boris Gunjević, *God in Pain: Inversions of Apocalypse* (New York: Seven Stories Press, 2012), 167.

31. Žižek, *Plague of Fantasies*, 226–27, inspired the discussion of these four types of response.

32. Immanuel Kant, *Critique of Judgment*, trans. James Meredith (New York: Oxford University Press, 1973), 24, 21.

33. Slavoj Žižek, "The Most Sublime of Hysterics: Hegel with Lacan," trans. Rex Butler and Scott Stephens, accessed July 10, 2015, http://www.lacan.com/zizlacan2.htm; see also Žižek, *Most Sublime Hysteric*, 118.

34. Agamben, *Profanations*, 86.

35. G. W. F. Hegel, *Phenomenology of Spirit*, trans. A. V. Miller (Oxford: Oxford University Press, 1977), 210.

36. See also Slavoj Žižek, *The Puppet and the Dwarf: The Perverse Core of Christianity* (Cambridge: MIT Press, 2003), 81–85.

37. Giorgio Agamben, *The Kingdom and the Glory: For a Theological Genealogy of Economy and Government*, trans. Lorenzo Chiesa with Matteo Mandarini (Stanford: Stanford University Press, 2011), 246.

38. Agamben, *Kingdom and the Glory*, 221.

39. Agamben, *Kingdom and the Glory*, 226.

40. Agamben, *Kingdom and the Glory*, 245.

41. Agamben, *Kingdom and the Glory*, 200–1, 211.

42. Agamben, *Kingdom and the Glory*, 245.

43. Giorgio Agamben, *Nudities*, trans. David Kishik and Stefan Pedatella (Stanford: Stanford University Press, 2011), 98.

44. I am deploying the term *apparatus* in its Agambenian sense. See Giorgio Agamben, *"What Is an Apparatus?" and Other Essays*, trans. David Kishik and Stefan Pedatella (Stanford: Stanford University Press, 2009). It is not in the Foucauldian sense of "a set of strategies of the relations of forces supporting, and supported by, certain types of knowledge." Michel Foucault, *Power/Knowledge: Selected Interviews and Other Writings, 1972–1977*, ed. Colin Gordon (New York: Pantheon, 1980), 196, quoted in Agamben, *"What Is an Apparatus?,"* 2.

45. Agamben, *"What Is an Apparatus?,"* 14.

46. Nimi Wariboko, *Nigerian Pentecostalism* (Rochester: University of Rochester Press, 2014).

47. Slavoj Žižek, "Only a Suffering God," 171.

Chapter 7

1. Jacques Derrida, *Positions*, trans. Alan Bass (Chicago: University of Chicago Press, 1982), 71.

2. Gerhard Richter, *Thought Images: Frankfurt School Writers' Reflections from Damaged Life* (Stanford: Stanford University Press, 2007), 1.

3. This chapter is a revised version of "West African Pentecostalism: A Survey of Everyday Theology," in *Global Renewal Christianity: Spirit-Empowered*

Movements, Past, Present and Future, Vol. III: Africa and Diaspora, ed. Vinson Synan, Amos Yong, and Kwabena Asamoah-Gyadu (Lake Mary: Charisma House, 2016), 1–18.

4. See Nimi Wariboko and Amos Yong, *Paul Tillich and Pentecostal Theology: Spiritual Presence and Spiritual Power* (Bloomington: Indiana University Press, 2015).

5. John Fiske, *Understanding Popular Culture*, 2nd ed. (London: Routledge, 2011), 22.

6. John Fiske, *Reading the Popular*, 2nd ed. (London: Routledge, 2011), 1.

7. Fiske, *Understanding Popular Culture*, 56.

8. Birgit Meyer, "Aesthetics of Persuasion: Global Christianity and Pentecostalism's Sensational Forms," *South Atlantic Quarterly* 109, no. 4 (2010): 742; italics in the original.

9. Annalisa Butticci, "Crazy World, Crazy Faith! Prayer, Power and Transformation in a Nigerian Prayer City," *Annual Review of Sociology of Religion* 4 (2013): 254.

10. Butticci, "Crazy World," 256.

11. J. Kwabena Asamoah-Gyadu, *Contemporary Pentecostal Christianity: Interpretation from an African Context* (Eugene: Wipf and Stock, 2013), 33.

12. Fiske, *Reading the Popular*, 116.

13. Fiske, *Understanding Popular Culture*, 86, 88.

14. Jacques Rancière, *Dissensus: On Politics and Aesthetics*, ed. and trans. Steven Corcoran (London: Continuum, 2010).

15. Fiske, *Reading the Popular*, 13–16, 27, inspired this paragraph.

16. Matthews Ojo, *The End-Time Army: Charismatic Movements in Modern Nigeria* (Trenton: Africa World Press, 2006), 89.

17. I have adapted the four modes of exchange as described by Kojin Karatani for my purposes here. See his *The Structure of World History: From Modes of Production to Modes of Exchange* (Durham: Duke University Press, 2014), 1–28.

18. Annalisa Butticci, *African Pentecostals in Catholic Europe: The Politics of Presence in the Twenty-First Century* (Cambridge: Harvard University Press, 2016).

19. Birgit Meyer, "Aesthetics of Persuasion," 741–63, quote on 754.

20. See Afe Adogame, *The African Christian Diaspora: New Currents and Emerging Trends in World Christianity* (London: Bloomsbury Academic, 2013), 118, 137.

21. Adogame, *African Christian Diaspora*, 118; italics mine.

22. Adogame, *African Christian Diaspora*, 98–99.

23. Adogame, *African Christian Diaspora*, 84–85.

24. By "academic theology" I mean systematic or constructive theology that functions around classical doctrines and their receptions and interpretations over time. Logos here means a theology that functions in this way and does not involve the daily meanings people draw from practices of their faith or the philosophical/religious significance of the mundane narratives of their everyday lives. But our

discourse does not reject logos, and as stated later; microtheology brings together both the signs of logos and meaning. For it is obvious that to make sense of the everyday form of theology we have used critical theory as a frame to interpret practices of ordinary Pentecostals. Note that in the preceding paragraph I stated that there are two issues in the statement: methodology of extracting everyday form of theology (microtheology) and the philosophical grounding of theoretical constructs of ordinary folks (some philosophy of existence). The problem with "academic theology," as I see it, is that its starting points for theological construction are doctrines and their past interpretations instead of practices of folks on the ground.

25. This way of putting the matter is informed by Enrique Dussel, *Ethics of Liberation in the Age of Globalization and Exclusion*, trans. Eduardo Mendieta, Camilo Peréz Bustillo, Yolanda Angulo, and Nelson Maldonado-Torres (Durham: Duke University Press, 2013).

26. Margery Perham, *The Colonial Reckoning* (London: Collins, 1962), 87, quoted in Karen E. Fields, *Revival and Rebellion in Colonial Central Africa* (Princeton: Princeton University Press, 1985), 31–32.

27. Adogame, *African Christian Diaspora*, 86.

28. Adogame, *African Christian Diaspora*, 87–92.

29. See Adogame, *African Christian Diaspora*, 94–99, for a view of the world as a battlefield.

30. Adogame, *African Christian Diaspora*, 18.

31. Adogame, *African Christian Diaspora*, 85.

32. Erving Goffman, "On Face Work: An Analysis of Ritual Elements in Social Interaction," *Psychiatry* 18 (1955): 213–31; Erving Goffman, *The Presentation of the Self in Everyday Life* (New York: Doubleday, 1959).

Conclusion

1. I am indebted to Eric L. Santner, *On the Psychotheology of Everyday Life: Reflections on Freud and Rosenzweig* (Chicago: University of Chicago Press, 2001), for inspiring this thought.

2. Santner, *Psychotheology of Everyday Life*, 5.

3. Santner, *Psychotheology of Everyday Life*, 5.

4. Nimi Wariboko, *Nigerian Pentecostalism* (Rochester: University of Rochester Press, 2014), 268–73.

5. Slavoj Žižek, "The Abyss of Freedom," in F. W. J. Schelling, *Abyss of Freedom/Ages of the World* (Second Draft, 1813), trans. Judith Norman (Ann Arbor: University of Michigan Press, 1997), 49–50.

6. Žižek, "Abyss of Freedom," 50.

7. Santner, *Psychotheology of Everyday Life*, 6–7.

8. Santner, *Psychotheology of Everyday Life*, 7.
9. Santner, *Psychotheology of Everyday Life*, 60–66.
10. Santner, *Psychotheology of Everyday Life*, 66.
11. Franz Rosenzweig, *The Star of Redemption*, trans. William W. Hallo (Notre Dame: University of Notre Dame, 1985), 332.
12. Rosenzweig, *Star of Redemption*, 332.
13. Rosenzweig, *Star of Redemption*, 333–34.
14. Rosenzweig, *Star of Redemption*, 334.
15. Santner, *Psychotheology of Everyday Life*, 66.
16. Santner, *Psychotheology of Everyday Life*, 97.
17. Santner, *Psychotheology of Everyday Life*, 105.
18. Aristotle, *Nicomachean Ethics*, 1097b 25–30. The translation is from *Nicomachean Ethics*, trans. Martin Oswald (Indianapolis: Liberal Arts Press, 1962).
19. Jean-Luc Nancy, *The Inoperative Community*, trans. Peter Connor, Lisa Garbus, Michael Holland, and Simona Sawhney, foreword Christopher Fynsk (Minneapolis: University of Minnesota Press, 1991).
20. Giorgio Agamben, *Means without End: Notes on Politics*, trans. Vincenzo Binetti and Cesare Casarino (Minneapolis: University of Minnesota Press, 2000), 115–16.
21. See Rosenzweig, *Star of Redemption*, 65–70; Santner, *Psychotheology of Everyday Life*, 72–73.
22. Rosenzweig, *Star of Redemption*, 69.
23. Santner, *Psychotheology of Everyday Life*, 73.
24. Rosenzweig, *Star of Redemption*, 65, 72, 79.
25. Rosenzweig, *Star of Redemption*, 71.
26. Santner, *Psychotheology of Everyday Life*, 75.
27. Slavoj Žižek, *The Indivisible Remainder: On Schelling and Related Matters* (London: Verso, 2007), 59.
28. Slavoj Žižek, *How to Read Lacan* (New York: W. W. Norton, 2006), 43.
29. Richard Wagner, *Jesus of Nazareth and Other Writings* (Lincoln: University of Nebraska Press, 1995), 303.
30. Rosenzweig, *Star of Redemption*, 300–1, 404–5.
31. Rosenzweig, *Star of Redemption*, 409.
32. Jürgen Moltmann, *The Spirit of Life: A Universal Affirmation*, trans. Margaret Kohl (Minneapolis: Fortress Press, 2001), 51.
33. Franz Kafka, *The Trial*, trans. Willa Muir and Edwin Muir (New York: Schocken, 1984), 220.
34. Santner, *Psychotheology of Everyday Life*, 102.
35. For ex-citation as calling forth, see Eric L. Santner, "Miracles Happen: Benjamin, Rosenzweig, Freud, and the Matter of the Neighbor," in Slavoj Žižek, Eric L. Santner, and Kenneth Reinhard, *The Neighbor: Three Inquiries in Political Theology* (Chicago: University of Chicago Press, 2005), 86–92.

36. May we suggest that one of the functions of Paul's "as-if-not" is aimed at suspending this obscene underside of the incorporation of glossolalia into the symbolic network?

37. This paragraph was inspired by Santner, "Miracles Happen," 104–5.

38. Santner, *Psychotheology of Everyday Life*, 102.

39. Santner, *Psychotheology of Everyday Life*, 102.

Bibliography

Achebe, Chinua. *Things Fall Apart*. New York: Anchor Books, 1994.
Adogame, Afe. *The African Christian Diaspora: New Currents and Emerging Trends in World Christianity*. London: Bloomsbury Academic, 2013.
Agamben, Giorgio. *The Kingdom and the Glory: For a Theological Genealogy of Economy and Government*. Translated by Lorenzo Chiesa with Matteo Mandarini. Stanford: Stanford University Press, 2011.
Agamben, Giorgio. *Means without End: Notes on Politics*. Translated by Vincenzo Binetti and Cesare Casarino. Minneapolis: University of Minnesota Press, 2000.
Agamben, Giorgio. *Nudities*. Translated by David Kishik and Stefan Pedatella. Stanford: Stanford University Press, 2011.
Agamben, Giorgio. *Potentialities: Collected Essays in Philosophy*. Edited and translated by Daniel Heller-Roazen. Stanford: Stanford University Press, 1999.
Agamben, Giorgio. *Profanations*. Translated by Jeff Fort. New York: Zone Books, 2007.
Agamben, Giorgio. *The Time That Remains: A Commentary on the Letter to the Romans*. Stanford: Stanford University Press, 2005.
Agamben, Giorgio. *"What Is an Apparatus?" and Other Essays*. Translated by David Kishik and Stefan Pedatella. Stanford: Stanford University Press, 2009.
Aristotle. *Nicomachean Ethics*. Translated by Martin Oswald. Indianapolis: Liberal Arts Press, 1962.
Asamoah-Gyadu, J. Kwabena. *Contemporary Pentecostal Christianity: Interpretation from an African Context*. Eugene: Wipf and Stock, 2013.
Badiou, Alain. *Being and Event*. Translated by Oliver Feltham. London: Continuum, 2005.
Badiou, Alain. *Theoretical Writings*. London: Continuum, 2004.
Barrera, Albino. *God and the Evil of Scarcity: Moral Foundations of Economic Agency*. Notre Dame: University of Notre Dame Press, 2005.
Bataille, Georges. *The Bataille Reader*. Edited by Fred Botting and Scott Wilson. Oxford: Blackwell, 1997.

Blount, Brian. *Then the Whispers Put on Flesh: New Testament Ethics in an African American Context*. Nashville: Abingdon Press, 2001.
Bowie, Andrew. *Schelling and Modern European Philosophy*. New York: Routledge, 1993.
Buchanan, James. *What Should Economists Do?* Indianapolis: Liberty Fund, 1979.
Burrus, Virginia. "The Heretical Woman as Symbol in Athanasius, Epiphanius and Jerome." *Harvard Theological Review* 84, no. 3 (1991): 229–48.
Butticci, Annalisa. "Crazy World, Crazy Faith! Prayer, Power and Transformation in a Nigerian Prayer City." *Annual Review of Sociology of Religion* 4 (2013): 243–62.
Butticci, Annalisa, ed. *Na God: Aesthetics of African Charismatic Power*. Rubano: Grafiche Turato Edizioni, 2013.
Butticci, Annalisa. *African Pentecostals in Catholic Europe: The Politics of Presence in the Twenty-First Century*. Cambridge: Harvard University Press, 2016.
Campbell, Colin. *The Romantic Ethic and the Spirit of Modern Consumerism*. London: Blackwell, 1987.
Caputo, John. *The Weakness of God: A Theology of Event*. Bloomington: Indiana University Press, 2006.
Chesterton, G. K. *Orthodoxy*. San Francisco: Ignatius Press, 1995.
Chow, Rey. *The Protestant Ethnic and the Spirit of Capitalism*. New York: Columbia University Press, 2002.
Connolly, William E. *Capitalism and Christianity: American Style*. Durham: Duke University Press, 2008.
Connolly, William E. *The Fragility of Things: Self-Organizing Processes, Neoliberal Fantasies, and Democratic Activism*. Durham: Duke University Press, 2013.
Cox, Harvey. *Fire from Heaven: The Rise of Pentecostal Spirituality and the Reshaping of Religion in the Twenty-First Century*. Reading: Addison-Wesley, 1995.
Crockett, Clayton. *Interstices of the Sublime: Theology and Psychoanalytic Theory*. New York: Fordham University Press, 2007.
Cross, Terry. "Tillich's Picture of Jesus as the Christ: Toward a Theology of the Spirit's Saving Presence." In *Paul Tillich and Pentecostal Theology: Spiritual Presence and Spiritual Power*, edited by Nimi Wariboko and Amos Yong, 71–83. Bloomington: Indiana University Press, 2015.
Deleuze, Gilles. *The Logic of Sense*. Translated by Mark Lester with Charles Stivale. New York: Columbia University Press, 1990.
Derrida, Jacques. *Positions*. Translated by Alan Bass. Chicago: University of Chicago Press, 1982.
Dussel, Enrique. *Ethics of Liberation in the Age of Globalization and Exclusion*. Translated by Eduardo Mendieta, Camilo Peréz Bustillo, Yolanda Angulo, and Nelson Maldonado-Torres. Durham: Duke University Press, 2013.
Fenn, Richard. *Key Thinkers in the Sociology of Religion*. London: Continuum, 2009.

Fenn, Richard. *The Return of the Primitive: A New Sociological Theory of Religion*. Aldershot: Ashgate, 2001.
Fenn, Richard. "Sociology and Religion: Searching for the Sacred." In *The Oxford Handbook of Religion and Science*, edited by Philip Clayton and Zachary Simpson, 253–70. Oxford: Oxford University Press, 2006.
Fields, Karen E. *Revival and Rebellion in Colonial Central Africa*. Princeton: Princeton University Press, 1985.
Fiske, John. *Reading the Popular*. 2nd ed. London: Routledge, 2011.
Fiske, John. *Understanding Popular Culture*. 2nd ed. London: Routledge, 2011.
Goffman, Erving. "On Face Work: An Analysis of Ritual Elements in Social Interaction." *Psychiatry* 18 (1955): 213–31.
Goffman, Erving. *The Presentation of the Self in Everyday Life*. New York: Doubleday, 1959.
Gourgouris, Stathis. "Paul's Greek." In *Paul and the Philosophers*, edited by Ward Blanton and Hent de Vries, 354–80. New York: Fordham University Press, 2013.
Hamza, Agon. "A Plea for Žižekian Politics." In *Repeating Žižek*, edited by Agon Hamza, 226–39. Durham: Duke University Press, 2015.
Hamza, Agon, ed. *Repeating Žižek*. Durham: Duke University Press, 2015.
Hatch, Nathan. *The Democratization of American Christianity*. New Haven: Yale University Press, 1989.
Hegel, G. W. F. *Elements of the Philosophy of Right*. Cambridge: Cambridge University Press, 1991.
Hegel, G. W. F. *Phenomenology of Spirit*. Translated by A. V. Miller. Oxford: Oxford University Press, 1977.
Hegel, G. W. F. *Hegel's Science of Logic*. Translated by A. V. Miller. Atlantic Highlands: Humanities Press International, 1989.
Heidegger, Martin. *Poetry, Language, Thought*. Translated by Albert Hofstadter. New York: Harper and Row, 1971.
Horton, Robin. "A Hundred Years of Change in Kalabari Religion." In *Black Africa: Its People and Their Cultures Today*, edited by John Middleton, 192–211. New York: Macmillan, 1971.
Horton, Robin. *Kalabari Sculpture*. Lagos: Department of Antiquities, Federal Republic of Nigeria, 1965.
Horton, Robin. "The Kalabari Worldview: An Outline and Interpretation." *Africa* 32, no. 3 (July 1962): 197–219.
Horton, Robin. *Patterns of Thought in Africa and the West: Essays on Magic, Religion and Science*. Cambridge: Cambridge University Press, 1993.
Johnson, Adrian. " 'Freedom or System? Yes, Please': How to Read Slavoj Žižek's *Less Than Nothing: Hegel and the Shadow of Dialectical Materialism*." In *Repeating Žižek*, edited by Agon Hamza, 7–42. Durham: Duke University Press, 2015.

Johnson, Adrian. *Žižek's Ontology: A Transcendental Materialist Theory of Subjectivity*. Evanston: Northwestern University Press, 2008.

Kafka, Franz. *The Trial*. Translated by Willa Muir and Edwin Muir. New York: Schocken, 1984.

Kant, Immanuel. *Critique of Judgment*. Translated by James Meredith. New York: Oxford University Press, 1973.

Kant, Immanuel. *Critique of Practical Reason*. New York: Macmillan, 1956.

Karatani, Kojin. *The Structure of World History: From Modes of Production to Modes of Exchange*. Durham: Duke University Press, 2014.

Keller, Catherine. *Cloud of the Impossible: Negative Theology and Planetary Entanglement*. New York: Columbia University Press, 2014.

Keller, Catherine. *On the Mystery: Discerning God in Process*. Minneapolis: Fortress, 2008.

Keller, Catherine. "The Entangled Cosmos: An Experiment in Physical Theopoetics." *Journal of Cosmology* (September 2012): 1–18.

Keller, Catherine. *Face of the Deep: A Theology of Becoming*. London: Routledge, 2003.

Kolozova, Katerina. *Toward a Radical Metaphysics of Socialism: Marx and Laruelle*. Brooklyn: Punctum Books, 2015.

Kotsko, Adam. "The Problem of Christianity and Žižek's 'Middle Period.'" In *Repeating Žižek*, edited by Agon Hamza, 243–55. Durham: Duke University Press, 2015.

Kripal, Jeffrey. *Authors of the Impossible: The Paranormal and the Sacred*. Chicago: University of Chicago Press, 2010.

Lacan, Jacques. *The Ego in Freud's Theory and in the Technique of Psychoanalysis 1954–1955*. Bk. 2, of *The Seminar of Jacques Lacan*. Edited by Jacques-Alain Miller, translated by Sylvana Tomaselli. New York: Norton, 1991.

Lacan, Jacques. *The Ethics of Psychoanalysis 1959–1960*. Bk. 7, of *The Seminar of Jacques Lacan*. Edited by Jacques-Alain Miller, translated by Dennis Potter. New York: Norton, 1992.

Lacan, Jacques. *The Four Fundamental Concepts of Psycho-Analysis*. Edited by Jacques-Alain Miller, translated by Alan Sheridan. New York: Norton, 1977.

Lazzarato, Maurizio. *The Making of the Indebted Man*. Los Angeles: Semiotext(e), 2012.

Levinas, Emmanuel. *Totality and Infinity*. Translated by Alphonso Lingis. Pittsburgh: Duquesne University Press, 1961.

Macchia, Frank D. "Glossolalia." In *Encyclopedia of Pentecostal and Charismatic Christianity*, edited by Stanley M. Burgess, 223–35. New York: Routledge, 2006.

Madigan, Kevin, and Jon D. Levenson. *Resurrection: The Power of God for Christians and Jews*. New Haven: Yale University Press, 2008.

Maimonides, Moses. *Guide to the Perplexed*. Bk. 1. Chicago: University of Chicago Press, 2010.
Marshall, Ruth. *Political Spiritualities: The Pentecostal Revolution in Nigeria*. Chicago: University of Chicago Press, 2009.
McNemar, Richard. "The Mole's Little Pathways." In Nathan Hatch, *The Democratization of American Christianity*, 81. New Haven: Yale University Press, 1989.
Meillassoux, Quentin. "Potentiality and Virtuality." *Collapse: Philosophic Research and Development* 2 (2007): 55–81.
Meyer, Birgit. "Aesthetics of Persuasion: Global Christianity and Pentecostalism's Sensational Forms." *South Atlantic Quarterly* 109, no. 4 (2010): 741–63.
Moltmann, Jürgen. *The Spirit of Life: A Universal Affirmation*. Translated by Margaret Kohl. Minneapolis: Fortress Press, 2001.
Nancy, Jean-Luc. *Being Singular Plural*. Translated by Robert D. Richardson and Anne E. O'Byrne. Stanford: Stanford University Press, 2000.
Nancy, Jean-Luc. *The Inoperative Community*. Translated by Peter Connor, Lisa Garbus, Michael Holland, and Simona Sawhney, foreword by Christopher Fynsk. Minneapolis: University of Minnesota Press, 1991.
Nancy, Jean-Luc, and Federico Ferrari. *Being Nude: The Skin of Images*. Translated by Anne O'Byrne and Carlie Anglemire. New York: Fordham University Press, 2014.
Norton, Anne. "Pentecost: Democratic Sovereignty in Carl Schmitt." *Constellations* 18, no. 3 (2011): 389–402.
Nussbaum, Martha. *The Fragility of Goodness: Luck and Ethics in Greek Tragedy and Philosophy*. Cambridge: Cambridge University Press, 2007.
Obadare, Ebenezer. "The Spirit of Yoruba Liberalism." *Marginalia*, February 16, 2017. Accessed February 17, 2017. http://marginalia.lareviewofbooks.org/spirit-yoruba-liberalism.
Olukoya, Daniel. *Prayer Passport to Crush Oppression*. Lagos: Mountain of Fire and Miracles Ministries Press, 2006.
Ojo, Matthews. *The End-Time Army: Charismatic Movements in Modern Nigeria*. Trenton: Africa World Press, 2006.
Peterson, Erik. "Theology of Clothes." In *Selection*, edited by C. Hasting and D. Nichol, vol. 2, 56–64. London: Sheed and Ward, 1954.
Rancière, Jacques. *Dissensus: On Politics and Aesthetics*. Edited and translated by Steven Corcoran. London: Continuum, 2010.
Raschke, Carl. "The Monstrosity of Žižek's Christ." *Journal of Cultural and Religious Theory* 11, no. 2 (2011): 13–20.
Richter, Gerhard. *Thought Images: Frankfurt School Writers' Reflections from Damaged Life*. Stanford: Stanford University Press, 2007.
Robert, William. "Nude, Glorious, Living." *Political Theology* 14, no. 1 (2013): 115–30.

Rosenzweig, Franz. *The Star of Redemption*. Translated by William W. Hallo. Notre Dame: University of Notre Dame, 1985.

Ruda, Frank. "How to Repeat Plato: For a Platonism of the Non-All." In *Repeating Žižek*, edited by Agon Hamza, 43–57. Durham: Duke University Press, 2015.

Santner, Eric L. "Miracles Happen: Benjamin, Rosenzweig, Freud, and the Matter of the Neighbor." In Slavoj Žižek, Eric L. Santner, and Kenneth Reinhard, *The Neighbor: Three Inquiries in Political Theology*, 76–133. Chicago: University of Chicago Press, 2005.

Santner, Eric L. *On the Psychotheology of Everyday Life: Reflections on Freud and Rosenzweig*. Chicago: University of Chicago Press, 2001.

Schelling, F. W. J. *Abyss of Freedom/Ages of the World* (Second Draft, 1813). Translated by Judith Norman. Ann Arbor: University of Michigan Press, 1997.

Schelling, F. W. J. *The Ages of the World: Third Draft* (c. 1815). Translated by Jason M. Wirth. Albany: State University of New York Press, 2000.

Schelling, F. W. J. *Philosophical Investigations into the Essence of Human Freedom*. Translated by Jeff Love and Johannes Schmidt. Albany: State University of New York Press, 2006.

Smolin, Lee. *The Trouble with Physics: The Rise of String Theory, the Fall of a Science, and What Comes Next*. Boston: Houghton Mifflin, 2006.

Sohn-Rethel, Alfred. *Intellectual and Manual Labor: A Critique of Epistemology*. Translated by Martin Sohn-Rethel. London: Macmillan, 1978.

Sölle, Dorothee. *Beyond Mere Obedience*. Translated by Lawrence W. Denef. New York: Pilgrim Press, 1982.

Taylor, Mark C. *About Religion: Economics of Faith in Virtual Culture*. Chicago: University of Chicago Press, 1999.

Taylor, Mark C. *Altarity*. Chicago: University of Chicago Press, 1987.

Taylor, Mark C., and Carl Raschke. "About *About Religion*: A Conversation with Mark C. Taylor." Accessed June 14, 2015. http://www.jcrt.org/archives/02.2/taylor_raschke.shtml.

Tillich, Paul. *The Protestant Era*. Chicago: University of Chicago Press, 1948.

Tillich, Paul. *Systematic Theology, Volume 1: Reason and Revelation, Being and God*. Chicago: University of Chicago Press, 1951.

Tillich, Paul. *Systematic Theology, Volume 3: Life and the Spirit, History and the Kingdom of God*. Chicago: University of Chicago Press, 1965.

Vaughan, Henry. "The World." Accessed June 24, 2015. http://www.poetryfoundation.org/poem/174701.

Verene, Donald Phillip. *Hegel's Recollection: A Study of Images in the Phenomenology of Spirit*. Albany: State University of New York Press, 1985.

Vernant, Jean-Pierre. *Mortals and Immortals: Collected Essays*. Princeton: Princeton University Press, 1991.

Wagner, Richard. *Jesus of Nazareth and Other Writings*. Lincoln: University of Nebraska Press, 1995.

Walker, Gavin. "Žižek and Marx: Outside in the Critique of Political Economy." In *Repeating Žižek*, edited by Agon Hamza, 195–212. Durham: Duke University Press, 2015.
Wariboko, Nimi. *The Charismatic City and the Public Resurgence of Religion: A Pentecostal Social Ethics of Cosmopolitan Urban Life*. New York: Palgrave Macmillan, 2014.
Wariboko, Nimi. *The Depth and Destiny of Work: An African Theological Interpretation*. Trenton: Africa World Press, 2008.
Wariboko, Nimi. *Economics in Spirit and Truth: A Moral Philosophy of Finance*. New York: Palgrave Macmillan, 2014.
Wariboko, Nimi. *Ethics and Time: Ethos of Temporal Orientation in Politics and Religion of the Niger Delta*. Lanham: Lexington Books, 2010.
Wariboko, Nimi. *God and Money: A Theology of Money in a Globalizing World*. Lanham: Lexington Books, 2008.
Wariboko, Nimi. *Nigerian Pentecostalism*. Rochester: University of Rochester Press, 2014.
Wariboko, Nimi. *The Pentecostal Principle: Ethical Methodology in New Spirit*. Grand Rapids: Eerdmans, 2012.
Wariboko, Nimi. "West African Pentecostalism: A Survey of Everyday Theology." In *Global Renewal Christianity: Spirit-Empowered Movements, Past, Present and Future, Vol. III: Africa and Diaspora*, edited by Vinson Synan, Amos Yong, and Kwabena Asamoah-Gyadu. Lake Mary: Charisma House, 2016.
Wariboko, Nimi, and Amos Yong. *Paul Tillich and Pentecostal Theology: Spiritual Presence and Spiritual Power*. Bloomington: Indiana University Press, 2015.
Williams, Tennessee. "The Timeless World of a Play." In Tennessee Williams, *The Rose Tattoo*, 4–7. New York: New Directions, 1951.
Yong, Amos. "Spiritual Discernment: A Biblical-Theological Reconsideration." In *The Spirit and Spirituality: Essays in Honor of Russell P. Spittler*, edited by Wonsuk Ma and Robert P. Menzies, 84–101. London: T. and T. Clark, 2004.
Zimeri, Sead. "Islam: How Could It Have Emerged after Christianity?" In *Repeating Žižek*, edited by Agon Hamza, 256–68. Durham: Duke University Press, 2015.
Žižek, Slavoj. *Absolute Recoil: Towards a New Foundation of Dialectical Materialism*. London: Verso, 2014.
Žižek, Slavoj. "The Abyss of Freedom." In F. W. J. Schelling, *Abyss of Freedom/Ages of the World* (Second Draft, 1813), translated by Judith Norman, 3–104. Ann Arbor: University of Michigan Press, 1997.
Žižek, Slavoj. "Christianity Against the Sacred." In Slavoj Žižek and Boris Gunjević, *God in Pain: Inversions of Apocalypse*, 43–71. New York: Seven Stories Press, 2012.
Žižek, Slavoj. *In Defense of Lost Causes*. London: Verso, 2009.
Žižek, Slavoj. *Event: A Philosophical Journey Through a Concept*. London: Penguin Books, 2014.

Žižek, Slavoj. *The Fragile Absolute: Or, Why Is the Christianity Legacy Worth Fighting For?* London: Verso, 2008.
Žižek, Slavoj. *How to Read Lacan.* New York: W. W. Norton, 2006.
Žižek, Slavoj. *The Indivisible Remainder: On Schelling and Related Matters.* London: Verso, 2007.
Žižek, Slavoj. *Less Than Nothing: Hegel and the Shadow of Dialectical Materialism.* London: Verso, 2012.
Žižek, Slavoj. *The Most Sublime Hysteric: Hegel with Lacan.* Translated by Thomas Scott-Railton. Malden: Polity Press, 2014.
Žižek, Slavoj. "The Most Sublime of Hysterics: Hegel with Lacan." Translated by Rex Butler and Scott Stephens. Accessed July 10, 2015. http://www.lacan.com/zizlacan2.htm.
Žižek, Slavoj. "The Necessity of a Dead Bird: Paul Communism." In *Paul and the Philosophers*, edited by Ward Blanton and Hent De Vries, 175–85. New York: Fordham University Press, 2013.
Žižek, Slavoj. "Only a Suffering God Can Save Us." In Slavoj Žižek and Boris Gunjević, *God in Pain: Inversions of Apocalypse*, 155–92. New York: Seven Stories Press, 2012.
Žižek, Slavoj. *Organs without Bodies: On Deleuze and Consequences.* New York: Routledge, 2012.
Žižek, Slavoj. *The Parallax View.* Cambridge: MIT Press, 2009.
Žižek, Slavoj. *The Plague of Fantasies.* London: Verso, 2008.
Žižek, Slavoj. *The Puppet and the Dwarf: The Perverse Core of Christianity.* Cambridge: MIT Press, 2003.
Žižek, Slavoj. *The Sublime Object of Ideology.* London: Verso, 2008.
Žižek, Slavoj. *Violence: Six Sideways Reflections.* New York: Picador, 2008.
Žižek, Slavoj, and John Milbank. *The Monstrosity of Christ.* Edited by Creston Davis. Cambridge: MIT Press, 2009.

Index

abject, 11, 129, 147
Absolute, xvii, 17, 35–36, 38, 97–98, 105, 107
abstract, xvi, xviii, xix, 2, 19, 30, 38–39, 118, 123–125
abstract universal notion, 123–124
abstraction, 5–6, 118, 124, 134
abundant life, 17, 86
abyss, xiv, 46, 51, 126, 189
Achebe, 78
Adam, 61–63
Adogame, Afe, 79, 170, 179
adultery, 190
aesthesis, 168
aesthetics, xvii, 69–70, 105, 155, 159–160, 168–169
affectivity, 103–104, 110
Africa, xv, xx, 54, 80, 121, 153, 156, 159, 164–166, 174, 179
African Traditional Religion (ATR), 48, 52, 54, 176–177
Africans, ix, 105, 153, 165
Agamben, Giorgio, xi, xiii, 1, 4, 29, 39, 40, 42–43, 117, 119, 125–127, 138, 149, 151–153, 188
airiness, 142
alienness, 183, 185, 191, 192
All, xiv–xvi, 101, 109
alterity, 181–183, 191, 193
Althusser, Louis, 129

amateme-so, 88
anarche, 25
ancestors, 49
angel, 61
anointing, xviii, 14, 36–37, 40, 59, 62, 69, 71, 77, 114, 128–129, 146, 159–160, 163–164, 168, 182
antifragility, 115, 119
apocalypse, 75
Apollonian, 32
apparatus, 15, 18, 46, 106, 129, 131, 148, 152, 153, 155, 163, 174
appearance qua appearance, xix, 69, 76
arche, 25, 33
argōs, 187, 188
argōs-being, 187
Aristotle, 125, 187
arrow of time, 173
as if not, 28, 29, 43, 218
Asamoah-Gyadu, Kwabena, 160
assets, 127
attachment, 84, 92, 106, 119, 193
attributes, of God, xii, xix, 4
Azusa, 22, 25

Babel, 31
Bacchanalian, 31, 115
background dependent, 96
background independent, 96

Index

Badiou, Alain, xi, xiii, 107, 110
bathroom, 17, 45, 57, 60, 61
be-ginnan, 67
Being, 7, 22, 24, 53, 67–68, 90, 96, 104, 107–108
being-in-Christ, 138
being-in-the-Spirit, 138
being-in-worship, 136
being-with, 68, 141
Benjamin, Walter, 9, 173
Bethlehem, 42
between-ness, 141
bibibari, 89, 90, 92
Bible, 5, 12, 16, 17, 26, 28, 63, 160, 190
   1 Corinthians, 28
   1 Timothy, 128
   2 Kings, 48
   Acts, 15, 21–22, 26–28, 32, 39–40
   Ephesians, 67, 69
   Ezekiel, 152
   Genesis, 31, 63
   Hebrew, 53, 59, 190
   I John, 192
   Isaiah, 42
   Job, 167
   John, 11, 23, 54, 59
   Luke, 54, 111
   Matthew, 190
   Philippians, 11, 111
   Revelation, 42, 75
   Romans, xi, 48, 56, 66, 78, 142
Big Other, 27, 70, 115, 168, 193
bills, *see also* witches, 121, 122, 125
bios, 43
bird, 48, 79, 115
black holes, 100
bodies, xvii, 15, 17, 20, 36, 38, 46–47, 62, 69–71, 76–78, 97, 103–105, 129, 137, 148, 157–161, 163, 166–169, 180

bone, 31, 151
born-again, 30, 43, 65, 72–73, 136, 139, 154, 161, 164, 166–167
born-again shopping, 164, 166–167
boundaries, x, 13, 32, 67, 85–86, 91, 106, 128, 155–156, 158, 160, 170
Brooklyn, 162, 195
Butticci, Annalisa, 70–71, 105, 159, 168

cages, 161
Calvary, 5
Campbell, Collins, 129
canoe, 48
Cantor, Georg, 107
capitalism, 111, 113–131
capitalo-parliamentary institutions, 123
castration, 192
causal network, 83–84, 102
causality, 12–13, 18, 22, 33, 49, 107
chain, 13, 35, 54, 74, 102, 136, 142, 149, 179
chain of causality, 12–13, 18, 22, 33
chairs, 69
Charismatic movement, 106, 165
Chesterton, G. K., xvi, 5, 37
Chief, 130, 166
choices, 151
Chow, Rey, 129
Christianity, 165, 177
Christo-marketistic religion, 122
Christo-nationalistic religion, 122
church, 8, 15–16, 20, 22, 26–28, 41, 65, 111, 115, 121, 129–130, 139, 150, 157–158, 162, 163
circulation of money, 118
clothing, 62–63
coincidentia oppositorium, 96–97, 102–103, 140
collective effervescence, 87

collectivity, 73, 138
commodities, 6, 163
commodity exchange, 59, 124, 143, 166
commodity fetishism, 6, 124
communion, 49, 139–140, 144, 162, 170, 187
community, 13, 16, 23, 25–28, 30, 39, 50, 53, 55, 59, 85, 87–89, 91, 94, 100, 110, 139, 142, 157, 160, 174, 179, 187
compearance, 187
conation, 145
concrete, xviii, xix, 2, 29–30, 38–39, 47, 55, 59, 90, 98, 105, 118, 124, 134, 149, 156, 165, 171, 173, 179–180
Connolly, William, 116, 118, 128
conscience, 127
consciousness, 5, 35, 76–77, 86, 93–94, 137, 182, 188
consumerism, 129, 130
consumerist religion, 122
context, xx, 1, 3, 11, 30, 57, 59, 84, 90, 95, 138–139, 153, 157, 164, 167, 182–183, 189
contexture, 57
contraction, 33–34
contractor-prayer warriors, 59
cooked sacrament, 164
Copernican Revolution, xxi
core, xiv, 10–11, 15, 17–18, 30–31, 46, 48, 92, 97–98, 103, 134, 143, 182, 186–187, 189, 191
cosmos, 37, 38, 109, 185
crack, xiv, 13, 15, 17, 36, 37, 41, 44, 46–47, 54, 56, 73, 144, 106, 151, 191
creatable, 97, 100
creative destruction, 119
creativity, xx, 93, 96–98, 100, 162
Creator, 34–35
critical theory, xi–xiii, 1, 2
Crockett, Clayton, 39
culture, xx, 26, 28, 29, 51, 103, 128, 157, 161, 166, 180, 182–183

dancing, 13, 143, 163
danger, 9–10, 13–14, 51, 155, 177, 191
dark energy, 17
das ding, 190
De Certeau, Michel, 105
deactivates, xii, 5, 66, 101, 138, 184
death of God theology, 5, 8
debts, 122
decision tree, 48
defiant character, 189
deity, xvii, 87, 96, 107–108, 167
Deleuze, Gilles, 104–105
demonic, 37, 57, 159, 177, 179
demos, 23
deontologization, 8
Derrida, Jacques, 11, 13–14, 22–23, 29, 57, 63, 66–67, 78, 113, 116, 154
desire, 123–124, 131, 138, 143–147, 174, 186, 190, 192–193
destiny, 53, 55, 68, 75, 88, 90, 92, 170–171, 191–192
desubstantialization, 146–148
devil, 179
difference, 17, 23–24, 31, 36, 54, 77, 95, 99, 103, 115, 137, 146–147, 193
discernment, xix, 3, 14, 16–17, 19, 45–61, 63
discernment, categories, xix, 3, 14, 16, 17, 19, 45–51, 53–61, 63
disciples, 22, 23, 27, 31–32, 39–41
discourse, xi, 1, 28, 31, 56, 69, 79, 102–103, 118, 153, 156, 161, 174, 177

distribution, 48–49, 71, 105, 118, 130, 163, 166
divine machine, 37
divine voice, 193
divine-human relation, xvi, 5, 7–8, 11, 15, 19, 29, 41, 74, 103, 134, 136, 142, 191
diviner, 47, 50, 89
divorce, 123
doxa, 40–41
drive, xvi, 23, 73, 113–114, 128, 148, 150, 187
dualism, xiv, 2, 104, 105
dunamis, 39
dung, 11
Durkheim, Emile, 87
dynamis, 39

E *Tamuno oke*, 176–177
economy of exchange, 78, 151
Eden, garden of, 61
egg, 176
Emmanuel, 162–163
Eneke, 79
energies, 17, 46, 84, 105, 110, 135, 141, 160, 163, 169–170, 175
engine, 40
enigma, 5, 29, 182–183, 189, 191, 193
enjoyment, 41, 63, 85, 113, 122, 128, 130, 139, 193
enkinaesthetic theology, 104
enspirited matter, 83
epistemological, xiv, xix, 6, 8, 32–33, 54, 58, 106, 139, 183
epistemological quest, 54, 58
epistemology, xi, 12, 44, 55, 58, 84
ergon, 187
eschaton, 41, 113, 202
essence, xiv, xvi, xviii, xix, 5, 41–42, 67–68, 76–77, 141, 152, 181, 187–188
extimate, 9, 155

eternal past, 75, 90, 92
eternity, xix, 34, 35, 37, 83, 86, 92, 133, 142, 185
ethical substance, 28, 30, 131, 181
ethos, 54, 59, 85, 109, 115, 127, 185
Eucharist, 156
eudaimonia, 68
Europe, 70, 79, 170–171
evangelical-capitalist-resonance machine, 118, 128
Eve, 61–62
event, 15, 22, 24–25, 27, 32, 39–43, 48, 51, 55, 65–66, 68, 71, 72, 80, 84, 92, 94, 96, 103, 107, 136
everyday theology, iv, xii, xix, 8, 9, 12–13, 15, 19, 69, 80, 155, 157–158, 161, 163–168, 172–175
evil, 35–37, 61, 110, 176, 179, 190
ex-citation, 192
excess, 10, 15, 18, 25, 31–32, 65, 99, 107, 113, 115, 118–119, 149–150, 173, 181, 186, 188, 191, 193
exchange, 6, 10–11, 41, 59, 67, 78, 113–114, 123–124, 131, 134, 143, 149, 151, 163, 166–167
excrement, 11
existence, xii, xiv–xvi, 2, 7, 10, 13–15, 26, 33–37, 43, 49, 53, 55, 57–58, 66–68, 70, 73, 80, 90, 91–96, 98, 100, 102, 111, 116, 117, 125, 128, 133, 136, 139, 153, 156, 163–165, 170–175, 177–178, 180–181
existential, 3, 18, 56, 113, 119, 156, 160, 171–172, 174, 180, 181–182
expansion, 17, 33, 34, 67–68, 70
expected unexpected, 170
explanation, prediction, and control (EPC), 49, 50
exposition, 8, 187
expressionist picture, 17
external difference, 182–183
extravagance, 31

face, 3–4, 6, 20, 45, 46, 59–61, 71, 80, 99, 108, 117, 119, 121, 140, 147, 157, 168, 175, 190
failures, 68, 131, 150–151, 213
faith, 2, 10, 11–12, 27, 46, 58, 69, 71–72, 77, 79, 85, 155, 166–167, 175
fantasy, 193
fasters, 59
Fenn, Richard, 84, 86, 89, 108, 185
fetishistic inversion, 7
fidelity, 13, 15, 71–72, 80
finance capital, 115, 118–119, 122
fire, xv–xvi, 21, 38–39, 55, 63, 126, 158, 167
fireworks, 40
fisherman, 48
Fiske, John, 157
flesh, 23, 45, 48, 54–55, 63, 70, 98, 103, 168, 180, 188
flourishing, xvi, 14–15, 32, 68, 70, 80, 92, 105, 111, 112, 116, 156, 157, 170, 172, 177, 179
form, iv, x, xii, xv, xix, 1, 2–5, 7–8, 10–11, 14–15, 18–19, 27–30, 32–34, 43, 47–51, 54, 57, 59–60, 65, 69, 73, 78–81, 91, 98–99, 108, 112, 115, 116, 122, 126, 129–131, 134–135, 142–145, 151, 153, 155–161, 163–177, 179, 185, 191–192
foaming ferment, 93, 118, 131, 137
founding heroes, 49
fragility, 115–119, 125, 160, 204, 210, 220, 223
freedom, 18–19, 22, 30, 33–35, 37, 54, 66–68, 74, 92, 112, 116, 119–120, 122–123, 125–128, 149, 161, 171
Freud, 189–190
functionings, 170, 171

gaming of the self, 112, 115

gap, xiv, xvii, 1, 3–4, 7–8, 12, 23, 29, 31, 36, 40–41, 46, 56, 71–72, 74, 77, 99, 106, 113, 124, 130, 146, 151–152, 167–168, 173, 182, 188, 191
garment, 62
gaze, 6, 55, 59, 62–63, 112
generative forces, 149–150
gentrified, 107
gesturality, 134
Ghana, 160
ghosts, 180
gift, 27, 62–63, 78, 140, 164, 166
Glory, xv, xvi, 39, 40–43, 63, 71, 151–152, 168, 170, 178, 196n.6
Glory-God, xvi, 196n.6
glossolalia, 22, 24–29, 31, 69, 182, 192–193
God, xi–xviii, xix–xx, 1–8, 10–19, 23, 25–26, 28–44, 46, 48, 50, 52–56, 58, 60–62, 64–72, 74–76, 78–81, 83–84, 86–88, 90, 92–100, 102–106, 108, 110–112, 114, 116, 118, 120–124, 126, 128, 131, 133–143, 146, 150, 152–153, 155–156, 158, 160–162, 164, 166–172, 174–176, 178, 180–184, 186–187, 190–193
God dey, 170, 178
God's subjectivity, 10–11
Godhead, xvi, 34, 73, 138, 182
Godness, 7–8
Gods, 6, 48–49, 53–54, 86, 89
Godself, xii–xiii, 4, 16, 103, 197
Goffman, Erving, 177–179
goods, 11, 118, 128, 130, 149, 163, 164, 166, 188
grace, xix, 4, 14–19, 29–30, 55, 62–81, 85, 92, 96, 111, 135, 137, 140, 143, 150, 178
grassroots, xii, 1, 16
grotesque, 58, 160
guilt, 31, 66, 116

232 Index

Gyges, myth of, 62

hand, xv–xvii, 8, 14, 57, 61, 84, 91, 125, 145, 161, 166–167, 176–177, 196
Hand-God, xvi, 196n.6
handkerchiefs, 69
hearing ears, 52
heaven, xvii, 10, 21, 40, 70, 74–75, 113, 143, 168, 190
Hegel, xix, 12, 51, 76, 93–94, 106, 137, 151, 195n.4
Heidegger, Martin, 23, 144–145
heresy, 13
hole, 19, 25, 38, 61, 74, 99–100
holiness, 78, 138, 156, 158
holism, 5–6
Holy Communion, 162
Holy Ghost, 63, 156, 160–161
Holy Spirit, xvii, 7, 10, 13 16–18, 21, 23, 27, 30, 39–42, 54–56, 58, 62, 66–67, 70, 72, 74, 78, 112, 137–139, 142, 145, 147, 151, 158–159, 161, 165–166, 168–169, 175, 182, 192
homo sacer, 63
horizon, 37, 85, 91, 117, 153
Horton, Robin, 33, 49, 87
Humean concept, 80
hypertext, 95
hyphenation, xvi

I-can-do-it, 122
I-It, 112
I-Thou, 112
idealism, xvii
identity, xiii, xvi–xvii, 1, 10, 23–24, 26–27, 30–31, 35, 40, 73, 87, 124, 131, 137, 141, 157, 160–161, 178, 182, 186, 189, 193
ideology, 122–123, 161
Ifa, 79

images, xviii, 45, 52, 61, 161
imaginary, xiii, 26–27, 39, 70, 161, 167–168, 170
imagination, 50–52, 61, 79–80, 99, 108–109, 130, 133, 185
imaginative hedonism, 130
immigrants, 121, 167, 170, 171, 172
impassibility, 192
impossible gift, 78
impotentiality, 116–117, 119, 125–127
impressionist painting, 16
incompleteness, xiv–xv, 2–3, 5, 19, 30, 56, 74
inconsistency, 12, 73
incorporation, 28, 192–193
inequalities, 130
inoperativity, 39, 41–43, 63, 152, 181, 187, 189
inoperoso, 187
insemination, 151
instrumental faith, 166–167
intelligibility, 186, 193
intercultural understanding, 183
interiority, 52, 76–77
internal disciplining, 129
interpellation, 55, 116, 124, 126, 129, 193
interstitiality, 95, 110
intimacy, 7, 24, 52, 139
intrinsicness, 6
invisibility, 45, 62, 63, 161
iron, 160–161
Israel, 27
Italy, 70, 105, 167–168

Japanese, 141
Jehovah, 71, 111, 161, 168
Jerusalem, 21–22, 27, 40, 114
Jesus Christ, 3, 11, 17, 27–28, 38–39, 138, 142, 146, 173
Johnson, Adrian, 6, 198–199

jouissance, xv, 11, 13, 61, 71, 91, 93, 112–113, 137, 139, 143, 159, 168, 175
Judaism, 21, 27, 196
jug, 144–145

kabhod, 41, 152
Kafka, Franz, 184, 192
Kalabari, 33, 49, 50–53, 86–90, 93, 101–102, 176
Kant, Immanuel, 30, 37, 92, 144, 149, 195
Kantian duty, 148, 149–150
Kedem grape juice
Keller, Catherine, ix, 84, 95–96, 98, 100, 102–105
kenosis, 192
kernel, xvi, 11, 31, 189
Kierkegaard, Soren, 9
King James Bible, 160
knowledge, x, xiv, 8, 16, 31, 41, 42, 44, 46–47, 52–54, 58–60, 62, 83–85, 99, 111–112, 153
Kripal, Jeffrey, 94–95
krokro eyes, 50

Lacan triad, 27
Lacan, Jacques, xi, 1, 22, 143, 190
laceration, 7
lack, 5, 10, 20, 23, 25, 99, 101, 114, 147, 181
lack proper, 99
Lagos, 20, 65, 195
language, 7, 21–26, 28, 31, 59, 61, 66, 75, 85, 95, 101, 103, 107, 127, 160–161, 166, 172, 174, 177, 189–190, 192–193
law, 28–29, 33, 37, 56, 65–67, 80, 85–86, 101, 108–110, 112, 149, 190
law of worship, 149

Lazzarato, Maurizio, 118, 122
legislature, 85, 94
lepers, 48
less than nothing, 143, 152
Levinas, Emmanuel, 62, 189
life-in-the-spirit, 22, 67, 148–149
light, 1, 14–15, 41, 46–47, 58, 60–61, 72, 84, 89, 101, 103, 105, 126–127, 133, 167, 173–174, 189
luminal, 136, 160
livingness, xiii, 56, 142
logocentric, 12
logos, 39, 58, 172–173
love, xx, 11, 41–42, 66–67, 83, 114, 181, 190–192
loyalties, 170

machine, 40–41, 78, 112, 118, 128, 152, 163, 186
Malebranche, Nicholas, 114
manifest presence, 69
market, 4, 6, 10, 59–60, 115–120, 122, 124, 126–127, 130, 141, 164
Maroko, 65
marriage, 190
Marshall, Ruth, 18, 79
Marx, Karl, 6, 118, 195
Marxist, xi, 2
Mascall, Eric L., 41–42
master, 5, 60, 115, 126–127, 135, 143
materialism, xvii, 94, 198–199
matter, xvii, 2, 17–18, 29, 49, 53–54, 70, 79–80, 83, 86, 88, 114–115, 139, 146, 153, 159, 168, 178
meaning structure, 165
meanings, 15, 26, 88, 118, 142, 156–158, 160, 162–164, 174–175, 180, 183
mediality, 15, 18, 74, 134, 136–137, 142, 145, 187

Meillassoux, Quentin, 84, 101–102, 109–110, 185
Messiah, 43
messianic, 29, 43, 173–174
messianic gap, 173
metaethical self, 188–189, 191
metaphysics, xiv, 76, 95, 102, 109
methodology, xx, 1, 33, 53, 98, 172, 174
Meyer, Brigit, 158, 169
microaffirmations, 176, 193
microaggressions, 176, 177, 193
microtheologies, xx, 1–2
midst of life, 181, 183–184, 186–187, 191
migrants, 181, 183–184, 186–187, 191
Milbank, John, xi
miracles, xiv–xv, 1, 2, 5, 14, 15, 78, 83–84, 107, 109–110, 158, 169–170
mirror, xvii, 17, 45–47, 56–57, 59–61, 140
modes of exchange, 166–167
Moltmann, Jürgen, 192
money, 79, 114, 118, 203, 121, 164, 166
monotheism, xiv, 38
monstrosity, 10, 17–18, 65, 67, 69, 71, 73–75, 77, 79, 81, 108, 189–190, 191
Most Moved Mover, 97
Mountain of Fire and Miracles Ministries, 158–195
mouth, 7, 60, 116, 193
mysticism, 84, 95, 106
myths, 184, 100

Na God, 80, 170
Name-it-and-claim-it theology, 10
Name-of-the-father, 33
Nancy, Jean-Luc, xi, 1, 187
narratives, 57, 72, 169–170, 178

nationalism, 122
native doctor, 47
nature, 22, 32, 35–39, 43, 46–49, 51–55, 57, 62–64, 66–67, 78, 83, 89, 98–99, 102, 117, 123–124, 134–135, 139, 141, 142, 149, 158–160, 163, 173, 183, 187, 189
necessity, xv, 12, 33, 72, 75, 90, 92, 96, 131
negative theology, 95–99
neighbor, 56, 62–63, 182–183, 187, 189–191
neoconservatives, 122
neoliberal capitalism, xii, 47
New York, ix, 121, 162
Nicholas of Cusa, 140
Nietzsche, Friedrich, 3
Niger Delta, 49, 86, 88
Nigeria, 20, 49, 65, 86, 88, 158, 176
night of the world, xvi, 51–52, 58–59, 72, 196n.6
Nimi, 52
nomos, xv, 2, 85, 109, 123, 185
nonbeing, xiv, 95
Norton, Anne, 23
not-All, xvi, 5, 6, 102
noumenal, xv, xvii, xix, 3, 5, 8, 15, 37, 44, 46–48, 51, 53–55, 57–61, 76–77, 92, 106, 111, 169, 184
noumenal Thing, xv, xvii, xix, 3, 5, 8, 15, 37, 44, 46–48, 51, 53–55, 57–61, 76–77, 92, 106, 111, 169, 184
novum, 93, 100
nudity, 62–63
null, 57
numen, 87–88

obedience, 46, 80, 122–123, 128
objet petit a, 143, 146–147
obscene supplement, 193
obstacle, xix, 8, 31, 38, 76, 150–151, 182

Odu, 79
oikonomia, 39–41, 152
Ojo, Matthews, 165
Olive oil, 69, 163
omega point, 100
omnipotence, 11, 197
omnivoyant, 37
ontologization, 8
ontology, xi, 8, 12, 84, 101
orthopraxis, xvi, 36
Other, 15, 22–26, 70, 115, 168, 181–183, 186–187, 189–193
Otherness, 34
ought to speak, 30
out-of-jointness, 183, 186, 191

pagan pleasures, 11
paleonomy, 13, 155
panoptic, 158
para-site, x, 95
parallels, xvi
paranormal, 94
part of no part, xiii, 114
parthenogenesis, 135
partial organs, xv, xvi, xix, 2, 196n.6
participation, 16, 58, 120, 139, 158
particularity, 73, 143, 144
pastor, 37, 40, 57, 60, 121, 135, 162
Paul, xi, 26, 27–29, 43, 56
pentecocapitalism, 128–129
Pentecost, 15, 21–25, 27–29, 31, 33, 35–43, 55
Pentecostal leaders, 37
Pentecostal logic of sense, 17, 104–105
Pentecostal principle, 9–10, 18, 65, 175
perceptual apparatus, 106
performative, 72, 161
periodization, 109
personhood, 48, 87
perverse core, 11, 18, 92
Peter, 21, 27–28, 40, 75

Peterson, Erik, 63
phallus, 151
phantasy, 106, 128
phenomenal, xv–xviii, xix, 3, 5, 12, 14–15, 19, 36–37, 39, 46–48, 51, 53–55, 59, 62–63, 74, 76, 79, 83–84, 92–93, 106, 111–112, 169, 184
photograph, 16
piano, 141
piety, 9–10, 13, 155, 159
Plato, 62, 199
play, xx, 60, 65–68, 94, 99, 101–102, 104, 112–114, 135, 139–141, 144, 150, 159, 161, 175–176
pleasure, 68, 112, 116–117, 122, 130, 149, 157–159, 161, 164, 166
plunder, 166
pluralism, 181, 184
pneuma, xiii, 39
pneumatological imagination, 130
poem, 133
polis, 187
pollutions, 176
potential to not-do, 119–120
potentiality, 34, 41, 100–101, 110, 119, 123, 125–128, 139, 184
potentiality to-do, 123, 126, 127–128
potentiality, to not-do, 123
poverty, 65, 114
power, xv, xvi, xix, 2, 10–11, 13, 15, 17–18, 29–30, 33, 35–36, 42, 48, 50–51, 53–54, 62, 65–66, 68–69, 71–72, 78, 83–87, 95–96, 98, 100, 102, 107–110, 116, 118, 120–122, 125–126, 129, 131, 135, 137–138, 141, 147, 151–153, 158–161, 163–169, 171, 176, 179, 185–186
Power-God, xvi, 196n.6
praise, 40–43, 87, 134, 140, 144–146, 152, 156, 159, 173
praxis, xx, 39–41, 53, 126, 139, 149, 151, 177, 179, 187, 197–198

prayer, xv, 1, 59, 61, 76, 79, 156, 158, 160–161, 167, 173
Prayer City, 158
predestination, 75, 92
priest, 47, 176, 192
probabilities, 48
production, 9, 13, 16, 52–53, 59, 96, 118, 119, 129–131, 135, 139, 157, 159
profanation, 73, 138, 148, 184
progressives, 122
prophecy, 26, 32
prophetism, 58
prosperity gospel, 113–114, 148–149
Protestant ethic, 129
psalmist, 32
psychoanalysis, 60
pulpit industry, 157
pupils, 60
pure gift, 140, 166
pure means, 18–19, 41–42, 65, 71, 74, 115, 130, 131, 133–153, 187–189, 212n.10

quantity, 6
quantum, 99, 102

radical love, 181
Rancière, Jacques, 163
randomness, 48, 119
rationality, 79, 143
reading, 161
Real, 12, 31, 38, 93, 103, 105, 118, 140, 146, 167
real presence, 16, 36, 38–39, 69–70, 76–78, 103, 105, 140, 167, 169, 192
reality, xi, xiii–xix, 2–6, 8, 10, 12–14, 17, 19, 26, 29, 34, 37, 41, 44–49, 51, 53–54, 56–57, 59–60, 63, 70, 74–75, 77, 83–84, 90, 93–95, 99–101, 105–108, 110, 111, 118, 120, 139–140, 143, 153, 157, 168–169, 172, 174, 178, 182
reciprocity, 10, 104, 149, 166
reflexivity, 14
relationalism, 97, 103
religio, 100
religious machine, 163
remainder, 40, 147, 186
Renri, 141
repetition, 9, 69
Resolute, 97–98
reveilation, 25
revelation, 25, 51, 59, 61, 63, 96, 122, 184, 186
rites, 100, 178, 184
rituals, xvi, xviii, 15, 22, 70, 94, 175, 176, 178–179
Roman Catholicism, 105
Romans, xi, 48, 56, 66, 78, 142
roof, 17, 19–20
Rosenzweig, Franz, 184–186, 188–189, 191
Rotary, xvii, 33–34, 73

sacrality, 15, 96, 111
sacrament, 140, 164
sacred, xi, xvi, xix, 4, 14–17, 19, 49–50, 55, 63, 70, 78–79, 81, 83–105, 107–113, 118, 129, 138–139, 164, 170, 178, 184–186
salvation, 14, 18, 50, 66–67, 69, 71, 73–75, 86, 89, 108, 129, 158
Santner, Eric, 182–184, 186, 188–189
saving grace, 66, 71
Schelling, F. W. J., xvii, 33–36, 39, 73, 75, 92, 145–146
Schmitt, Carl, 85
science, 9, 33, 94–95
Scott, James, 105, 179

secernere, 25
secrets, 25, 46, 60, 62, 130
secularity, 108–109
secularum, 138
seduction, 192–193
seeing eyes, 47, 52, 57, 59
seers, 63
self, xv–xvi, 2, 11, 15, 25, 31, 48, 54, 56, 58, 62, 68, 70, 77, 79, 86, 90, 112–113, 115–116, 124–125, 129, 147, 169, 176, 178, 182, 188–189, 191
self-alienation, 74
self-emptying, 77, 146–147
self-identity, xvii
self-interpretation, 156, 166, 180
self-presentation, 156
self-reflection, 77
selfhood, xvii, 189, 191–192
senses, 29, 69, 70–71, 104–105, 138, 159, 167–169
sensorimotor, 69
sensory organs, 49, 52, 54
sets of possibilities, 66, 85, 89, 107
sex, 128, 133
shear, 160, 161, 167
Shekhina, 191–192
sign, xxi, 19, 56, 78–79, 102, 138, 143, 165, 172
signatures, 33, 79
signification, 28–29, 96, 109, 142
signifier, 5, 114, 142–143
sin, 62, 190
singular-plural, xvi, 141
skin, 17, 38, 45, 62, 65, 67, 69, 71, 73, 75, 77, 79, 81, 139
slain, 159
sleeper, xxi
So, 49–50, 53, 88–90, 93
social suffering, 113–115
Sölle, Dorothee, 127–128

Sollen, 30
soul, x, xvii, 2, 18, 54, 88, 120, 141, 187, 190
soup, 85
sovereignty, 11, 18, 185
spacing, 7
speaking in tongues, 22, 25–27, 31, 147
spectacles, xii, 4, 160
Spirit, 159, 163, 168–169, 180, 182, 184, 192–193
Spirit-led, 127
spiritual warrior, 161
split, xii–xix, 1–20, 22–28, 30–50, 52, 54–56, 58, 60, 62, 64, 66, 68, 70, 72, 74, 76–78, 81, 106–107, 124, 135, 146, 148, 151–153, 155, 167, 169, 174–175, 181–184, 186–187, 191–193
spontaneity, 18, 127–128
stain, 6
Stoics, 104
strangeness, 182–183, 189, 191, 193
street seminary, 66
subject, xvi, 2, 6–7, 11–12, 16–18, 22, 26, 30–31, 34, 37, 58, 72, 74, 97, 111–112, 124, 137, 141–142, 146–147, 181, 192–193
subjectivation, 4
subjectivity, xiv–xv, xix, 2, 10–11, 14, 15, 17, 19, 22, 51, 58, 71, 111–113, 115, 128, 130, 135, 146, 147
substance, 6–7, 10–11, 28, 30, 98, 104, 111–112, 117, 131, 152–153, 181
substractive process, 27
superego, 116
surplus, 65, 84, 130, 150, 173, 181, 186–187, 193
surprises, 13, 65, 67, 80, 100, 170, 185–186
sword, 61, 160, 161, 166–167
symbol, 23, 138, 152, 163, 172–173

symbolic, 22, 26–29, 31, 51, 53, 61, 70, 72, 85, 112, 146–148, 151, 164, 168, 178, 186, 189, 192–193
symbolic order, 22, 26, 28–29, 112, 148, 186, 189
synthesis, xv, xviii, 4, 31

tarrying, 41, 51, 54, 55
tax, 129
Taylor, Mark C., 23, 84, 95, 145
Taylor, Mark Lewis, v, xx
tears, 4–5, 92, 147, 169
technique of the self, 129
technology of the self, 48, 129, 169
teleoaffectivity, 165
telos, 51, 88, 133
temple, 23, 42, 114
temporalization, 184–186
testimonies, 20, 72
textflesh, 180
textual, 56–57, 174
theism, 86, 99, 110, 196n.7, 203n.57
theologia, 40
theological spirit, 180
theopoetic, 97
theorein, 135
theory, xi–xx, 1–2, 12–13, 15, 19, 42, 47, 96, 103, 111, 129, 135, 173, 177, 184–185
thighs, 159
Thing, 29, 37, 39, 189
thing-in-itself, 39, 55, 58, 111, 163
things-in-themselves, 5, 8, 14, 76, 106
throne, 152
throwness, 192
Tillich, Paul, xx, 13, 38, 157
time, x, xiii, xvi, xx, 3, 8, 10, 13, 19, 28–29, 33–36, 38–40, 43, 48, 50, 60, 75, 86, 87, 96, 101, 107–110, 137, 142, 150, 156, 162, 166, 169, 171, 173–174, 179, 184–186
tithe, 79, 121, 129

too-muchness, 15, 181, 193
Topeka, 22, 25
totality, xx, 12, 29, 37, 73, 100–101, 107, 136, 175, 186, 193
traces, xvi, 70–71, 98, 168
tradition, xi–xii, 1–2, 10, 13, 18, 20, 27–28, 30, 63, 72, 87, 155–156
transcendent, 7, 83–84, 100–102, 106, 153, 184
transcendental matrix, 134
transcripts, 179
transgression, 5, 22, 66, 91, 123
translation, 28–30, 192–193
transphysical, 54–55, 61
transubstantiates, 147
traumatic kernel, 31
triad, 26–27, 70–71, 168
Trinity, xiv, xix, 38, 40–41, 43, 161
Truth, ix, xix, 7, 12, 23, 27, 31, 33, 47, 52, 61, 63, 76–77, 105, 113, 115, 117–118, 133, 136, 139, 145, 150, 163, 182
truth procedure, 12, 77

ultimate concern, 38, 156
uncanniness, 182, 183, 211n.36
unChristianity, 17
Unconditional, 29–30, 75, 149
unfathomable X, 46, 146–147, 189
unfinishedness, 80, 182
unfulfilled possibilities, 85–86, 89
ungrund, 25, 35
United States, xx, 122, 128
universal singularity, 124
universality, xviii, 73, 124, 127
unknowability, xix, 63
urination, 151
urn, 50, 89
utilitarianism, 135
utopia, 114, 127

Vaughan, Henry, 133

veil, xvii, 14, 37, 46, 48, 59, 62–63, 76, 92, 108, 111, 139
Vernant, Jean-Pierre, 45
Victoria Island, 20, 65, 111
virtuality, 9, 100–102, 184
virtualizing power of time, 107, 109–110, 185
virtue, 33, 122, 127, 131, 187
visa, 79
vision, xv, 5, 32, 42, 49, 55, 65, 76, 140, 152
vocation, 29, 126
void, 29, 31, 60, 72, 92, 99, 144–147, 152

Wagner, Richard, 190
Wall Street, 118
walls, 4, 19–20, 59–60
wari-temeso, 88
water-spirits, 49
wearable theology, 15, 157
wearable theology, 15, 157
Weber, Max, 129
West Africa, 80, 153, 156, 163–166, 174
Western democracies, 125
Western societies, 124–125
will, 141, 145, 146, 197
will to power, 135
wind, xiii, 21, 38–40, 139
window shopping, 164

witchcraft, 48
work, 55, 67–68, 70, 72–75, 79, 123, 172, 187, 203–204
worldview, xv, xvi, 2–3, 9–10, 36, 76, 80, 88–89, 94–95, 108, 117, 136, 139, 155, 161
worship, xiii, xiv, xix, 1, 4, 14–15, 17–19, 23, 41–43, 53, 65, 69, 70, 71, 74, 86–87, 104–105, 113, 130–131, 133–153, 156, 158–160, 166, 168, 173, 187–189, 196n.7, 212n.10
Worship as pure means (WPM), 41, 130, 212n.10
worship-fed prayers, 156
WPM (worship as a pure means), 136, 142–143, 212n.10

xenololia, 24, 26–27, 38

yada, 53
Yong, Amos, iv, 130
Yoruba, 79, 198, 223

zero-point, 188
Žižek, Slavoj, xi, xiii, 1, 3, 9, 30, 34, 36, 70, 73, 84, 92–93, 100, 102, 116, 120, 124, 148, 153, 168, 182–183, 189
zōē, 43
Zoe Ministries, 65

www.ingramcontent.com/pod-product-compliance
Lightning Source LLC
Chambersburg PA
CBHW030537230426
43665CB00010B/922